In this book TINBERGEN's publi-
cations are classified into five
groups :

1. business cycle theory and policy
2. international economics
3. long-term economic development
4. distribution of income
5. economic systems

IN THE FIELD of social and economic
sciences Professor Tinbergen is of
great renown. He has pioneered in
many fields, which has recently been
proved again by his stimulating
study on the Theory of Optimum
Regimes. In all fields he demonstrated an extraordinary inventiveness
in stating problems and unsurpassed
clarity and simplicity in setting out
their solutions.

Professor Tinbergen's books have
been translated into several languages and are accessible to practically
all students of economics. Apart
from this a large number of articles
were published in various periodicals
in Dutch, English, German, Danish,
French and in other languages.
These articles contain some of his
most important contributions.

JAN TINBERGEN – SELECTED PAPERS

Professor Tinbergen with one of his students

JAN TINBERGEN
SELECTED PAPERS

EDITED BY

L. H. KLAASSEN
L. M. KOYCK
AND
H. J. WITTEVEEN

1959

NORTH-HOLLAND PUBLISHING COMPANY - AMSTERDAM

PRINTED IN THE NETHERLANDS

To Tine, whose love
and thoughtfulness
give flavour to my work
and happiness to my life

PREFACE

Professor Tinbergen is of great renown in the social and economic fields and has pioneered many ideas correlative to these fields. His books have been translated into several languages and are accessible to practically all students of economics.

He has also authored a great many articles which were published in various periodicals in Dutch, English, German, Danish and French among other languages. Contained in these articles were some of his most important contributions.

The editors of this volume were of the opinion that these articles would prove extremely valuable to anyone interested in economics. Their idea was to make a careful selection of these scattered papers, which as aforementioned were executed originally in sundry languages, and publish them in one volume in the English language with the articles which were originally published in other languages appropriately translated.

Twenty-five years have elapsed since Professor Tinbergen was first appointed Professor at the Netherlands School of Economics at Rotterdam and this fact offered the editors an opportunity to align the papers to show the development of Tinbergen's scientific activities over a long period of years.

In the execution of this plan the editors of this book have divided the field covered by Tinbergen into five groups.

   i. Business Cycle Theory and Policy
  ii. International Economics
 iii. Long-term Economic Development
 iv. Distribution of Income
  v. Economic Systems.

Relative to each of these groups one or more articles have been selected that contain an original approach to a certain problem or represent an important instance in the development of Tinbergen's scientific activities. The selections were difficult and of course remain subjective. On the subject of the first group, "Business Cycle Theories and Policy", Tinbergen did pioneering work in the beginning of his academic career. The article "An Economic Policy for 1936" can be considered as the first econometric business cycle model. It is the forerunner of Tinbergen's work at the League of Nations in 1938 which resulted in the well-known books: "Statistical Testing of Business Cycle Theories I, II".

In the article "An Economic Policy for 1936" it is not without interest to note that a number of ideas, especially those on the consumption function and its role in problems of employment policy, anticipated the Keynesian theory. At the same time Tinbergen developed a method for economic policy using econometric models. Along with the above-mentioned articles, studies on special cycles, the shipbuilding cycle and reinvestment cycles were selected in this group.

In the group "International Economics" a short article is selected in which the importance of long-term trade elasticities and a method for the statistical estimation of these elasticities is considered. The fact that Tinbergen always has a great interest in problems of current interest and always tries to bring the discussion of these ideas on to a scientific level, can be seen from the studies on customs unions and the theory of economic integration.

In the group "Long-term Economic Development" three articles have been selected in which Tinbergen discusses the effects of technical progress on employment and economic welfare. His model on "Long-term Economic Development" published in the "Weltwirtschaftliches Archiv" is still, notwithstanding the large amount of work subsequently done on the subject, an important and stimulating study on economic growth.

From the beginning of his scientific career Tinbergen has always been highly interested in social problems and the problem of the distribution of income has especially and continuously occupied him. It is to his great credit that he has brought this problem out of the sphere of popular political discussion and on to a scientific level. The articles selected in the fourth group, in which a precise description of the mechanism of income formation in terms of the usual instruments of economic analysis is given, may prove this.

The book closes with a recent and as yet not published study on

"The Theory of the Optimum Regime". It is not by accident that the group "Economic Systems" in which this study is classified comes at the end of the book. In a certain sense it is an indication of the development of Tinbergen's activities. Prior to the second world war these activities were mainly centered around business cycle problems. In the forties and fifties it was problems of long-term economic development, especially development programming for under-developed countries, which occupied Tinbergen's activities. The study of these problems against the background of a broad international viewpoint has now led Tinbergen to study the economic aspect of one of the most important controversies that presently divides the world – the controversy between different systems of economic organization. Just as with his contribution to the theory of income distribution, Tinbergen keeps himself away from popular black-white slogans and tries to give a scientific analysis of the problem of the best economic system from an economic point of view.

All the students from the passing parade of his period of 25 years of lecturing wish to express their gratitude to Professor Tinbergen by offering to him this selection of his papers.

The Editors:
L. H. KLAASSEN
L. M. KOYCK
H. J. WITTEVEEN

CONTENTS

III. Long-Term Economic Development

A SHIPBUILDING CYCLE?*

The basic problem of any theory on endogenous trade cycles may be expressed in the following question: how can an economic system show fluctuations which are not the effect of exogenous, oscillating forces, that is to say fluctuations due to some "inner" cause? Or if we take the simplest case, that of a single, isolated market, how can price and turnover fluctuate in this manner in a market which is considered isolated?

We are greatly indebted to MOORE[1] for his example of an "elementary cycle", and to HANAU[2] for his statistical elaboration of such an "elementary cycle". I refer to the so-called "pork cycle". The very interesting examples quoted by MOORE and others where this "elementary cycle" plays a part are much more complicated insofar as they show disturbances of the cycle which stem from exogenous influences and therefore interrupt the cycle, in most cases even before one period has come to an end. The most important cause for disturbance from the outside is the different yield per acre of the agricultural products in question.[3]

In this article I should like to demonstrate a relationship between shipbuilding and freight rates which will bring us to another type of "elementary fluctuation", a type which, it seems to me, displays interesting characteristics of consequence to the theory of economic fluctuations in general, and also are not without meaning for the field of shipbuilding in particular.

---

* Ein Schiffbauzyklus? Weltwirtschaftliches Archiv, 34. Band (1931 ii), p. 152–164.
[1] H. L. MOORE, *Synthetic Economics*, New York 1929.
[2] A. HANAU, "Die Prognose der Schweinepreise", *Vierteljahreshefte zur Konjunkturforschung*, Sonderheft 18; 3., vollst. neu bearb. Aufl. des Sonderheftes 2, Berlin 1930.
[3] With most agricultural products, the acreage is connected with the prices of the previous year. If the yields per acre were constant, an entirely analogous cycle of prices and production would be the result. Now and then parts of such cycles can be observed, *e.g.* for cotton about the year 1906.

In addition to a thorough treatment of this type of fluctuations I will deal briefly with the relationship between the "shipbuilding cycle" and the "pork cycle" and in conclusion add a few related remarks on the latter cycle.

1. SOME STATISTICS ON THE SHIPBUILDING CYCLE

Fluctuations in shipbuilding determine to a large extent the fluctuations in the increase in total tonnage of a country's merchant marine, since the number of sunk and scrapped ships is relatively small. This fact is illustrated by the lower portion of Fig. 1 in which curve C represents the annual increase in the total tonnage of Great Britain, the United States and Germany (deviation from trend) and curve D the total world launchings (idem, reduced). In much the same way the volume of shipbuilding is largely dependent on the level of freight rates. These in turn are clearly correlated with total available tonnage. It will be understood that both relationships are subject to a certain lag so that, for example, freight rates will be high if total tonnage was low shortly before. An increase in tonnage will appear about one year after the occurrence of increased rates because one year is approximately the construction time of a new ship Such retarded relations (lag correlations) are shown in the two top portions of Fig. 1. Line A shows the fluctuations in freight rates, derived from the index of homeward freights published by "Fairplay",[4] in deviations from a parabolic trend of the second degree; while curve B represents the fluctuations in the total tonnage of the three big sea-faring countries (Great Britain, United States, Germany) in terms of percentages of deviation from a parabolic trend of the second degree.

The two relationships described here are the basis for a third which is the most significant to us: the relationship between the increase in total tonnage and the volume of the total tonnage of about two years earlier. The two curves are remarkably similar, as will be seen from the centre portion of Fig. 1.

Before we consider the consequence of this relationship I should like to state briefly its social and economic significance.[5] This is, obviously,

---

[4] *Fairplay*, London, Vol. 67 (1916 II), No. 1754, p. 946

[5] See also: J. TINBERGEN, "Scheepsbouw en conjunctuurverloop", *De Nederlandsche Conjunctuur*, 's-Gravenhage, Jg. 1931, Afl. 1, p. 14.

that the volume of shipbuilding is primarily a function of the ship-owners' demand for freight capacity—costs seem to be less variable —and furthermore, that the level of freight rates, at least during the period under review, depends mainly on the shipowners' supply of freight capacity. The demand of importers and exporters considered as an aggregate appears to fluctuate much less. We do by no means want to deny the influence of these other factors, but their effect is probably secondary.

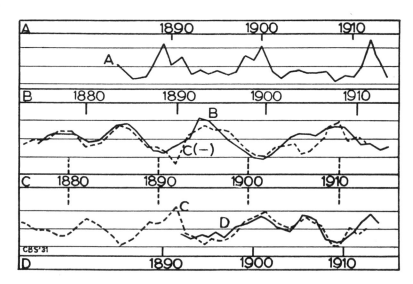

Fig. 1

Index of freight rates (A), total tonnage of British, American and German merchant marines (B), increase in tonnage (C), world launchings (D) prior to 1913 (deviations from trend).[6]

We have seen that an increase in the total tonnage is in the first place dependent upon the volume of tonnage of about two years earlier. At this point emerges an interesting theoretical problem: how great would the total tonnage and its rate of increase have been if the relationship described above had had no exceptions? This relationship,

---

[6] For the figures compare: *De Nederlandsche Conjunctuur*, Jg. 1931, Afl. 1, p. 22.

this "reaction mechanism", will in most cases and at any rate in the present one, prove to result in a cyclical movement which I have briefly called the "shipbuilding cycle". The following paragraphs reveal the characteristics of this shipbuilding cycle. The only successful method in my opinion is a strictly mathematical approach to the problem because this is the only way to arrive at a determinate solution.[7]

2. DETERMINING THE PROBLEM

We want to obtain the development over time of total tonnage; time will be expressed as t, tonnage as $f(t)$, so that the function f is our unknown quantity.

The data given are in the first place the abovementioned relationship between "increase" and "tonnage some time ago". The rate of increase will be expressed here as $f'(t)$, the tonnage θ years ago—we are stating the problem generally at first—as $f(t-\theta)$. The intensity of the reaction, *i.e.* the volume of the increase which corresponds to a tonnage level of one unit above the trend, shall be expressed as a. Since a high level corresponds with a low increase, the relationship discovered may be expressed in the following equation

(1) $$f'(t) = -af(t-\theta) \qquad (a>0).$$

Apart from this equation which defines the law according to which the subsequent conditions develop from the present condition, something should also be indicated about the initial conditions, since naturally the shape of the development is influenced by them. It will be understood that not only should the total tonnage at some initial moment be given but also the development during the total initial period of length θ. It is only then that the further development will be defined since the increase will in each case be determined by the conditions given θ years earlier. Another given quantity, therefore, must be the development in an interval of, shall we say $0 \leq t < \theta$, which will be expressed here by the equation:

(2) $$f(t) = g(t) \qquad 0 \leq t < \theta,$$

---

[7] Readers who are not versed in mathematics can omit paragraph 3 without losing the line of reasoning.

Finally the solution should meet another requirement in order to have economic significance: it must be real and finite.

In the following paragraph we will first try to find the solution to the general equation (1) and subsequently work out the particular form of the result which corresponds to the value of the constant in our particular case. These values are as follows: in the shipbuilding cycle, the value of θ is 2 (in years), the value of a in the period under review lies between 1 and 1/2.[8] The development in the course of two years may generally be assumed to be a simple curve (that is it may be illustrated as either a parabola or a sinusoid or an exponential curve etc. with only minor deviations).

3. THE MATHEMATICAL SOLUTION OF THE PROBLEM[9]

The solution of equations of this kind (functional equations) in analytical mathematics is, as will be known, usually not found "methodically" but experimentally. If a solution has been found and we can prove that only one solution is possible, then we may conclude that we have found the correct solution.

In the case of equation (1) the most obvious way to obtain a solution is in the following manner: assume

(3) $$f(t) = e^{\alpha t + \beta} = C e^{\alpha t},$$

where the two constants are still to be defined and must be assumed *a priori* in as general a form as possible, in other words we assume that they are complex quantities. Substituting (3) into (1) we get:

(4) $$a\, C e^{\alpha t} = -\, a\, C e^{\alpha(t-\theta)},$$

which after dividing by $C e^{\alpha t}$ reads:

(5) $$a = -\, a e^{-\alpha \theta}.$$

From (4) and (5) it follows that C can be chosen arbitrarily, whereas

---

[8] In fact, that the value decreases slowly in the period under review. Strictly speaking, a is therefore also a function of t. Because of its slow variability, however, the best way is to assume a to be constant for the time being and substitute it as variable in the solution found. In physics this is known as the method of adiabatic variables. (*Cf.* P. EHRENFEST, *Ann. der Physik*, Bd. 51, 1916, p. 327.

[9] The author is greatly indebted to Dr. J. DROSTE, Professor of Mathematics at the University of Leiden, for some critical remarks on this paragraph.

a depends on equation (5). To solve this last equation we substitute thus

(6) $$-a\theta = z = x + iy,$$

or

(7) $$a = -\frac{x + iy}{\theta},$$

and then write for (5)

$$\frac{z}{a\theta} = e^z,$$

which for $a\theta = b$ turns out to be

(8) $$z = be^z.$$

Splitting this complex equation into its real and its imaginary components we get:

(9A,B) $$x = be^x \cos y \qquad y = be^x \sin y,$$

Eliminating x we get:

(10) $$x = \frac{y}{\text{tg } y}$$

(11) $$\frac{y}{\sin y} = be^{\frac{y}{\text{tg } y}}$$

or

(11′) $$b\frac{\sin y}{y} = e^{-\frac{y}{\text{tg } y}}$$

A graphical solution of equation (11′) is made possible by the graph in Fig. 2. The drawn curves represent the right-hand and the dotted curves the left-hand side of different values for b, namely $b = 0.25$; 1; 2.
The following conclusions may be drawn from the figure:
1. The intersections for $y = 2\pi$, 4π etc. cannot be used as solutions because they lead to infinite values for a.
2. The other intersections are acceptable solutions which shall be expressed as y_k ($k = 1$ in the first interval of length 2π, $k = 2$ in the second interval etc.).
3. The solution for y_1 is missing if $eb < 1$, i.e. if

(12) $$b(\equiv a\theta) < \frac{1}{e} \sim 0.37.$$

4. All y_k increase if b increases.

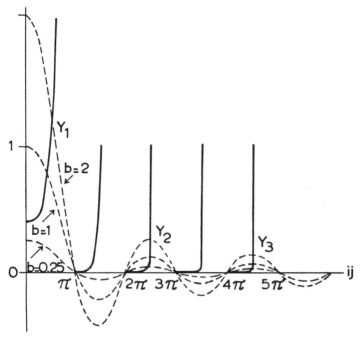

Fig. 2.

It will be seen that we have found a number of particular solutions which take the form of:

$$f = C_k e^{+a_k t},$$

in which a_k is given through equation (7) if x and y in this equation have the subscript k. From equations (10) and (11') it follows further-more that also — y_k and x_k form a pair of roots. The corresponding a_{-k} is conjugate to a_k.

Since the original equation is linear, each sum of two or more solutions is again a solution so that the general form of the solutions found now reads:

(13)
$$f(t) = \sum_{-\infty}^{+\infty} {}^k C_k e^{\alpha_k t}, \quad \text{where } C_0 = 0.$$

Only those solutions that are real have an economic significance, from which it may be concluded that also C_{-k} is conjugate to C_k. Each pair of terms from (13):

$$C_k e^{\alpha_k t} + C_{-k} e^{\alpha_{-k} t}$$

represents a sine wave with an arbitrary phase and initial amplitude, but with a fixed period and a fixed damping degree, since the last two quantities are defined by a_k.

If it were possible to represent any development of function $f(t)$ for the interval $0 \leq t < \theta$ by the proper selection of C_k, then (13) would be the general solution of the equation quoted above. In the following we shall proceed as if this assumption were proven already. For those cases which are of interest to us any possible errors will be small. However, the proofs which should be made at this point will be omitted because of their length. We will proceed as if they have been included. This means that equation (13) presents a solution to the problem only when $b \geq 1/e$ (compare (12)).

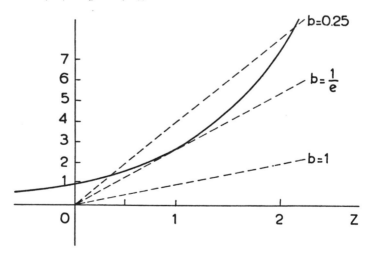

Fig. 3.

We must not forget that the solution of equation (8) which has been attempted with the help of equations (10) and (11′), is correct only if $y \neq 0$, *i.e.* if z is actually a complex figure.

If $y = 0$ and hence z is real, the division of equation 9B by 9A to get equation (10) is not permissible and the solution of (8) must be made directly. In this case it can be done quite simply (see Fig. 3).

If we write (8) thus

(8′)
$$\frac{z}{b} = e^z,$$

then the right-hand side in Fig. 3 is again represented by the drawn line and the left-hand side by the several dotted curves where b takes the values 1, $1/e \sim 0.37$ and 0.25. The figure shows that (8) has a real solution in cases where $b < 1/e$ applies, in other words where the complex solution does not exist. In general the equation actually has two roots: z' and z'', which coincide only for $b = 1/e$ in $z = 1$. In the above cases the following two terms take the place of the solution with $y < 2\pi$:

(14)
$$C'_1 e^{-\frac{z'_1}{\theta}t} + C''_1 e^{-\frac{z''_1}{\theta}t},$$

except for the border-line case of $b = 1/e$ where, according to a familiar theorem of linear differential equations, a in (14) reads instead:

(15)
$$(C'_1 + C''_1 t)e^{-\frac{t}{\theta}}.$$

With the same reservation made for equation (13) we will further assume that for cases where $b < 1/e$ or $b = 1/e$ the general solution is given through (13) except that instead of the terms for $k = 1$ we must read the terms under (14) and (15) respectively.

4. THE ECONOMIC SIGNIFICANCE OF THE SOLUTION

In the following we shall try to give an explanation of the most important features of equations (13), (14), (15) for economic theory and, in particular, the theory of trade cycles in nonmathematical terms. The fluctuations following the law of the "shipbuilding mechanism" are determined by:

1. the lag θ,
2. the intensity of reaction a,
3. the movement during an "initial period" from which point onward the mechanism has been undisturbed.

The movement is actually a combination of several elementary fluctuations from which it results by superposition. These elementary fluctuations are partly of a cyclical nature and partly consist of a unilateral approximation to a state of equilibrium. If the product (b) of lag period and reaction intensity exceeds 0.37, all components are cyclical.

The period of the cyclical components, *i.e.* the interval between two consecutive zero levels with equidirectional movement of the com-

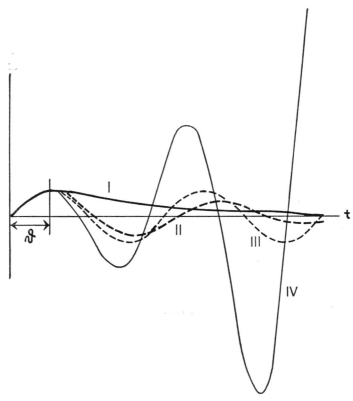

Fig. 4.

ponent in question, is dependent on only θ and a. One may say that it is inherent in the mechanism. There are a whole number of cycles beginning with the maximum period, whereas all further components show steadily decreasing periods. The length of the maximum period is at least equal to 2θ for cases where $b > 1/e$. The second lies always between θ and $\frac{2}{3}\theta$, the third between $\frac{1}{2}\theta$ and $\frac{2}{5}\theta$, the one in the order of $k+1$ between θ/k and $2\theta/2k+1$. For $b > 1/e$ the maximum period already lies between θ and $\frac{2}{3}\theta$, the one in the order of k between θ/k and $2\theta/2k+1$. The "initial development" (see under 2 above) determines the relative importance of the components. The importance of the bigger cycles will be greater if the smaller ones in the initial development are not recognizable. In the present case of shipbuilding the periods which are shorter than θ (= 2 years) in connection with the "mechanism" are probably insignificant.

Since, in general, the periods which are shorter than the lag period are of little interest we shall leave them out of our discussion.

The movement therefore presents itself as follows: if (1) b is smaller than $1/e$ (0.37) or equal to $1/e$ (0.37), in other words in the case of short lags and/or small intensity of reaction there is no cyclical motion, just a unilateral adaptation to the state of equilibrium $f(t) = 0$, i.e. to the trend. If (2) b lies between 0.37 and $\pi/2 \simeq 1.57$, then we get a damped sine wave, i.e. a gradual approximation to the state of equilibrium by the steadily decreasing amplitude of the fluctuations.

If (3) $b = \pi/2$, we get a pure sine wave, that is to say, a cyclic motion with constant amplitude. Finally, if (4) $b > \pi/2$, in other words exceeds 1.57, we get sine waves with amplitudes increasing in time. In the latter two cases therefore there is no approximation to a state of equilibrium.[10] Fig. 4 is a diagrammatical representation of a number of possible cases which are all based on the same initial development. The length of the period is for:

$$b < \frac{1}{e} : \infty,$$

$$\frac{1}{e} < b < \frac{\pi}{2} : > 4\theta,$$

[10] See also: U. RICCI, "Die synthetische Ökonomie von Henry Ludwell Moore", *Zeitschrift für Nationalökonomie*, Vienna, I (1929/30), p. 649 *sq.*

$$b = \frac{\pi}{2} : 4\theta,$$

$$\frac{\pi}{2} < b \quad : \; < 4\theta, \text{ but } > 2\theta,$$

that is four times the lag period in the case where we have pure sine waves, larger than four times the lag period in case of damped sine waves, and smaller (but not smaller than twice θ) in case of steadily increasing amplitudes. It seems to me that this result is of vital importance to the theory of economic dynamics. It permits remarkable conclusions about the relationships between the constants quoted above, particularly the significance of the intensity of reaction for the type and length of the waves. Moreover, it gives us a clue to a method of judging the stability of an economic system in general.

Its importance in the field of shipbuilding is in my opinion expressed in the statement that in shipbuilding an "endogenous" cycle of about eight years (since b is a value of between 2 and 1 which results in cycles of between 7.5 and 8.7 years) exists and that development showed a tendency to quieten down during the pre-war period (about 1900 when $b < \pi/2$, that is the second example given above).[11]

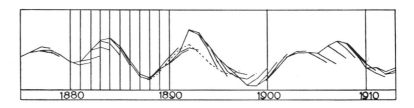

Fig. 5.

The reason why in the course of history this fact has not been recognized at all or at least only vaguely is explained on the one hand by the slow rate of decrease in amplitude and on the other hand by the fact that exogenous disturbances appear which change the total tonnage level. This is made clear in Fig. 5, where the thin curve represents

---

[11] This also means that at the same time the period of the fluctuation has a tendency to increase.

total tonnage during the years 1875 to 1913, and the thick curves indicate individual developments during a period of two years, which would for any given year be the combined result of the past two years' development and of the lag mechanism. The dotted curve illustrates the development over a period of 12 years which would have resulted from developments between 1885 and 1887 if during this entire period the mechanism had had an undisturbed effect.

As one can see from this figure, developments dependent on the mechanism and real developments coincide satisfactorily in most years, whereas in some years, *e.g.* in 1882, 1892 and 1905, there are distinct outside disturbances which can be attributed chiefly to general trade fluctuations. At the same time the graph permits an estimation of the relative importance of the "proper" shipbuilding cycle as opposed to general business cycles which are exogenous for shipbuilding.[12]

5. COMPARISON BETWEEN THE "SHIPBUILDING CYCLE" AND THE "PORK CYCLE"

After the discussion of the characteristics of the "shipbuilding cycle" it is profitable to draw a comparison between this cycle and the "pork cycle". The common feature of these two cycles is an endogenous movement which is caused by supply lagging behind price and influenced by the "reaction intensity" whereby supply responds to deviatons from the normal price.

The first difference lies in the relation between lag and period. In the pork cycle the period is exactly twice, in the shipbuilding cycle it is always more than twice, and in our example almost four times the lag. As can easily be seen, this difference is largely due to the fact that in the shipbuilding cycle it is the increase in tonnage which is significant. In the end the basic reason is that a ship is a durable good while a pig is more of a non-durable. Generally speaking we should therefore differentiate between durable good cycles

---

[12] The operation of the mechanism can also be detected fairly well in the postwar period (see other publications of the author) although not as distinctly as before the war. However, the time that elapsed since the war is a little too short to allow us to make a conclusive judgment.

and non-durable good cycles although the boundary is not clearly defined.[13]

Conceivably a second difference might be seen in the fact that in shipbuilding cycles the waves can be both undamped and damped. This difference, however, is not real; nor is another difference which could be mentioned, namely the existence of several periods in the shipbuilding industry compared to only one period in pork cycles. But if we analyse the pork cycle in a manner similar to the shipbuilding cycle, we will easily reach the conclusion that the "pork mechanism" corresponds to a damping or anti-damping as soon as the reaction intensity is smaller or larger respectively than the one causing the waves of constant amplitude. We also find that fluctuations with smaller periods can be generated by the mechanism, namely those with periods of $1/3$, $1/5$, $1/7$ *etc.* of the period of the "main cycle". These fluctuations, it seems to me, are of slight significance, just as in the case of the shipbuilding cycle. On the other hand, the interdependence between the rate of damping and the reaction intensity is of importance because it demonstrates that when the reaction intensity diminishes the amplitude can also diminish. This is already attempted in practice. Moreover, it can easily be proven that, contrary to what was demonstrated with regard to shipbuilding, the length of the lag is of no consequence to the degree of damping in the pork cycle.

---

[13] After writing the present article I also found that housing, *e.g.* in Hamburg, showed a similar durable good cycle. After 1900 the regular trade cycle is predominant. (*Cf.* K. HUNSCHA, "Die Dynamik des Baumarkts", *Vierteljahreshefte zur Konjunkturforschung*, Sonderh. 17, Berlin 1930).

TYPES OF EQUILIBRIUM AND BUSINESS-CYCLE MOVEMENTS*

1. In this article will be presented some remarks about the different types of positions of equilibrium between which we must distinguish in economic theory. The motive of these remarks can be found in the fact that business-cycle theory contains certain controversies, which —although actually existing—are seldom found clearly expressed. These controversies are caused by the important role that the position of equilibrium plays in business-cycle explanation; two viewpoints are in direct contradiction:

a. that business-cycle movement is a movement around a position of equilibrium;
b. that it is a movement between two consecutive positions of equilibrium.

The former opinion is implicit in many econometric business-cycle models;[1] the latter view is defended for instance, by GOUDRIAAN, although he makes only a casual reference to these problems.[2] On closer examination it appears that the different types of equilibrium must be analysed before a choice between these two viewpoints or a synthesis is possible.

2. Let us start with *the concept of equilibrium*. By a position of equilibrium we shall mean *an economic situation which remains unchanged, unless interference from outside takes place.* A priori *it is far from certain that any positions of equilibrium actually do exist.* Postulation of their existence assumes that all the characteristic magnitudes of the economy *can* actually be kept constant. Economic models can be

---

* Ligevægtstyper og Konjunkturbevægelse, Nordisk Tidsskrift for Teknisk Økonomi, 1944, pp. 45-63.

[1] I refer here to Kalecki's work and to my own contributions; there are many other examples as well.

[2] J. GOUDRIAAN, "De berekening van de omvang der werkloosheid als gevolg van prijsdaling in een gesloten economisch milieu", *De Economist* 83 (1934), p. 849.

constructed in which equilibrium appears to be impossible. An economy with a positive net investment can, in the most limited sense, never be in equilibrium. For, if the net investment is constant through time, the total stock of capital cannot also remain constant. These two conditions are incompatible with each other. We can take the liberty of assuming the existence of a position of equilibrium only if either the total stock of capital can be looked upon as irrelevant to the other economic magnitudes—and consequently need not be included in the model as a variable—, or if we are content with an approximation. In the following we shall assume the existence of a position of equilibrium.

The determination of the position of equilibrium of an economic system is based on certain *static* relationships between the variables that describe the system, *e.g.* static supply and demand functions. For example, if we put demand equal to supply in a single market, we obtain specific values for the price, p, and for the quantity sold, u. Once having assumed certain values, these magnitudes will remain constant as long as no interference from outside takes place.

3. What will happen, however, if a disturbance occurs? It may have different results, and it is by means of these results that we distinguish between different *types of position of equilibrium*. The distinction between *stable* and *unstable* equilibrium is generally known. However, there are other types which should be added to the list. We talk about a stable equilibrium in cases where, after a disturbance, there occurs a movement back towards the original position of equilibrium, and about an unstable equilibrium if the result is a further movement away from this position. Thus to determine the type of equilibrium we must know the movements of the system, *i.e.* we must know its dynamic characteristics. Static characteristics are not sufficient in this case. However, we often meet the opposite opinion in text books, where certain *assumptions* regarding the dynamics of the system are easily made. An example is the well-known sentence, that there will be stable equilibrium in the single market when and only when the slope of the supply curve with the p-axis is denoted by a *algebraically* bigger number than the slope of the demand curve. This statement is wrong, if we describe the dynamics of the market by

means of the well-known cob web theorem. For in this case it is essential, in order to obtain a stable equilibrium, that the absolute value of the slope of the supply curve is smaller than the absolute value of the slope of the demand curve.

Thus we must study the dynamics of the system more carefully in order to reach a better understanding of the types of equilibrium. By doing so it will become clear to us that even the simplest hypothesis regarding the movement will lead to an abundance of new possibilities. But as long as it cannot be settled empirically which among the possible assumptions corresponds best to the reality of a given problem, it is rather aimless to lose oneself in the consequences of the more complicated hypotheses.

4. Any movement in an economic system in a state of equilibrium arises by a departure from the original position of equilibrium. For it follows from our definition of the concept of equilibrium that no movement could possibly begin without such a departure. The best-known examples of such disturbances are those caused by abnormal agricultural crops, changes in economic policy, new technical inventions, *etc.* The further development of the movement until a new external disturbance takes place—the so-called *endogenous* part of the movement—is now dependent on the way in which the economic system will react. Thus a sequence of interdependent situations develops, every new situation being dependent upon the preceding. Dynamics is characterized in this way; without this interdependency the dynamic analysis would be superfluous and static theory would be sufficient to describe the phenomena.

5. The different forms of dynamic development depend upon the complexity of the assumptions. The simplest model is obtained, when every situation is dependent only on the proceding one. The next group of models are those where every situation is dependent on the two previous ones, and so on. This presupposes that we work with unit periods of a finite length, throughout which the economic magnitudes are assumed to be constant.

As an example we can choose the following simple model of a closed economy, where only two variables are of importance, *viz.* real income, y, and real expenditure (for consumption and net investment), u. We find that the income of the unit period of time t is equal to the expenditure; that is

(1) $y_t = u_t,$

while the expenditure u_t is directly dependent on the income of the proceding period, y_{t-1}:

(2) $u_t = ay_{t-1} + c,$

By analogy with the Keynesian concepts, we could now call a the marginal "propensity to spend". It is easy to express the position of equilibrium and the dynamic qualities of this model graphically (Fig. 1). If, for a moment, we disregard differences in time, we can measure y along the horizontal, u along the vertical axis and then draw both functions as straight lines. The straight line OR, which forms an angle of 45° with the axes, shows "the income-formation function" (1), while the straight line ST forms "the expenditure function" (2). As regards the latter function we can distinguish between several cases, according to whether $a \gtrless 1$ (with the limiting case $a = 1$) and according to whether the point of intersection S has got positive or negative co-ordinates (with the limiting case when the co-ordinates of S are 0,0). (In Fig. 1 only the two cases with positive co-ordinates are shown.) There exists only one point of equilibrium *viz.* the point of intersection S. As soon as another situation occurs, for instance if $y = y_1$, a movement will set in. The value of u_2 is obtained by substituting y_1 in equation (2), whereafter the value found for u_2 is used to obtain y_2 from equation (1); we then get u_3 from (2) by insertion of y_2 and so on.

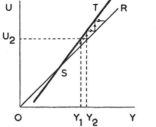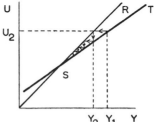

Fig. 1

If $a > 1$ the system will work itself away from the initial position; if, however, $a < 1$ it will gradually approach the point S. This can be easily shown algebraically, using the transformation:

$$y' = y - y_s \quad \text{and} \quad u' = u - u_s$$

when y_s and u_s are the co-ordinates of the point S. In this way the equations (1) and (2) are changed into

(1')
$$y_t' = u_t'$$
and

(2')
$$u_t' = a y_{t-1}'$$
so that

(3')
$$y_t' = a y_{t-1}'.$$

This equation, in which only one of the two variables occurs, we will term *the final equation*. It is, as we shall see, of decisive importance for determining how the system will react.

If we let y_0' denote the initial situation then:

(4)
$$y_1' = a y_0'; \quad y_2' = a^2 y_0' \ldots\ldots y_t' = a^t y_0'.$$

We thus see that an approximation to the equilibrium takes place for $a < 1$; the equilibrium is in this case *a stable* one. On the other hand a continued movement away from the initial position will take place if $a > 1$ (*unstable* equilibrium). In the intermediate case, when $a = 1$, we must distinguish between $c = 0$ and $c \neq 0$. For $c = 0$ the two functions (1) and (2) are identical; there are infinitely many points of intersection and each one of these constitutes a position of equilibrium. This is an indifferent equilibrium.

The formulae derived above have economic meaning only if they lead to positive values of the original co-ordinates (*i.e.* the co-ordinates before the transformation occurred). We shall not enter here into a discussion regarding the complications we should have to introduce if negative values appeared.

Furthermore, we must stress that the position of equilibrium S is characterized by the equivalence of income and expenditure, *i.e.* that there is neither positive or negative hoarding. This equilibrium we shall call *the Keynes equilibrium*.

6. The number of possibilities is increased considerably when we pass on to the second group of equations, *i.e.* when we assume that every situation is dependent on the *two* preceding situations. The final equation then assumes the form:

(5) $$y'_t = ay'_{t-1} - by'_{t-2}.$$

Several different economic interpretations of this equation are possible. The best one seems to us to be the following: expenditure is dependent on income and on the rate of increase of income, but with a certain time lag, that is

$$y'_t = a'y'_{t-1} + b(y'_{t-1} - y'_{t-2}).$$

This expression is identical with (5) if we put:

$$a = a' + b.$$

A dependence on the increase of income can occur not only directly, but also indirectly through the fact that expenditure is directly dependent on price increases (gains from speculation), while prices move parallel to income.[3]

It is easy to show that all sorts of movements now can take place. The solution of this difference equation is reached by putting:

(6) $$y'_t = Cx^t,$$

in which way (S) is changed into:

(7) $$Cx^t - a\,Cx^{t-1} + b\,Cx^{t-2} = 0.$$

We can thus choose the value of C arbitrarily; y' will be a solution only if x satisfies the "characteristic equation"

(8) $$x^2 - ax + b = 0.$$

This equation has two roots x_1 and x_2:

(9) $$x_1 = \frac{a}{2} + \sqrt{\frac{a^2}{4} - b} \quad \text{and} \quad x_2 = \frac{a}{2} - \sqrt{\frac{a^2}{4} - b}$$

which satisfy the original equation (5), but also every sum

(10) $$y'_t = C_1 x_1^t + C_2 x_2^t.$$

The reader can convince himself of this by carrying out the com-

---

[3] See also my analysis: *Business Cycles in the U.S.A.* 1919–1932, League of Nations, Geneva 1939.

putations. Furthermore, it can be proved that an expression with two arbitrary constants must be the most general solution of equation (5). For in this way we can freely choose two values of y' (*i.e.* by appropriate choice of the constants). A free choice of more y'-values is excluded, however. From the original equation we can immediately see that on the basis of any two values of y', for instance y'_0 and y'_1, all further values of y' are determined. For that reason (10) is the most general solution of (5).

Those types of movements that can be produced from the latter equation are dependent on the numerical values of x_1 and x_2, which are either both real numbers or both complex numbers; in the latter case they are conjugate complex numbers.

This occurs if

$$b > \frac{a^2}{4}.$$

In order that we can then obtain real y'-values, C_1 and C_2 must also have conjugate complex values; then we can write y' in the form:

(11)
$$y'_t = C \sqrt{b^t} \sin \frac{2 \pi (t - t_0)}{T}.$$

C and t_0 are now the arbitrary constants. T is dependent on the constants of the given equation in the following way:

(12)
$$T = \frac{2 \pi}{\text{arc tg} \dfrac{\sqrt{\dfrac{a^2}{4} - b}}{\dfrac{a}{2}}},$$

T is the period of the sinus function contained in (11). It can assume any value between 0 and ∞, depending on the pair of values a and b. The movements represented by (11) are strictly periodical fluctuations for $b = 1$, with a period T. For $b < 1$ they are damped periodical and for $b > 1$ they are negatively damped or "explosive".

If $b < a^2/4$, both x_1 and x_2 are real. It is now of interest whether these roots of the characteristic equation are negative, positive < 1 or > 1. A negative value corresponds to a zigzag movement, which can be either undamped, damped, or explosive, depending on whether

$x_1 \lesseqgtr 1$. However, negative values of either of the two roots never correspond to positive values of a and b. If one of the roots were negative, b would have to be negative, and if they were both negative, a would have to be negative. A positive value smaller than one corresponds to a unilateral movement towards an equilibrium, and a value bigger than one corresponds to a movement away from the equilibrium. In general, the values of x_1 and x_2 can fall in any one of these three intervals; thus any combination of the three types of movement mentioned above can occur, *e.g.* a damped zigzag movement and a movement away from the equilibrium, if

$$-1 < x_1 < 0 \qquad \text{and} \qquad x_2 > 1.$$

Here we must add that a combination of two movements of the latter type cannot have a single turning-point. In our case, however, (when a and b are positive) the zigzag components cannot occur, as we said before.

Finally we shall refer also to the case when

$$C = \frac{a^2}{4}.$$

The two roots x_1 and x_2 are equal in this case, and the movement of y_t' is described by

(13) $$y_t' = C_1 x_1^t + C_2 t x_1^t.$$

By the abundance of possible movements we can again classify the equilibria corresponding with them. Where only damped or equilibrium-directed components of movement occur the equilibrium is evidently stable; but if any one of the components shows a unilateral movement away from the equilibrium, the equilibrium is unstable, for eventually this component will lead to a movement away from equilibrium. The same holds true in the presence of an explosive periodical component. But here we get a new type with undamped periodical movement or oscillation. In this case neither a constant removal from nor any approach to the equilibrium occurs. We call this form a *semi-stable* equilibrium.

7. Till now our reflections regarded only cases with one single

equilibrium position. By introducing the possibility of several positions of equilibrium, we reach important new insight.[4]

This complication is indispensable for the discussion of our subject since our problem is whether the business cycle is a movement between two points of equilibrium, or movement about a single point of equilibrium as mentioned at the beginning. The possibility of several equilibrium positions is excluded as long as we work only with linear relations between the variables. If the straight lines in Fig. 1 had been curved, more points of intersection would have been possible, but

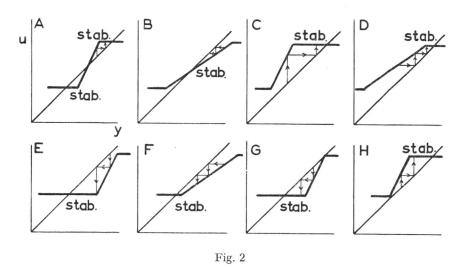

Fig. 2

not al all certain. But the main thing which interests us is whether such a plurality of equilibria actually occurs. Certain hints of such a supposition we find in GOUDRIAAN.[5]

His thinking might be summarized in the following way: real expenditure has both a certain maximum value and a certain minimum

---

[4] J. G. KOOPMANS has already indicated this possibility in his treatise: "De mogelijkheid van meervoudig economisch evenwicht", *De Economist* par. 1, (1932), p. 679, 766 and par. 41. A. WALD has contributed essentially to the solution of this problem in: "Über einige Gleichungssysteme der mathematischen Ökonomie", *Zeitschrift für Nationalök.* VII (1936), p. 637.

[5] *Op. cit.*

value. The maximum value is determined by the capacity limit of production, the minimum value by the subsistence level of consumption and the necessary capital replacement. Even if real income, for some reason or other, should exceed this maximum or fall under this minimum, real expenditure would still remain within these limits. If income does not cover the subsistence level, borrowing will be the result. In consequence the straight expenditure line ST will, in principle, change into a broken line with two horizontal parts (Fig. 2). We shall now investigate the consequences of this change of form for the movements of the system. This can be done by simple mathematical operations if we use the discontinuous form of the curve. In reality the curve is likely to be continuous, because not all firms reach their capacity limit, and not all families reach their minimum level of subsistence at the very same moment. But if we had to take this into account the mathematical treatment would become much more complicated, without changing the basic result.

8. Let us first see how the first model, shown in Fig. 1, now behaves. All possible cases are shown in Fig. 2. The direction of the movement is again denoted by arrows. We see that in case A three positions of equilibrium appear, two of which, the extreme ones, are stable, whereas the one in the middle is unstable. We shall call the stable positions the Goudriaan-equilibria. This case corresponds to the case of the unstable equilibrium in Fig. 1. The introduction of a maximum and a minimum has thus had important consequences.

Just as before we find only one position of equilibrium in case B, and that a stable one. In both these cases the Keynes-point lies between the Goudriaan-points. However it is also conceivable that it lies outside both of these. In that case the examples C–F will appear. Here we still get only one position of equilibrium, a stable one. In addition there are the two limiting cases G and H, where the Keynes-point coincides with one of the two Goudriaan-points. These are especially interesting because of the nature of these points of coincidence. For deviations to one side they are stable positions of equilibrium, for deviations to the other side unstable, and in such a way that the positions are unstable for disturbances in the direction of the other equilibrium, stable for disturbances in the opposite direction. This sort of equilibria, whose importance for business-cycle explanation has already been stressed by KALDOR,[6] we shall name *mixed* equilibria.

In spite of the enrichment of the picture of movements, which is obtained by the development of the theory of the Goudriaan-points, it is not possible to use the models of the first class for the explanation of business cycles, because in these theories every situation is dependent only on the one preceding situation. Thus is illustrated by Fig. 3, where the path of the several possible movements is shown. The letters correspond to those of Fig. 2. Thus not all cases of Fig. 2 have been taken into consideration; the reader might add the rest for himself. The dotted lines denote the position of the Goudriaan-points and the Keynes-point. In case A the Goudriaan-points are stable equilibria. The endogenous movements are thus steadily directed towards this equilibrium. Once the system is in equilibrium it can leave it again only if disturbed by outside forces, and if the disturbance is a small one the system will always return to the same equilibrium. A movement from one Goudriaan-point to the other will take place only if there occurs a disturbance strong enough to carry the system across the Keynes-point. We must think of a business cycle as a movement from the upper equilibrium to the lower one, and back again; we have

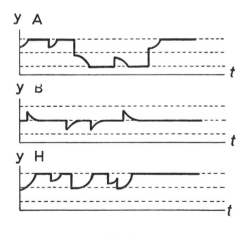

Fig. 3

[6] N. KALDOR, "A Model of the Trade Cycle", *Economic Journal*, L (1940), p. 79.

just seen that this only can happen if a sudden fall or rise occurs carrying the system over the Keynes-point. This sort of a movement is, however, unrealistic.

In case B matters are quite different, but also unrealistic. Only movements towards the Keynes-point can occur. After any disturbance from outside, the movement whether it is up or down, proceeds toward the dotted line in the middle. Thus this sort of model can not be used either as an explanation of business-cycle movements.

In the same way the reader can convince himself that none of the equations of the first group, shown in Fig. 2, contribute to the explanation of business cycles.

9. Consequently we must direct our attention to *the models of the second group, i.e.* those in which we assume that every situation is dependent on two preceding situations. We assume the existence of a Goudriaan-maximum and a Goudriaan-minimum and further it is assumed that *the maximum lies above and the minimum below the Keynes-point.* This means that income y_t is determined by equation (5):

$$(14) \qquad\qquad y_t = ay_{t-1} - by_{t-2},$$

as long as we do not get values above y^0 or below $y^{0\prime}$, where y^0 is the Goudriaan maximum and $y^{0\prime}$ the Goudriaan minimum. If we obtain such extreme values they must be replaced by y^0 and $y^{0\prime}$ instead of

$$ay_{t-1} - by_{t-2}.$$

In equation (14) we have removed the prime after y_{t-1}. That means that we measure income from the Keynes-equilibrium, or in other words, that the Keynes-equilibrium lies at the income level of 0. This is just a matter of measurement. For the moment we put $y^0 >$ and $y^{0\prime} < 0$.

We shall now systematically study the movements of our model, in relation to the values of the two coefficients a and b.

As mentioned above it is necessary to solve the characteristic equation (8); the roots are given by (9). These roots are apparently complex if, and only if, $b > a^2/4$ or $a < 2\sqrt{b}$; if we illustrate all possible pairs of values a, b graphically in the plane of Fig. 4, those pairs of values when $a < 2\sqrt{b}$ will be represented by all the points below the parabola OPN. Thus above this parabola we find only the a-b-values that lead to real roots. According to our previous assumption, for positive values of a and b the roots are also positive. It is also of importance whether the roots are $\leqq 1$; let us investigate in which sectors of the a-b-plane this is the case.

(15) $\qquad\qquad x \gtrless 1$, when $\sqrt{\dfrac{a^2}{4} - b} \gtrless 1 - \dfrac{a}{2}.$

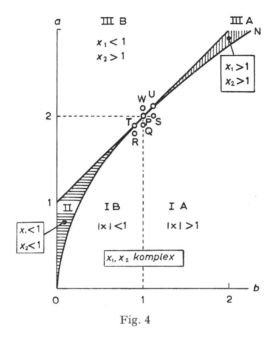

Fig. 4

Here we must distinguish between two cases, $viz.$ $a > 2$ and $a < 2$. For $a > 2$ we have $1 - \dfrac{a}{2} < 0$ and thus always $\sqrt{\dfrac{a^2}{4} - b} > 1 - \dfrac{a}{2}$ or $x_1 > 1$. For $a < 2$, however, we have $x_1 \gtrless 1$ depending on whether $\dfrac{a^2}{4} - b \gtrless 1 - a + \dfrac{a^2}{4}$ or $a \lessgtr b + 1$.

Thus all points above the line $a = b + 1$ represent, for a-values smaller than 2, pairs of values (a, b) with $x_1 > 1$; and all points below this line represent pairs of values with $x_1 < 1$; the latter is true, however, only as long as the points are lying above the parabola. The distribution of the points over the plane is shown by Fig. 4. In the same way we find the distribution of the x_2-values; all results are given in Fig. 4. In this we see that in sector II both roots are real and < 1 and thus both components of movements are directed towards the Keynes-equilibrium: this equilibrium is here a *stable* one. But in sector III at least one of the roots is > 1 (in sector IIIA even both), and consequently the movements are directed away from this equilibrium: the Keynes-equilibrium is *unstable*.

10. The next question is: are the Goudriaan-points also equilibrium positions?

In order to answer this question we must investigate whether the system, once having reached such a point, will stay there, *e.g.*, if first we have $y_{t-1} = y_{t-2} = y^0$ will we also get $y_t = y^0$.

This requires that either

(16)
$$ay^0 - by^0 = y^0$$

or

(17)
$$ay^0 - by^0 > y^0 \quad \text{if} \quad y^0 > 0$$

or finally

(18)
$$ay^0 - by^0 < y^0 \quad \text{if} \quad y^0 < 0.$$

These conditions are equivalent to

$$a - b \lessgtr 1 \quad \text{or} \quad a \lessgtr b + 1.$$

The equality holds good for the straight line; the inequality for all points above this line. *We thus find that the Goudriaan-points are equilibrium positions if the Keynes-equilibrium is unstable.* But this conclusion only holds good in the cases where the Keynes-point is lying between the two Goudriaan-points.

11. Eventually we shall investigate different kinds of the Goudriaan-equilibrium. Here we must first answer the following question:

Which movement sets in if the system makes a small departure δ from the point in question? The initial values of this movement are $y_0 = y^0$, $y_1 = y^0 - \delta$; which means that the constants A and B must satisfy the condition

(19)
$$y^0 = Ax_1^0 + Bx_2^0 = A + B$$

and

(20) $$y^0 - \delta = Ax_1^1 + Bx_2^1 = Ax_1 + Bx_2.$$

In principle the nature of the movement is the same for the Keynes- and the Goudriaan-equilibrium and only dependent on x_1 and x_2. In the cases when the Goudriaan-point represents a position of equilibrium, which thus means if $a \geq b + 1$, we always get $x_1 > 1, x_2 < 1$ (except for the case $a = b + 1$ to which we shall return later on) and as a rule the components corresponding to x_1 make the equilibria unstable. But the matter is actually changed for the Goudriaan-points, because certain movements are "prohibited", *viz.* movements upwards at the upper point and downwards movements at the lower point. If, for certain initial values of y_1 the components directed away from the equilibrium take the prohibited direction, they will fall away and they will—*for these initial values*—change the equilibrium into a stable one.

This state of affairs is characterized by A's assuming positive values in the foregoing formulae. But if A has a negative value the equilibrium remains stable. From (19) and (20) we find that:

(21) $$A = \frac{y^0 (1 - x_2) - \delta}{x_1 - x_2}.$$

In order to get $A \gtrless 0$, we must have either $y^0(1 - x_2) - \delta \gtrless 0$

or

(22) $$\frac{\delta}{y_0} \lessgtr 1 - x_2.$$

If thus the system gets a small deflection from the Goudriaan-equilibrium, a movement starts towards the equilibrium position and the original equilibrium is a stable one; for greater departures it is unstable, however. The critical value of this departure lies at $(1 - x_2)y^0$, and is thus proportional to the distance from the Goudriaan-point to the Keynes-point. The factor of proportionality $1 - x_2$ can assume all possible values between 1 and 0, and it assumes the smallest of these if $x_2 \sim 1$, which is in the neighbourhood of the line $a = b + 1$. Such an equilibrium—the nature of which is dependent on the size of the deflections—we shall call a *meta-stable* equilibrium, by analogy with the physical equilibrium of the oversaturated solution: this situation survives small departures but in case of greater departures a sudden crystallization takes place.

Further it is seen from (22) that no critical value exists for $x_2 > 1$, that means in sector IIIA; thus all movements are "unstable" in that sector.

12. Our results may be illustrated by the computation of a few examples, the graphical representation of which is to be seen in the Figs. 5 and 6. Fig. 5 refers to the movements of the different models the a-b-pairs of values of which are denoted by the letters Q, R, S, T, U, and W in Fig. 4.

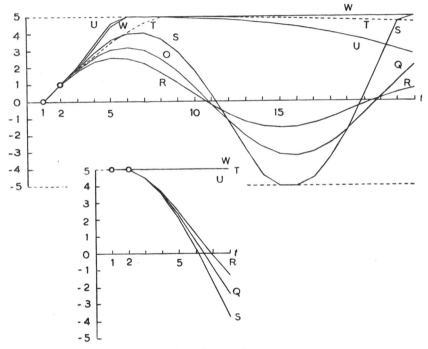

Figs. 5a and 5b.

The initial values are 0 and 1 for the curves of the upper half of Fig. 5, and 5, 5 for the curves of the lower half. For both halves the numerical value of 5 has been chosen for y^0 and $y_1^{0\prime}$ thus $y^0 = 5$ and $y^{0\prime} = -5$.

The *a-b*-values are :

Model	Q	R	S	T	U	W
a	1.9	1.8	2.0	1.899	2.098	2.04
b	1.0	0.9	1.1	0.9	1.1	1.0

The choice has been made in such a way that Q, R, and S lie in the first section, and also in such a way that Q shows an undamped, R a damped, and S an explosive movement; further T lies in section II, U in IIIA and W in IIIB. Accordingly, the curve W, for which the Goudriaan-point is a position of stable equilibrium, will lie in this level (since we assume that no shocks from outside occur). But the curves T and U, for which the point is not a position of stable equilibrium, will slowly return. Without the existence of the Goudriaan-maximum these curves would by degrees have moved away from the zero-point (the Keynes-point). But the curve S would have shown a periodical movement without the presence of the Goudriaan-points, although with a steadily growing amplitude. This latter, of course remains $\leq$ 5.

Fig. 6 shows the behaviour of model W after shocks of different sizes. For initial departures of the sizes 0.5 and 0.8, the system returns to its starting point. This is not the case for departures of the sizes 1.0 and 1.5.

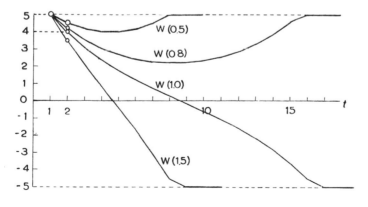

Fig. 6.

13. We shall now look at some *special cases*, the first of which is the case when $a = b + 1$. According to our results in section 10 any position is now a position of equilibrium; any position is stable as long as new shocks do not occur. The characteristic equation now runs: $x^2 - (b + 1)\, x + b = 0$ and we have:

$$x_1 = b \quad \text{and} \quad x_2 = 1 \quad \text{for} \quad b > 1$$
$$x_1 = 1 \quad \text{and} \quad x_2 = b \quad \text{for} \quad b < 1$$

for $b > 1$ we get $\delta/y^0 = A\,(1 - b) < 0$.

Thus no critical value exists here, *i.e.* all equilibria are *unstable*.

Whereas for $b < 1$ the general form of the movements is given by

$$(23) \qquad\qquad y = A + Bb^t$$

and any equilibrium is thus stable.

Next we shall study the still more particular case $a = 2$, $b = 1$. Here the two roots coincide and both are equal to one. Using equation (13) we now have $y = (A + Bt)x_1^t$, which in this case may be simplified to

$$(24) \qquad\qquad y_t = A + Bt.$$

This result is quite evident, for we can now write the difference equation:

$$(25) \qquad\qquad y_t = y_{t-1} + (y_{t-1} - y_{t-2}),$$

that is the increase $y_t - y_{t-1}$ is equal to the preceding increase $y_{t-1} - y_{t-2}$; it thus describes a straight line. This movement is of course broken only if a Goudriaan-point is reached. The movement is then changed into a horizontal one, until a new departure from the Goudriaan-point occurs. Then a straight-line movement to the other side continues until the next shock from outside occurs.

14. Till now we have assumed that the Keynes-point was lying between the two Goudriaan-points, corresponding to the sections A and B in Fig. 2. We shall now assume that *the Keynes-point is lying outside both the Goudriaan-points*. This is equivalent to the supposition that the signs of y^0 and $y^{0'}$ are equal. The condition that a point with a positive $y^{0'}$ is a position of equilibrium is now:

$$(26) \qquad\qquad ay^{0'} - by^{0'} \leqq y^{0'} \quad \text{or} \quad a \leqq b + 1.$$

We get the same condition that a point with a negative y^0 can be a position of equilibrium. This condition is thus not fulfilled if the condition of equilibrium is satisfied for the other Goudriaan-point, and *vice versa*. We thus find that in these models without any Keynes-point *only one of the two Goudriaan-points can be a position of equilibrium.*

Let us now see what sort of equilibrium this is. As we have seen earlier, the condition (26) is satisfied in the sectors I, II, and IIIA. These require a special treatment. In sector I any movement is periodic. If thus the system gets a shock from outside away from the position y^0, it will theoretically start a movement, which automatically returns to the lower Goudriaan-point, if the upper Goudriaan-point is not reached. If the upper point is reached the movement will also return, because the upper point is not a point of equilibrium. Since all movements setting out from the lower point will automatically return, it is a stable equilibrium.

For sector III somewhat the same holds true; here the movement returns immediately after the shock has been given, since we find here only movements directed towards the Keynes-equilibrium. Here the upper Goudriaan-point can only be reached if the shock carries the system directly to it.

But in sector IIIA we can also get movements directed away from the equilibrium. Here again we must analyse the movements more closely. If the system gets a shock δ away from the position $y_t = y^{0\prime}$ the initial values are $y_0 = y^{0\prime}$ and $y_1 = y^{0\prime} + \delta$ and we have

$$y^{0\prime} = A + B$$

$$y^{0\prime} + \delta = A x_1 + B x_2$$

which yields us:

(27) $\qquad A = \dfrac{-y^{0\prime}(x_2 - 1) + \delta}{x_1 - x_2} \quad$ and $\quad B = \dfrac{y^{0\prime}(x_1 - 1) - \delta}{x_1 - x_2}$

Here $x_1 - x_2$, $x_1 - 1$, and $x_2 - 1$ all are positive values, as well as $y^{0\prime}$ and δ. We must now distinguish between the three following cases:

a) $\delta < y^{0\prime}(x_2 - 1) < y^{0\prime}(x_1 - 1)$, which involves $A < 0$, $B > 0$:

b) $y^{0\prime}(x_2 - 1) < \delta < y^{0\prime}(x_1 - 1)$, which involves $A > 0$, $B > 0$ and

c) $y^{0\prime}(x_2 - 1) < y^{0\prime}(x_1 - 1) < \delta$ which involves $A > 0$, $B < 0$.

In case b) the movement is directed away from the equilibrium. A movement with a turning point can occur only if the negative component dominates in the long run; this is possible only for the component Ax_1^t, because $x_1 > x_2$ and thus in the long run we always get $|A| x_1^t > Bx_2^t$; a movement of this sort is thus possible only in case a). This means that in reality we have found another critical value of δ, viz.

(28) $$\delta = y^{0\prime} (x_2 - 1).$$

If the shock assumes values smaller than this, it will have as a consequence a movement automatically returning towards the equilibrium; values bigger than (28) result in a steady movement away from the equilibrium.

In the limiting case when $y^{0\prime} = 0$, *i.e.* where the lower Goudriaan-point coincides with the Keynes-point, the abovementioned results are changed as follows: the lower Goudriaan-point is now a general position of equilibrium, in sector iiiB, however, it is unstable. In the sectors iA and ii the equilibrium is always stable, and in sector iB the movements are certainly returning, but they are not damped. In sector iiiA, at length, the formula (27) is changed in such a way (y^0 falls away) that of the three possibilities *a*, *b*, and *c* only the last one is left, which means that we get an unstable equilibrium here also.

15. We are now able to take a survey of the abundance of possible movements that are derived from the theories of the second group, under the assumption of Goudriaan-points. We shall thus have to distinguish between models with:

    i. Keynes-Point Between the Goudriaan-Points and
    ii. Keynes-Point Outside the Goudriaan-Points.

i. Here we have models with:

a) *a stable Keynes-point*. In that case the Goudriaan-points are not equilibrium positions. These systems always have a tendency to reverse the direction of the movement as soon as they have reached a Goudriaan-point. If they belong to sector ii, the Goudriaan-points can be reached only by shocks that take the systems all the way to these positions, because all endogenous movements are directed towards the

Keynes-point. If the system belongs to sector I then automatic turning-points can also occur before the Goudriaan-points are reached; in sector II this can only take place because of shocks from outside which make the movement turn. In addition we have:

b) *models with an unstable Keynes-point.* Here the Goudriaan-points are meta-stable equilibria. These models thus have a tendency to remain in the Goudriaan-points. A lasting movement out from these points can occur only as a result of bigger shocks which carry the system over to the other equilibrium. There is no automatic return from the boom or the slump.

The models in I all have a similarity between boom and depression; this is lacking in the models in II. Here only one of the two positions is stable or meta-stable; the other is not an equilibrium at all. If both Goudriaan-points lie above the Keynes-point the position of equilibrium is the upper point in sector IIIB and the lower point in the other sector. In sector IIIB this position is meta-stable, stable in the sectors I and II, and again meta-stable in IIIA. If, however both Goudriaan-points are located under the Keynes-point, the upper and the lower Goudriaan-points change roles.

If we look at the historical data of business cycles, it is difficult to assume the existence of an evident asymmetry between the upper and the lower turning points. We cannot assert that there is a general tendency to remain in the upper points and no such tendency for the lower points; neither can we assert the opposite. In my opinion it is better to conclude that a significant tendency to remain in equilibrium does not appear at all. This leads us to the models in I, *i.e.* the models in which the presence of the Goudriaan-points is only of secondary importance. Here their only function is to set a limit to the amplitude of the movement in the cases in which—due to abnormally strong shocks or antidamping—there is a tendency to excessive deviation.

We think, that this opinion is also stressed by attempts to base models on statistically discovered relationships. However, it would lead us too far afield to discuss this point of view in this article. In conclusion we must add some final remarks about *the explanation of the turning-points.* Summarizing our reasoning, there are three types of turning-points, *viz.*:

1. *the perfectly endogenous:* those that occur without any shocks from outside and without the presence of a Goudriaan-point;
2. *the extended endogenous:* those that occur without any shocks from outside as a consequence of the presence of a Goudriaan-point;
3. *the exogenous:* those that are caused by shocks from outside.

Formulated mathematically the perfectly endogenous turning-points can occur if all relations are linear, and no shocks take place; the extended endogenous turning-points can be obtained if certain relations are non-linear, and the exogenous ones only if shocks occur. For laymen the exogenous turning-points are the easiest to "explain"; the shock is "the cause". After these the extended endogenous types are the simplest for laymen and non-mathematical economists; in explanation we can always refer to the economic phenomena which lead to the Goudriaan-points, for instance the existence of a limited capacity and so on. The most difficult ones to "explain" verbally are the perfectly endogenous turning-points. This is perhaps the reason why they have claimed so little attention in literary theory, in spite of the fact that they are likely to be of the utmost importance for the understanding of economic dynamics.

AN ECONOMIC POLICY FOR 1936*

1. INTERPRETATION OF THE PROBLEM

As the question submitted indicates we wish to ascertain whether a recovery in the domestic economic situation is liable to occur in this country as a result of certain causes and conditions which we will discuss later. The general expression "economic recovery" can be interpreted in various ways. In the following we will mean by this expression an expansion of employment unless otherwise expressly stated. Undoubtedly other interpretations are also possible. Several of these would lead to approximately the same conclusions regarding the question to be answered in this report. Employment was chosen as the symptom of economic recovery because, in my opinion, it is particularly important that employment should expand. In the present social system the highest employment possible is the best guarantee that prosperity will be as great as possible and as widespread as possible.[1] If we are concerned only that prosperity be as great as possible, the level of the consumption of consumer goods could be used to indicate economic progress. It is still possible, however, that consumption can be at a relatively high level but also be very unequally distributed between families.

The improvement in the economic situation discussed above, if it does occur, will be the consequence of either the conscious aim of certain governmental measures or of the economic actions of the private entrepreneurs. Apparently it is not the intention

---

* This chapter is a translation of the paper read before the Dutch Economic Association (Vereeniging voor de Staathuishoudkunde) on the question: "Is a recovery in the domestic economic situation of this country possible, with or without action on the part of the Government, even without an improvement in our export position? What can be learned about this problem from the experience of other countries?"

[1] This expression is somewhat inaccurate because usually it will not be possible to make prosperity both as great and as widespread as possible. I adhere to the existing terminology for convenience's sake because no great damage ensues.

of the Committee of our association to pay a great deal of attention to the method by which the improvement is to be achieved. The method which we will develop here makes it possible to analyse both of these cases. The most important point, however, is to determine whether an improvement which begins domestically will be able to continue, more particularly whether the need to maintain a favourable balance of payments is an obstacle. Accordingly the original cause of the revival is of less importance than the side conditions under which it can occur. It seems to me that the primary task of this report is to indicate the measures which, playing the part of a side condition, give the strongest support to the recovery once it has begun.

With regard to the first it is taken for granted that it consists of carrying out public works on a large scale, *e.g.* as is now taking place by means of the Working Fund but conceivably that "activating" can be accomplished by other methods; *e.g.* by means of a further wage reduction, by devaluation or by the state borrowing on a larger scale for its ordinary expenditures. Without commenting on their efficacy I just mention a few measures which have been recommended by others. Also these activating measures can be analysed by means of the method we will develop. A few examples will also be given. Furthermore the reader will be able to combine a number of cases himself with the aid of the tables.

In the question one side condition has already been imposed, *i.e.* that the export position does not improve. For convenience's sake I assume that it remains at the same level. However, we must outline exactly what we mean by the term future export position. I see two interpretations: In the first place that, at an unchanged price level of our export products, the demand for them abroad remains the same. This means that, if that price level is reduced, more products can be sold on the free markets. Another interpretation would be that the quantity of goods which can be sold abroad would be fixed and no larger sales would ensue in spite of improved competitive potentialities. This might be the case if all countries were alloted quotas for all export products without exception and those quotas could not be increased. Although this assumption seems unrealistic it will also be briefly discussed in order to illustrate the most unfavourable case. As a rule we will take the first of these two interpretations as starting point.

2. OUTLINE OF THE DIRECTION WHICH OUR INVESTIGATION WILL FOLLOW

The background of the question as asked by the Committee is probably the widely prevailing opinion that any measure creating a domestic upturn has the tendency to render the continuation of the improvement impossible. These objections against such measures are formulated in several ways; first, greater imports of raw materials are only possible through larger exports, otherwise they endanger the balance of payments and in consequence the credit system. Secondly: the domestic revival increases the price level at home and thus creates difficulties for the export industries. In answer to the first objection we propose the following alternative methods of ensuring the continuation of the improvement in the level of employment:

a) additional imports of raw materials are paid for by means of sales of gold and securities abroad; thereby maintaining free enterprise in production and trade at the existing level and also the existing gold parity of the guilder;

b) additional imports of raw materials are paid for by compulsorily limiting imports of finished products, either by quotas or by increasing domestic production efficiency to such an extent that certain domestic products become considerably cheaper and oust the foreign products. In this case the gold parity of the guilder will also be maintained;

c) additional quantities of raw materials are paid for, without any further compulsory measures in the field of trade or production, by reducing the gold parity of the guilder. We will assume this reduction to be around 25%.

In the following we now must investigate what will be the course of employment in each of the cases indicated above. Each case will be broken down into several possibilities. A number of problems arise in this connection which are summarized here for orientation's sake.

In the first place we must determine the optimum size of the measures above and the maximum length of time over which they must be extended. For example, how much gold will have to be sold and how long a time period is this to be used? Or again: if by means of organized action on the part of the government it is possible to rapidly increase the efficiency of industry, how great an improvement in efficiency can then be reached? Also: if the imports of consumer goods are to be limited, how far can we go in this respect? When surveying this and similar questions a few characteristic differences between a, b en c immediately become obvious. The process in a) can only be continued for a limited period before the gold reserves and the funds which can be liquidated are exhausted. Gold sales of Hfl 100 million a year would, for example, be technically possible but under the present circumstances might create psychological difficulties. However, if the earning capacity of the Dutch industry would no longer be below that of foreign industry and accordingly there was not so much capital exported, then the other items could theoretically burden the balance of payments even more. Furthermore the unfavourable psychological effects would also be reduced and the balance of the current items might be considerably more unfavourable than now. Yet there are limits in all cases, and a yearly withdrawal of over Hfl 500 million more than at present through the current items of the balance of payments, should be considered impossible at present.

As far as the other measures are concerned : the maximum annual increase in the efficiency of industry as a whole would be 10% at the most. This was the average rise in efficiency in the United States under the pressure of a crisis year such as 1931.

Limiting the imports of finished consumption goods by more than 25%—with the substitution of domestically manufactured goods— should also be considered impossible.

These and similar considerations are taken into account, in the determination of some "constants" in section 5.

The second kind of problem which must be kept constantly in mind when carrying out the purpose of this report, are the problems connected with the repercussions of one economic variable on another. In other words, what will be the effect of our measures on the economic system as a whole. An example is the increase in prices resulting from a rise in employment. In this case we must study the repercussion of rising employment on prices. In just the same way there will be a repercussion of rising employment on wages; and of rising wages and prices on the demand for consumer goods, *etc., etc.* I consider this type of problem to be essence of the argument we are going to unfold here. The sum of such repercussions will give us the answer we seek and moreover will show us the course followed by the level of employment in each of the cases to be discussed.

We are dealing with a complicated subject. Complicated in two respects: In the first place with respect to time. The relationships between present variables and variables four months hence work along numerous different channels. All sorts of differing lag phenomena play a part in these relationships. Secondly, the subject is complicated even if we leave time out of the picture, because many different variables in the economic mechanism are interconnected. This doubly complicated aspect is one of the reasons why it is so necessary that, when economic theory is applied, experts in many fields should co-operate. Moreover it means that a great deal of study has to be "invested" in an analysis of the details. However useful and necessary this study of detail may be, we also need a general view, especially in this report. What we want to find out is the result of the complicated economic process. In order to get our general view, generalization is indispensable. The numerous phenomena have to be grouped in such a way that the picture can be viewed without obscuring its characteristic lines. The so-called macro-economic approach must be introduced where for example we do not consider each article separately but in groups such as raw materials, finished products, *etc.* As a matter of course every attempt to generalize or stylize is a venture. The artistry in the work of the social economist lies in this stylizing. Some attempts have been made which could not be handled, some proved to be unrealistic. We have to steer clear of these rocks. Stylizing is necessary however and the alternative is sterility. It almost goes without saying that the identity of those elements which play a major part in the current economic discussions should be preserved as much as possible.

Qualitative stylizing, *i.e.* the classification of people, goods, *etc.* in large groups is not yet sufficient. We also have to work with figures and stylize quantitatively. We must know by how many percentage points wages will go up as the price of consumer goods rises by one per cent. This has to be done if only because evaluating contrary influences is not otherwise possible. Another example is the price increase argument which was already mentioned. Undoubtedly certain prices will go up during the upward phase of a domestic business cycle. Accordingly, the export industries will have to face difficulties. The question is whether these difficulties will reduce employment, immediately and later on, to a greater extent than the other causes will be able to increase it. An evaluation of these effects is necessary. In this connection a rough figure is better than no figure at all, but we must mention that it is a rough figure because this uncertainty remains. But if we only point out the uncertainties, we come not nearer to solving the problem. The latter is regrettably the customary manner of discussing this subject.

My conclusion points to the necessity of quantitatively stylizing the economic process. An initial attempt in this direction is presented in the following section. The space available does not allow me to say everything about this subject that ought to be said. Accordingly I will only be able to make an outline. Perhaps I may refer the reader to a pamphlet regarding this working method which will be published later. Perhaps I may also request an opportunity to clarify this subject in subsequent discussions.

3. THE QUANTITIES UNDER CONSIDERATION AND THEIR MEASUREMENT

It is desirable to break down the economic variables under consideration into three groups.

I. PHYSICAL QUANTITIES

In this group we distinguish the following quantities which, preceded by their symbol, have been collected in the list given below. All quantities pertain to a period of one year.

a quantity of labour performed;

b labour performed for new investment;

u consumer goods finished (or other goods to the extent they were for export);

u'_x finished consumer goods consumed domestically;

u_A consumer goods exported;

u'_A consumer goods imported;

v'_A production equipment imported;
x'_A raw materials imported for consumer goods;
y'_A raw materials imported for production equipment.

II. Prices (Index Numbers) of:

p consumer goods in retail trade (cost of living) in guilders;
p_A export products at the frontier, in guilders;
q production equipment, domestically, in guilders;
p'_A imported consumer goods, in guilders (frontier);
q'_A imported production equipment, in guilders (frontier);
r'_A imported raw materials for consumer goods, in guilders (frontier);
s'_A imported raw materials for production equipment, in guilders (frontier);
l wage index figures (daily wage).[2]

III. Value Figures (in Guilders)

U value of: Dutch production of consumer and export goods;
U' consumer goods, consumed in the Netherlands;
U_A exports;
U'_A imported consumer goods;
V'_A imported production equipment;
X'_A imported raw materials for consumer goods;
Y'_A imported raw materials for production equipment;
L wage income of labour;
E all remaining income, taken at the moment received;
Z same, at the moment when earned, together with non-distributed profits;
E' the part of E spent on consumer goods and services.
E'' the saved or hoarded part of E.

The units used for the measurement of the variables are the following:

---

[2] It is assumed that the length of working days does not alter and has not altered since 1923.

The monetary unit selected is Hfl 1,754 million which is the average of the total wage sum over the period 1923-1933. This has been used as far as possible as the basis for the calculations.

All prices are expressed in index numbers using 1923–1933 = 100 as basis.

Using both these principles, the units of all physical quantities are automatically determined, because a physical unit is typified by the fact that its value and its price are equal. A unit of every kind of goods is therefore the quantity whose price over the period 1923–1933 was equal to Hfl 1,754 million. The same applies to the labour unit.

The choice of these somewhat strange units gave certain advantages when carrying out the calculations.

The symbols indicated have furthermore been used to indicate the deviations shown by the variables concerned in respect of their trend values (linear trend over the period 1923–1933); those trend values themselves will be indicated with a horizontal bar above the symbol, e.g. $\bar{a}$.

Measuring the variables mentioned was obviously possible only in a general manner. In many aspects therefore our conclusions should be considered as provisional. In view of the available data, it is hardly possible to improve these figures, even though, for some of them, the gaps in the basic data are considerable. A number of cross-checks, however, gave me the impression that the model of Dutch economic life given hereafter is sufficiently accurate to give a more concrete shape to the discussions concerning the problem on which our country is now concentrating.

For the figures themselves and for a short description of the manner in which they were calculated, we refer the reader to Table I and its commentary.

The time path of each of the variables can be found in the graphs given in 1 (dotted line).

Finally we may remark that it was not determined *a priori* whether or not a certain economic variable ought to appear in this list. This was decided by asking whether the variable concerned was essential to explain the course of employment, either directly or indirectly. In this connection the following section should be consulted.

4. THE RELATIONS BETWEEN THE VARIABLES: THE ELEMENTARY RELATIONS

The economic variables included in the model are constantly changing, in a mutually interdependent way for the greater part. The changes in each of the variables are partly determined by non-economic and partly by economic influences. By the latter we mean only that the changes are determined as to size and direction by the changes in other economic variables. Thus the prices of consumer goods can rise 1 per cent owing to a bad harvest and 2 per cent owing to a rise in costs or a rise in the incomes of the consumers. The influences first mentioned we will call non-economic and, the last mentioned influences we will call economic. In general the non-economic influences will often have a random character, *i.e.* at times they will work in one direction and at other times in another direction, unpredictable and without regularity. If a non-economic influence can be indicated which does not meet these requirements of randomness, then it could, by way of exception, be classified with the systematic influences. For the reasons mentioned, however, the systematic influences will generally also be economic ones. In all discussions of economic policy, but particularly cyclical policy, it is more efficient to start with the assumption that only the systematic relations exist. Thus we obtain a picture, which, in the average over a longer period, will correspond well with reality. In this report we will follow this procedure.[3] Furthermore no attention will be paid to the influences which cause only seasonal fluctuations or very slow changes which are significant only at very long term (the secular movements). The elimination of these influences can take place, by approximation, by considering only the deviations from the trend[4] of all variables and trying to explain the movements which are shown by their annual averages. This has been undertaken in the following pages.

Viewed more closely from the theoretical angle, what really matters

---

[3] For a further explanation of this train of thought I refer to my article "Quantitative Fragen der Konjunkturpolitik", *Weltw. Archiv.* November 1935, page 366.

[4] For a further comment on the significance of the trend in this I refer to my article "La détermination statistique de l'équilibre cyclique", *Revue de l'inst. Int. de Stat.* 1936, page 173.

TABLE I
SURVEY OF THE BASIC MATERIAL

Nr.	Description	Symbol	Unit	1923	1924	1925	1926	1927	1928	1929	1930	1931	1932	1933	1934	1935
	Prices															
1.	Wages	$\overline{l} + l$	1923/33=100	103	100	99	99	99	100	102	103	102	99	95	91	
2.	Cost of living	$\overline{p} + p$	,,	107	109	109	103	103	104	103	99	93	86	85	86	84
3.	Prices of production equipment	$\overline{q} + q$	,,	122	114	106	108	101	101	102	98	91	80	72	71	68
4.	Export prices	$\overline{p}_A + p_A$	,,	120	120	121	110	108	109	110	100	81	62	57	56	25
5.	Import prices: finished consumer goods	$\overline{p}_A' + p_A'$	,,	107	117	122	115	114	114	111	100	82	64	55	53	47
6.	Import prices: finished production equipment	$\overline{q}_A' + q_A'$	,,	119	111	108	105	98	98	100	99	95	86	80	77	73
7.	Import prices: raw materials for consumer good	$\overline{v}_A' + v_A'$	,,	122	142	134	124	119	119	110	88	60	45	42	42	40
8.	Import prices: raw materials for production equipment	$\overline{s}_A' + s_A'$	,,	130	118	117	113	114	111	111	98	80	56	56	56	42
I.	World price level	$\overline{p}_w + p_w$	1926/30=100	106	107	108	102	102	103	101	92	79	68	63	60	60
	Physical quantities															
9.	Employment, total	$\overline{a} + a$	1923/33=100	88	91	94	98	101	107	111	113	107	95	94	96	
10.	Same, in investment works$_s$	$\overline{b} + b$	as $\overline{a} + a$	20.2	21.1	21.9	23.1	23.8	26.2	28.4	29.4	25.8	21.0	21.4	22.6	
11.	Total production	$\overline{u} + u$	Quantity which averaged 1923/33	282	292	312	333	340	358	366	358	348	342	358	362	
12.	Export quantity	$\overline{u}_A + u_A$		62	79	85	91	100	104	103	98	93	77	72	73	73
13.	Consumption quantity	$\overline{u}' + u'$		221	229	230	235	242	249	253	262	270	271	274	264	
14.	Import quantity: finished consumer goods	$\overline{u}_A' + u_A'$	cost Hfl 1,754 million=100	51	55	51	56	56	59	60	63	66	63	66	51	48
15.	Import quantity: finished production equipment	$\overline{v}_A' + v_A'$		6.9	7.3	10.3	12.8	14.8	18.7	20.6	19.4	14.1	11.1	11.9	12.1	11.6
16.	Import quantity: raw materials for consumer goods	$\overline{x}_A' + x_A'$		33	34	39	39	44	45	47	46	47	40	40	40	43
17.	Import quantity: raw materials for production equipment	$\overline{y}_A' + y_A'$		8.2	10.2	11.4	12.2	13.3	14.8	16.6	16.7	14.2	11.6	13.2	13.9	13.5
II.	Volume of world exports		1929 = 100	70	70	84	86	92	95	100	93	96	75	76		

TABLE I (continued)

Nr.	Description	Symbol	Unit	1923	1924	1925	1926	1927	1928	1929	1930	1931	1932	1933	1934	1935
	Value figures															
18.	Wage sum	$\overline{L}+L$	f. 17.54 mln	92	92	94	97	101	106	112	115	108	93	88	86	
19.	All other income, at the moment of earning, incl. non-distributed profits . . .	$\overline{Z}+Z$	,,	201	210	208	203	213	224	215	196	158	150	155		
20.	All other income, at the moment of payment, incl. non-distributed profits . .	$\overline{E}+E$	,,	185	192	192	192	196	204	204	190	167	156	156		
21.	Part of aforementioned income spent . . .	$\overline{E}'+E'$	,,	134	142	141	138	137	137	138	135	132	128	130		
22.	Part saved (incl. part put by) .	$\overline{E}''+E''$	,,	23	26	29	43	40	49	37	46	32	13	12	10	
23.	Value of exports . . .	$\overline{U}_A+U_A$	,,	74	95	103	100	108	113	113	98	75	48	41	41	38
24.	Value of consumption . . .	$\overline{U}'+U'$	,,	226	234	235	235	238	243	250	250	240	221	218	210	
25.	Value of imports of finished consumer goods . . .	$\overline{U}'_A+U'_A$	,,	54	64	63	64	64	67	67	63	54	39	37	27	23
26.	Value of imports of finished production equipment .	$\overline{V}'_A+V'_A$	,,	10.5	11.2	12.1	12.6	14.0	16.8	19.7	18.7	14.3	9.1	8.9	8.2	7.3
27.	Value of imports of raw materials for consumer goods . .	$\overline{X}'_A+X'_A$	,,	40	48	52	49	52	54	52	40	28	18	17	17	17
28.	Value of imports of raw materials for production equipment	$\overline{Y}'_A+Y'_A$	,,	10.6	12.1	13.4	13.8	15.2	16.4	18.4	16.3	11.4	6.5	7.4	7.8	6.4
III.	Income from enterprises operating abroad	$\overline{L}+L$	,,	17	27	37	42	39	37	33	27	21	14	12	10	

Short Commentary on Table I. Sources and Methods of Calculation:

No.

Prices

1. Average daily wage according to the State Insurance Bank.
2. Index of the cost of living, workers' families, Amsterdam.
3. Calculated from the new index figures for wholesale prices of the Central Bureau for Statistics and re-calculated 1923–'26 with the aid of the statistics of production and consumption (C.B.S.).
4. Calculated from a sample of Dutch exports, comprising about half of all exports.
5. Calculated from a sample of the Dutch imports of finished consumer goods.
6. Calculated from the new index figure for wholesale prices of the C.B.S. and re-calculated for 1923–'26 on the basis of import data.
7. Ratio of the value of imports of various raw materials for consumer goods based on a sample and the quantity index of the C.B.S. for imports of those raw materials.
8. Prices of metals and timber from the C.B.S. index figure for raw materials.
I. De Ned. Conjunctuur May 1936, page 18, with re-calculation according to Stat. Jahrbuch f.d. deutsche Reich, 1935, page 118*.

Physical quantities

9. Number of unit-workers according to the State Insurance Bank.
10. Same in building and metal industry.
11. Own calculation from the known production indices for man industry and a few agricultural series.
12. C.B.S. index figure for exports of manufactured and agricultural products (sample includes half the total exports).
13. Own calculation including about 2/3 of all consumption; by adding a constant term we have seen to it that the value of consumption (series 24), calculated similarly, is approximately equal to the product of the quantity and the index figure of the cost of living.
14. Calculated from the ratio of value and price (see 5); the latter was calculated from a sample of value and quantity.
15. Imports are weighted according to their price in a fixed year determined from a sample. The entire figure has been expanded to correspond to the total of all import production equipment during the period 1923–33.
16. Calculated in the same way as 14.
17. From value and price.
II. League of Nations figure for the period 1923/24, revised with figures borrowed from the source mentioned under I.

Value figures

18. Figures concerning insured workers subject to the accident law, the agricultural and the marine insurance law.

19. Calculated as follows: estimated national income of persons + estimated non-distributed income of enterprises — wage sum. The estimated national income is calculated from the taxed income with allowance for tax evasion and taking the incomes below the tax limit into account (the method of Bonger). The non-distributed income of enterprises is calculated from a sample of about 90 large enterprises, by comparison with paid-out dividends and gratuities, the latter being also known in total.

20. Deduced from 19 by subtracting the non-distributed incomes and by shifting dividends and gratuities one year.

21. Value of consumption, from which wage income has been subtracted.

22. Estimated from issues and mortgage loans.

23, 25–28. Own calculation from trade statistics.

24. See 13.

iii. Calculated for the years 1931-1934 from the balance of payments figures for the Netherlands (Maandschrift C.B.S.); estimated for earlier years on the basis of Dutch East Indies balance of payments and dividends.

is not so much the ordinary (mathematically established) trend but a consecutive series of figures which I would like to call an "equilibrium development". The latter would then be characterized by two features; first, that it, just as the actual movement, satisfies the (dynamic) equations. This implies in the economic sense that it also is a possible time path (not conflicting with the reactions of the economic subjects, the institutional and other ties); and second that it runs as gradually as possible. I have given my thoughts in this respect more exhaustively elsewhere[5] and I refer the reader to this passage.

Here we may note in passing that in "quiet times" the difference between the equilibrium curve and the trend will not be very great. Since 1931, however, a few shifts have occurred in the economic world which have brought about sudden changes in several equilibrium positions. For this reason difficulties are encountered when attempting to determine the equilibrium situation in 1935 (see section 5).

The fact that certain influences determine the systematically and cyclically important changes of some economic variable, can be expressed in an algebraic equation. By way of documentation the equations which will be mentioned here are summarized in Table ii. For the reader without mathematical background the following description is

---

[5] *Revue de l'Institut Intern. de Statistique,* July 1936.

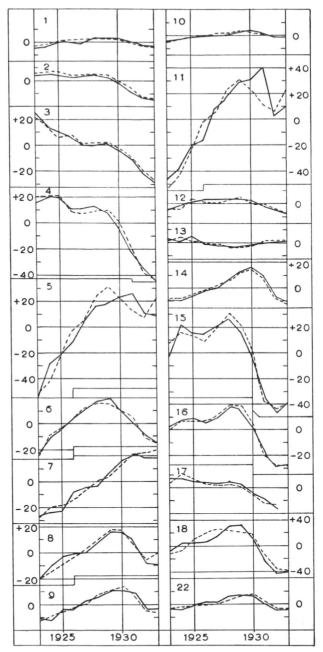

Fig. A. Survey of the result of the correlation calculations, to control the equations which establish the main economic quantities of the Netherlands ("Barometer" for the Netherlands, 1923–1933). The numbers correspond to the relative equations and figures.

given. In order to use sentences which do not prove too unreadable, the relationships have not always been expressed in a mathematically exact manner. The foremost aim has been to make them easy to understand. As the reader will understand, all criticism of the economic thinking in this report must be directed mainly at the assumptions which will be made in the next paragraph. The conclusions which will be reached and discussed in the later paragraphs follow logically from these assumptions. After the assumptions have been made and have been expressed mathematically in the form of equations, they are inserted, as it were, in the mathematical machine which immediately supplies the result.

EXPLANATION OF THE MOVEMENT OF THE PRICE QUANTITIES

(1)[6] Wages: It is assumed that the change in the wage level from year to year, is influenced by the changes in the cost of living and by the state of employment. A price increase will occasion a rise in wages and so will a state of above normal employment. It is moreover assumed that a price decrease will give rise to a wage decrease, just as will a subnormal level of employment. It is further assumed that the full effect of price changes on wages requires ample time to be felt (one year). The slowness of response of wages is well known.

Fig. 1 shows that the real movement in wages (the dotted line represents the change, from the previous year) as a percentage of the former wage level can actually be explained graphically by the top line which represents a combination of the two causes mentioned. The two lower solid lines represent the components of the top one. Thus the significance of each of the factors is shown separately. The middle one of the drawn lines represents, year by year, the price rise or drop from the level of the previous year; multiplied however, by a certain constant. In this case this figure is 0.27 as mentioned in the chart. This means that the wage increases and decreases on the average amount to only 1/4 of the price increases and decreases which cause them. The bottom line shows the employment situation multiplied by 0.16. The figures 0.27 and 0.16 which can not be determined a priori have been assigned arbitrary values in order to ensure that "things work out as well as possible", i.e. that the actual course of wages and the "calculated" course should correspond as closely as possible.

---

[6] The numbers preceding each part of this discourse correspond to the equations and to the corresponding graphs.

The significance of the equation discussed here for the entire line of reasoning is that, unless the contrary is expressly stated, it is always taken for granted that the price changes which occur lead a year later to wage changes of the indicated size. Furthermore when employment exceeds the value which is considered normal wages will rise, while a subnormal level of employment leads to wage decreases.

(2) PRICES OF CONSUMER GOODS FOR DOMESTIC CONSUMPTION (the cost of living). It is assumed that the prices of these goods are determined primarily by the following three factors:

A. the prices of consumer goods abroad;
B. the cost of domestic consumer goods and
C. the level of sales of consumer goods.

The latter factor is used to measure the strength of competition; when sales are high, competition will be relatively slight and accordingly prices will have the tendency to be on the high side. In the case of low sales the opposite will be the case. Here again, of course, it is not possible to know in advance what the extent of such an influence of sales on prices will prove to be. For this reason once again a coefficient has been mathematically determined which ensures as much conformity as possible to reality.

Costs (B), obviously, are not known exactly. Here, however, we are concerned with only the fluctuations in costs and not with their absolute level. Fluctuations have been estimated in a simple manner by adding together in certain proportions the price of raw materials for consumer goods, wages and a trend series (see the formula in Fig. 2). A trend series is a series of figures which rises or falls gradually and regularly with time: in our example it falls. This trend series serves to indicate the estimated influence of technical improvements *etc.*

In Fig. 2 the actual course of the cost of living has been represented graphically by means of a dotted line; the four solid lines represent the values of the cost of living and the three components of these values, calculated in the way just discussed. The components are A: $0.04 \times$ the cost of the consumer goods[7] and C: $0.08 \times$ the sales of consumer goods. From this graph we can see,

---

[7] Costs are $1/3 \ (r'_A + 2l - 6t)$; if we multiply this by 0.45 then we obtain the amount indicated in the formula.

e.g., that the main influence can be attributed—according to our calcula-tions)—to costs. The influence of foreign competition and domestic sales (as a standard for extra competition) is small.

(3,4). With regard to the prices of domestically manufactured pro-duction equipment and of export articles, similar hypotheses have been set up and calculations have been made. Thereby we found the follow-ing differences with consumer goods: the influence of foreign compe-tition is much greater with the latter two groups. The influence of domestic competition measured in sales can be ignored in these cases. The influence of costs is as large in the case of production equipment as in that of consumer goods and is much smaller for export articles. The influence of costs, however, is in the case of the two kinds of goods first mentioned only about 0.5; that is to say that if competing prices are not altered only fifty percent of a rise or reduction in costs is passed on. How well our conclusions conform with reality can be seen in the Figs. 3 and 4 which have been set up in entirely the same way as the previous figures.

EXPLANATION OF THE MOVEMENT OF THE PHYSICAL QUANTITIES

In order to make a more or less systematic survey of the relations which are responsible for the immediate determination of the physical quantities, we will break down these relations into several groups. In the first place there are the four *sales equations* numbers (5) to (8).

Equation (5) states the fact that total production (which is assumed to be equal to sales) is equal to the sum of the production for the home market and the production for the foreign market.

Equation (6) expresses that *foreign sales* are determined by three factors:

A. the size of world exports z;
B. the foreign price level p_W;
C. the price level of export goods p_A.

As the reasoning used in this connection is approximately the same as in a corresponding analysis in "De Nederlandsche Conjunctuur" we may refer to it.[8] The solution attained can also be seen in Fig. 6. An elasticity of nearly 1.5 is found for total exports.

---

[8] *De Nederlandsche Conjunctuur*, May 1936, page 17.

Equation (7) (see Fig. 7) is an identity which relates to *domestic sales*. It is deduced from the identity: income spent on consumer goods = price × quantity of these goods. The income spent on consumer goods thereby consists of two parts: A) the total wage income L (where accordingly savings have been left out of consideration) and a part E' of the remaining income E. The full explanation of the domestic sales is not given in this way; it is partly shifted to be explanation of E', for which purpose equation (17) serves.

Finally equation (8) gives a rough idea of the main influence which effects the level of sales of *investment goods*. The volume of total

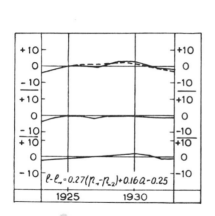

Fig. 1.

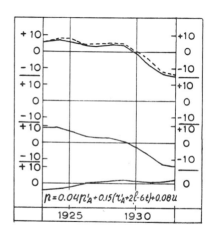

Fig. 2.

Figs. 1–4. Explanation and calculation of the movement of prices in the Netherlands. A broken line indicates the actual movement of the relevant variable. The solid line running through the broken one represents the calculated movement. This line is found by adding up the values indicated by the lines drawn underneath, which show the influence of the explanatory variables separately. The explanatory variables are given in the same order as in the formulae.

Fig. 1. Calculation of the annual increase in daily wages from the increase in the cost of living, and the level of employment.

Fig. 2. Calculation of the price level of consumer goods from the price level of imported consumer goods, production costs, and total sales.

sales (domestic production + imports) of production equipment changes mainly as a result of changes in the profit expectations, the latter (at least as far as their systematic part is concerned) are assumed to be parallel to the actual profits realized. In this equation a total lag of one year has been assumed, which can be interpreted as the sum of a psychological waiting period, a technical preparation period and a technical execution period. Domestic production is represented on the left side of this equation by the term $3\,y'_A$, which assumes that raw materials take up about $1/3$ of the value during the basic period (which was used, as we know, as basis for quantity measurement).

This equation raises the question whether other variables are not also immediately partly responsible for the volume of investments.

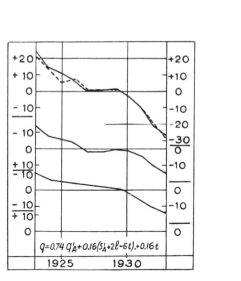

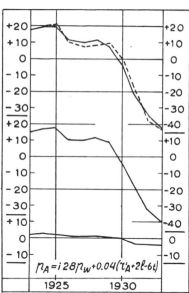

Fig. 3.   Fig. 4.

Fig. 3. Calculation of the price level of producer goods from the price level of imported producer goods, production costs, and a trend.

Fig. 4. Calculation of the price level of exports from the world price level and production costs. An explanation of the formulae used is given in the text.

It will undoubtedly be argued that the fact that new processes become known will exert a considerable influence on investment. This influence is not denied at all, but it is not considered to be one of the systematic influences. The fact that important new processes become known is related only in a very slight degree to the growth of economic variables and can often be considered as economically incidental.

Another factor which plays a part in determining the quantity of investment is, in the opinion of many, the rate of interest or the rates of interest at which money can be obtained. In this respect the following can be noted: In analysing the influence of the rate of interest on short-term loans, we find, by means of a statistical investigation car-

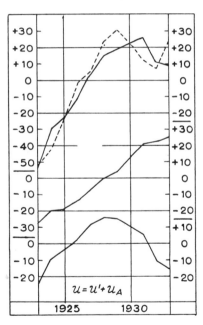
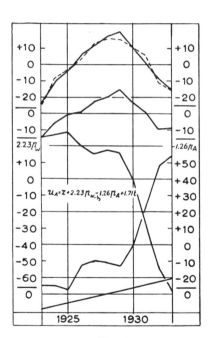

Fig. 5.   Fig. 6.

Fig. 5. Calculation of the production of consumer and export goods from domestic and foreign sales.

Fig. 6. Calculation of foreign sales from the volume of world trade, world price level, Dutch export price level and a trend.

ried out in the same way as for the other equations, that such an influence is very slight. This is a consequence of the relatively slight share
which this type of interest cost represents in total investment costs.
The same is found with regard to the rate of interest for long-term
loans, a fact which can probably be explained by the slight amplitude
of the fluctuations in this rate of interest. Finally, we might think of
the funds that are absorbed by the enterprises through the issuing of
shares. The "interest" which is obtained from this withdrawal of
capital cannot be indicated accurately. We could say, however, that this
capital is acquired the more "advantageously", the higher share prices

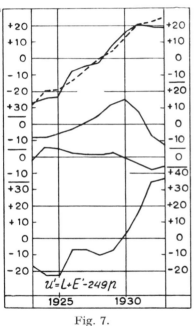

Fig. 7.

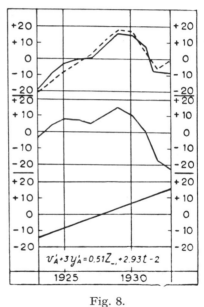

Fig. 8.

Fig. 7. Calculation of domestic sales from wage income, spent part of non-
labour-income and price level for consumer goods.

Fig. 8. Calculation of investment volume from profits of the previous year
and a trend.

(For a further explanation see the footnote to Figs. 1–4 and the text.)

are. High share prices, however, are always present when profits are high: there is a very strong parallelism between both these two variables. Therefore the influence of interest on the volume of investments cannot be separated from the influence of profits already mentioned. Accordingly the assumption which has been made with respect to this equation would seem acceptable to me. We can see from Fig. 8 that it is in reasonable accordance with the facts, if it is understood that we must add to the line which represents the influence of profit (the line $0.51 Z_{-1}$) a so-called "trend component" (the bottom line in the Figure). This line should probably be explained by the slow technical and structural changes. These give rise to the fact that, given equal earning power, increasingly larger investment quantities will be required.

The second group of equations which explain the fluctuations of the physical quantities could be called *technical equations*.

Equation (9) gives the relation between the *quantity of labour a—b* which is used in all stages for the production of consumer goods, and the quantities of raw materials imported for consumer goods used for finished consumer goods. In this connection it has been assumed that perhaps 5 times as much labour is used for domestic products as for imported finished products. The result is shown in Fig. 9; we see that a good correlation is obtained if we approach $a—b$ by means of the expression $0.2\ u'_A + x'_A$, and a trend component of very small significance.

Equation (10) gives a similar relation with regard to the *production equipment*. Only in this case, in view of the absence of retail trade it has been taken for granted, for simplicity's sake, that labour is required only to process raw materials (Fig. 10).

Equation (11) is a *technical relationship between raw materials and finished products in consumer goods*. The coefficients, which have also been found with the aid of correlation calculation, have a ratio which is quite acceptable: thus it would seem that about $2^1/_2$ times as much value is added to imported raw materials before they reach the consumer than is the case with finished consumer goods. The best correlation is obtained if the quantity of raw materials is multiplied by 4.35, and the quantity of products imported by the figure 1.72 which is about $2^1/_2$ times smaller. These figures moreover imply that the total value at retail prices is about 4.35 times as great as the

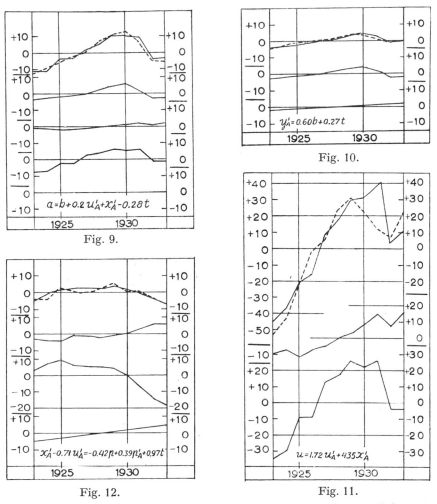

Fig. 9.

Fig. 10.

Fig. 12.

Fig. 11.

Fig. 9. Calculation of employment from "investment employment", imports of processed consumer goods, imports of raw materials for same and a trend.

Fig. 10. Calculation of imports of raw materials for the investment goods industry from the "quantity of investment labour" and a trend.

Fig. 11. Calculation of the production of consumer goods and export goods from the imports of finished consumer goods and the imports of raw materials for same.

Fig. 12. "Competition equation" for consumer goods. (See text; about equivalent to the calculation of the import ratio between raw materials and finished products from the ratio between domestic and foreign prices).

(For a further explanation please see the comments to Figs. 1–4 and the text).

value of the raw materials used in the manufactured products. With respect to imported goods, the value at retail prices is about 1.72 times as great as in the import value. It will perhaps give cause for surprise that we repeatedly speak of value here, while we are concerned with quantity indices. However, the average value over the entire period 1923–1933 is always meant. These figures are the ones which have been selected as a basis for the units in which the quantities have been measured.

Perhaps some readers will not find the correlation shown in Fig. 11 to be very satisfactory. It is indeed considerably smaller than in most other cases. This can be partly explained by the very large magnitude of the figures we are using (the average of the series u is over 300) which makes the relative errors not so very important. Furthermore the index u is fairly primitive, and a certain amount of deviation can easily occur through stock formation of raw materials.

The third group of equations we call the *competition equations*. They show how sales are distributed over the goods which are manufactured in this country and goods which have been imported. There is one for consumer goods and one for production equipment.

The first equation (12) states that the difference between the imported finished products and imported raw materials (converted into one single average quantity in order to make comparison possible) is inversely proportional to the Dutch price level and directly proportional to the price level of the imported consumer goods. A relation has not been assumed between the left side of this equation and the *difference* between both price levels because the p and the p'_A are not entirely comparable: the p is the index of the cost of living while the p'_A relates to the wholesale value of the articles imported (Fig. 12).

In the second competition equation (13) which relates to production equipment, this relation has been possible; the indices q and q'_A can thus be compared (Fig. 13).

EXPLANATION OF THE MOVEMENT OF THE VALUE VARIABLES

Equation (14) is nothing but an identity: the wage total is equal to the product of the wage rate and the quantity of labour performed. This would, written in full, have looked as follows:

$$\overline{L} + L = (\overline{a} + a)\,(\overline{l} + l)$$

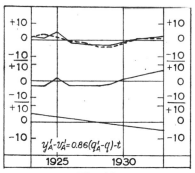

Fig. 13.

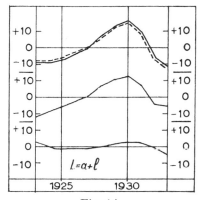

Fig. 14.

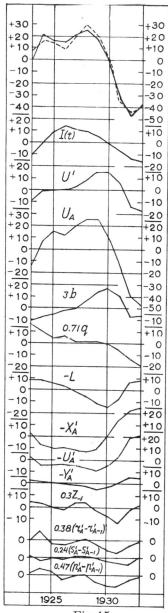

Fig. 13. "Competition equation" for production equipment (see commentary Fig. 12 and text).

Fig. 14. Calculation of total wages from employment and day wage.

Fig. 15. Calculation of profits (incl. other non-labour income) for the entire Dutch economy.

Fig. 15.

(Compare for a further explanation the commentary to Figs. 1–4 and the text.)

or elaborated

$$\overline{L} + L = \overline{al} + \overline{a}l + a\overline{l} + al.$$

As we find that the normal values of $\overline{L}$ and $\overline{a}\,\overline{l}$ also prove to be equal we are left with

$$L = \overline{al} + a\overline{l} + al,$$

in which $\overline{a} = \overline{l} = 1$, because of the choice of the units, while al has been omitted as a term of the second order; thus equation (14) is obtained (Fig. 14).

Equation (15) indicates how *profit (including all other non-labour income)* is calculated. In this connection the entire economy of the Netherlands is considered as one unit. We find first of all in the formula the terms representing the joint "static" incomes I, which are drawn from enterprises operating abroad (incl. those in the colonies) and to which are added bankers' and shippers' services rendered to foreigners. In the second place we find the "static" terms which pertain to domestic enterprises. These reflect only the value of all products, from which has been deducted the value of all raw materials (including consumer goods imported in a technically finished stage). With respect to all these goods, it has been assumed that the quantity of manufactured production equipment shows fluctuations proportional to the number b but 3 times as intensively (as the labour factor in the value of production equipment can be considered to be about 1/3). In the third place we find in the formula for Z also a number of "dynamic" terms; these represent calculated income derived from price and quotation movements during the past year. Examples of such income components are, on the one hand, speculation profits (speculation both in goods and securities) and, on the other hand, fictitious income arising from calculations based on historical cost price. Moreover, it has also been taken for granted that the quotations of domestic securities run parallel to Z, whilst quotations of foreign securities have been assumed to run parallel to the world market prices of raw materials. The mutual relationships between these several parts of "dynamic" income are difficult to determine with correlation analysis, because the movements of Z and of the prices of raw materials were almost parallel during the period 1923–1933. It is remarkable that the difference between Z and the "static" terms should show so closely the behaviour expected of the "dynamic" terms. This tendency, to a certain extent, renders the hypothesis of the dynamic terms acceptable, and even probable (equation Fig. 15).

An estimate of the relative influence of the dynamic terms for domestic or foreign income (*i.e.* whether speculation and calculation profits on raw materials and foreign securities on the one hand, or domestic securities on the other) has been attempted by trial and error in two ways. On the one hand rough estimates have been made of the size of the raw materials quantities on which these profits might have been made. It is almost impossible for these to be larger than half a year's consumption of imported raw materials for consumer goods and finished consumer goods, and one year's consumption with regard to imported raw materials to be used to manufacture production equipment. Therefore, they have been taken at that amount. The ratio of domestic speculation profits to speculation profits on foreign securities has been estimated in a very indirect manner. We find that if domestic securities were relatively important, Dutch economic life would show an extraordinarily heavy cyclical movement with a two-year period; but this has never been ascertained *de facto*. This is discussed further in section 5. However, if about 2/3 of the speculation profits on securities were obtained on foreign holdings, these heavy fluctuations would not be present. On this basis the ratio was assumed.[9]

The equations (16) to (18) relate to non-labour income and its utilization.

Equation (16) expresses the fact that total non-labour income actually earned shows the same fluctuations as Z, with two differences. The fluctuations are smaller (reservation policy), and they are somewhat delayed. (A period elapses between the "earning" of the income and paying the corresponding dividends, gratuities and interest). The delay averages about 4 months (the influence of the current year is 0.48, as against the one of the previous year 0.20) which is plausible when we think of the large number of small enterprises and of interimpayments and such like.

As far as the utilization of this income is concerned we have worked with a simple hypothesis. It is taken for granted that the amount of

---

[9] The concept domestic securities refers here to securities quoted exclusively domestically.

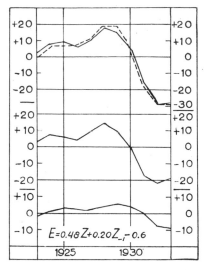

Fig. 16.

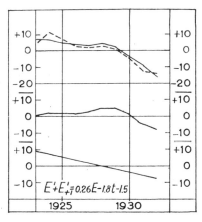

Fig. 17.

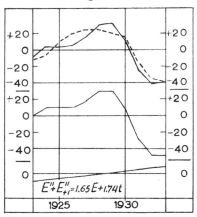

Fig. 18.   Fig. 19.

Fig. 16. Calculation of non-labour income (excluding the non-distributed profits) out of "profits" and the "profits" of the previous year.

Fig. 17. Calculation of the spent part of non-labour income out of the entire non-labour income (with six months' lag).

Fig. 18. Calculation of the part saved or hoarded in a manner analogous to the one shown in equation (17).

Fig. 19. Calculation of the value of imported production equipment from quantity and price.

(For further explanation compare the commentary to Figs. 1–4 and the text.)

income saved depends only on the amount of total non-labour income. The influence of the rate of interest has not been included because, in the first place, several influences which might be exercised by the rate of interest are conflicting and, in the second place, because the figures do not indicate the direction of the final influence. Naturally this part of the analysis is very rough and there is considerable need for detailed

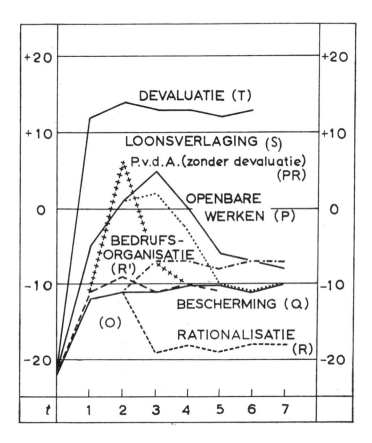

Fig. 20. Development of employment under different types of economic policy. The various policies are indicated by short and loose slogans or devices. A precise description (a definition) of these devices is given in the text (section 6) and in Table VI under the symbols indicated. Of course, the volume of the changes in employment depends upon the extent to which each of the measures adopted is applied. This is indicated and discussed in the text.

observations. Furthermore a lag of about six months[10] has been assumed between receipt of income and expenditure or savings.

The *expenditure equation* (17) and the *savings equation* (18) were originally determined separately by means of a correlation calculation. The coefficients thus found were slightly different from the values indicated here. The latter have been found by requiring that the sum of the coefficients for E appearing in both equations, should be equal to 2. This was achieved by a small increase in each coefficient (see Figs. 17 and 18).

The equations (19) and (20) up to (24) inclusive are all identities, illustrating the fact that the value of a certain kind of goods is equal to its quantity multiplied by its price. (These equations have also been expressed in linear form.) For four of the five product flows which have been studied, one of the three variables mentioned has been calculated with the aid of the other two (see the table concerning the manner of calculation). These equations thus are automatically fulfilled. With regard to the fifth goods flow (the one pertaining to raw materials imported for the manufacture of production equipment) we get a fair result (Fig. 19).

Equation (20) states that the value of all consumer goods is equal to the sum of wages and the spent part of the non-labour incomes. It could also in view of equation (7), be written in the same form as the five previous equations. It would then state that the value of the goods consumed is equal to the product of the quantity and the price of these goods.

5. THE RELATION BETWEEN THE VARIABLES: THE GENERAL PICTURE OF THE MOVEMENT

In the previous section we have recapitulated for all economic variables included in our analysis, the main immediate relations which cause the systematic changes in these variables. These relations could also have been summarized in a somewhat different manner. In section 4 an indication has been given of the other variables by which these economic quantities are directly influenced. One might also wonder on which other variables a given qyantity, *e.g.* wage, exercizes its influence. Then we have only to check in which equations wages appear

---

[10] The influence of this hypothesis however is very slight.

as (partly) determining factors. A glance at Table II shows this to be the case in the following equations:

2, 3, and 4 where wages influence prices as an element of cost; 14 where it influences the total wages (and therefore purchasing power).

Similar remarks could be made with regard to other variables. As economic reasoning is usually set up in this way, it seemed proper to me to demonstrate in this manner that there is no real distinction, in principle, between the method followed here and customary economic reasoning. There is only the difference that in this paper all relations are expressed in numbers and that only the chief immediate causal links (about forty) are included: these however are presented consistently!

The aim of this section is to step from the direct relations to the indirect ones, in order to find the result of a complete series of successive causal connections. This also takes place in economic reasoning. Moreover it is nothing but repeatedly applying the relations already mentioned in motley order. This process is complicated and, for the reasons already enumerated, will be done with the aid of mathematics. Let us put it in this way: the relations discussed in section 4 are now thrown into the mathematical machine and the result is ejected from the machine, more or less ready-made. The reader not versed in mathematics can be assured that this machine process is uninteresting, in so far that, economically speaking, nothing new is added. All economic premises are to be found in section 4 and economic criticism should therefore be directed towards that section. The non-mathematical reader will furthermore forgive me for discussing in this section a few more problems which, in my opinion, should not escape comment, in spite of the fact that they often sound more or less mathematical. The matters which follow here, however, cannot be omitted because they are in the nature of the problems we are dealing with here. The close relations we observe in an economy, between such a large number of variables, brings some need for a strictly logical arrangement, which naturally resembles some of the techniques applied in physics of complicated "systems". If they are given a starting impetus in certain points they show strange wave-like movements.

The economic model shows a certain similarity. If the initial situation is given, all subsequent systematical movements can be cal-

TABLE II

SURVEY OF THE ELEMENTARY EQUATIONS

1. $l - l_{-1} = 0.27\,(p_{-1} - p_{-2}) + 0.16\,a.$
2. $p = 0.04\,p'_A + 0.15)\,r'_A + 2\,l - 6\,t) + 0.08\,u.$
3. $q = 0.74\;q'_A + 0.16\,(s'_A + 2\,l - 6\,t)$
4. $p_A = 1.28\,p_W + 0.04\,(r'_A + 2\,l - 6\,t).$

5. $u = u_A + u'.$
6. $u_A = z + 2.23\,(p_W)_{-0.25} - 1.26\,p_A.$
7. $u' = L + E' - 2.49\,p.$
8. $v'_A + 3\,y'_A = 0.51\,Z_{-1}.$
9. $a = b + 0.20\,u'_A + 0.98\,x'_A.$
10. $y'_A = 0.69\,b.$
11. $u = 1.72\,u'_A + 4.35\,x'_A$
12. $x'_A - 0.71\,u'_A = -0.42\,p + 0.39\,p'_A$
13. $y'_A - v'_A = 0.86\,(q'_A - q).$

14. $L = a + l.$
15. $Z = I + U' + U_A + 3\,b + 0.71\,q - L - X'_A - U'_A - Y'_A +$
    $0.24\,[s'_A - (s'_A)_{-1}] + 0.38\,[r'_A - (r'_A)_{-1}] + 0.47\,[p'_A - (p'_A)_{-1}] + 0.3\,(Z - Z_{-1}).$
16. $E = 0.48\,Z + 0.20\,Z_{-1}.$
17. $E' + E'_{-1} = 0.26\,E_{-1}.$
18. $E'' + E''_{-1} = 1.74\,E_{-1}.$
19. $U_A = u_A + 0.88\,p_A.$
20. $U' = L + E'.$
21. $U'_A = u'_A + 0.58\,p'_A.$
22. $V'_A = v'_A + 0.13\,q'_A.$
23. $X'_A = x'_A + 0.41\,r'_A.$
24. $Y'_A = y'_A + 0.13\,s'_A.$

culated with the aid of the described system of equations. Thus, as we have already seen, a systematic movement is one which is created without new outside disturbances. The non-systematic movements must be superimposed. They will usually not take place in a previously determined direction. As stated already, I limit myself, in accordance with general usage, to a study of the systematic movements.

The initial situation which has to be taken as a basis for a study of the further movements of the system should, however, be known in such a way that we know—or at least approximately know—how large in this situation the deviations are, shown by a number of variables, from their equilibrium value. It is not sufficient that we know the value, expressed in the normal manner, we should also know how far it is above or below the equilibrium value. For all "external" quantities introduced we should know, in the first place, the following:

p'_A the price level of the consumer goods imported;

q'_A the price level of the production equipment imported;

r'_A the price level of the imported raw materials for consumer goods;

s'_A the price level of imported production equipment;

p_W the world price level in general;

z the size of world exports;

I the incomes from enterprises operating abroad, *etc.*

Moreover we should also know the deviation from equilibrium values for a few of the internal variables. Not of all, because there are relationships which we should not forget. Those internal variables which have to be known can be determined only after all purely simultaneous relations have been eliminated.

The reader is requested to assume that this has taken place according to the rules of mathematics.

This elimination takes place after the numerical values for the external variables have been supplied. This greatly simplifies the calculations.

Determining the equilibrium values on which our analysis is based does not take place without some arbitrariness. This arbitrariness, however, is not very serious with regard to the validity of the conclusions of this report.

Generally speaking the equilibrium value can only be determined when we know the relations applying at the moment of observation. The relations which we have taken as starting-point, however, are the relations which applied, on the average, during the years 1923-1933. With regard to a large part of the relations this will still be approximately true. In others some shifts have occurred.[11] These have resulted, at the same time, in a change of the equilibrium position.

---

[11] I have assumed that this affected only the constant term and not the coefficients of the equations concerned. Taken strictly this will be the case only if a number of the govermental measures to cope with the present slump were again removed.

We can now do two things. Either continue to measure in the old way but then add (additive) terms to a few of the equations which indicate the shifts. This shift presumes that all quantities for the year 1935 are already known, which is not the case, especially not with Z, E, U' and a few other quantities. It is also possible to start measuring from the new point of equilibrium in that case; the latter has to be determined by estimation. We have proceeded in this way here. The state of equilibrium assumed thereby is the situation which the writer —usually on the authority of others—assumes would be established as cyclical equilibrium by the present "data", if the forces at work had a sufficiently long period of influence.[12]

We now assumed that, at present, the following deviations from this new equilibrium are dominant (in the units assumed earlier for each quantity).

p'_A and q'_A prices of imported finished products: —5 %;

$r'_A\,s'_A$ prices of imported raw materials: —10 %;

p_W world price level: —5 %;

z volume of world trade: —5 (*i.e. ca.* —5 %);

I incomes from enterprises working abroad—10 (*i.e.ca.* 25 %).

We repeat, however, that with respect to the conclusions reached in our further argument it is not serious if these values should be chosen somewhat differently.

In accordance with the premises of the problem propounded, these quantities have been taken as constant figures. Furthermore, as stated, all variables have been eliminated which can be eliminated with the aid of simultaneous relations (relations in which no influence of the past is at work; *i.e.* where no lag has been assumed). This gives the possibility of expressing all internal quantities in the simultaneously prevailing wage rate as well as the 4 values of internal quantities which were applicable at earlier dates, namely the wage rate, the cost of living, the "profit" of the previous year, and the cost of living of two previous years. The equations obtained are those given in the following table (see Table III).

---

[12] We can also interpret in this way, at least in a number of theoretically important cases, the definition of equilibrium development given earlier. This is not the place to elaborate on this, however.

Nr		Coefficients of the terms with:				Constant terms in case:							
		l	l_{-1}	$(p_{-1}-p_{-2})$	Z_{-1}	O	P	Q	R	R'	PR'	S	T
*25	$p=$	3.12	− 2.77	− 0.75	−0.08	− 1.65	− 3.90	− 2.75	− 2.35	− 6.85	− 9.1	12.15	+ 3.0
26	$q=$	0.32				− 5.3							
27	$p_A=$	0.08	− 6.25			− 6.8	− 6.8	− 6.8	− 11.8	− 11.8	− 11.8	− 6.8	+32.8
28	$a=$	6.25	− 6.25	− 1.69								+31.2	
29	$b=$	−0.10			0.184	0.094	+ 5.17	0.094	0.094	0.094	5.17	0.094	+ 1.0
30	$u=$	35.2	−34.66	− 9.36	−1.02	+ 0.64	−27.46	−13.36	53.94	− 1.36	−29.46	172.2	−13.0
31	$u_A=$	−0.10				− 2.58	− 2.58	− 7.58	− 1.28	1.28	+ 3.7	− 7.58	9.4
32	$w'=$	35.3	−34.66	− 9.36	−1.02	+ 8.22	−24.88	− 5.78	55.2	− 0.08	−33.18	181.0	3.6
33	$u'_A=$	8.51	− 8.25	− 2.23	−0.243	+ 1.27	− 5.43	−15.63	12.07	1.13	7.83	42.5	−10.3
34	$v'_A=$	0.206			0.127	− 0.195	+ 3.20	− 0.195	− 0.195	− 0.195	+ 3.20	− 0.195	2.1
35	$x'_A=$	4.75	− 4.69	− 1.27	−0.14	− 0.36	− 4.16	+ 3.14	15.64	0.14	3.66	23.14	1.1
36	$y'_A=$	−0.07			0.127	0.065	3.565	0.065	0.065	0.065	3.565	0.065	0.7
37	$L=$	7.25	− 6.25	− 1.69								+31.2	
*38	$Z=$	44.4	−43.6	− 11.8	−1.37	−24.6	−50.3	−53.6	31.4	−52.9	−78.6	1.6	56.0[2]
39	$E=$	21.3	−21.0	− 5.7	−0.46	−11.8	−24.1	−25.7	15.1	−25.4	−37.7	+ 0.8	26.9[3]
*40	$E'=$	35.8	−35.3	− 9.5	−1.22	+ 4.1	−34.6	−13.6	49.4	−17.1	−55.8	179.4	3.9
41	$E''=$	[4]											
42	$U_A=$	−0.03			−1.22	−13.56	− 8.56	−13.56	−11.66	−11.66	− 6.66	−13.56	+19.4
43	$U'=$	43.1	−41.5	−11.2	−1.22	+ 4.1	−34.6	−12.6	+49.4	−16.1	−55.8	211.1	3.9
44	$U'_A=$	8.51	− 8.25	− 2.23	−0.243	1.63	− 8.33	−18.53	9.17	4.03	−10.73	39.6	4.2
45	$V'_A=$	0.206			0.127	0.865	+ 2.63	− 0.865	− 0.865	− 0.865	+ 2.63	0.865	+ 0.33
46	$X'_A=$	4.75	− 4.69	− 1.27	−0.14	− 4.46	− 8.26	0.96	11.54	3.96	7.76	19.04	9
47	$Y'_A=$	−0.07			0.127	− 1.225	2.275	− 1.225	− 1.225	− 1.225	2.275	− 1.225	3.3

[1] The purpose of the method of writing used in this table is that the first equation for case O reads: $p = 3.12\,l - 2.77\,l_{-1} - 0.75\,(p_{-1}-p_{-2}) - 0.08\,Z_{-1} - 1.65\ldots$; for case P the last term is replaced by −3.90, etc. [2] First year 78.0. [3] First year 37.6

[4] The values of E'' can be calculated more simply by another method, by using E' and E.

If we select from this table the equations shown with an asterisk in addition to the numbers (16) and (17) (Table II) of the original system, then we have five equations with five variables (Table V), whilst the remaining equations of Table II only serve to determine the other variables out of those five variables.

From this we find that, in order to know the further systematic movements of the system, we have to assume as given the values of a few quantities during the two years previous to the base year. The figures assumed in this report are mentioned below, together with some explanations.

TABLE IV

ASSUMED INITIAL VALUES

Variables	p_{-2}	p_{-1}	l_{-1}	l	Z_{-1}
Initial values	$+2$	$+2$	$+18$	$+16$	-40

When determining these values the following considerations have been taken into account. It is assumed that foreign countries are again just about in cyclical equilibrium, for which assumption there are several indications. Furthermore the price and wage figures when introduced into equation (1) should yield a reasonable figure for a and when introduced in (2) they should give a reasonable figure for u. In any case there is a certain arbitrariness in the choice which does not greatly affect the validity of the conclusions reached.

Once these values have been assumed, by means of repeated application of the equations of Table V, we can calculate the entire further development of the variables E', l, Z, E and p while with the aid of equations (26) to (47) we can find all other variables.

In Table V we have given an example of such a calculation; it is the case which would occur if no further measures of economic-political nature were taken or enforced by circumstances and, as will always be done in what follows, by applying the fictitious assumption that external circumstances will not change.

In the following part of this essay we will now show that the development which would occur in the case of certain other kinds of economic policy, can be calculated by making some relatively small changes in the formula equipment. Before we deal with this aspect, however, a few remarks

TABLE V

THE 5 EQUATIONS WITH FIVE VARIABLES WHICH SUCCESSIVELY DETERMINE EACH OTHER, THE GIVEN INITIAL VALUES, AND THE DEVELOPMENT OF THE CALCULATIONS IN A CONCRETE CASE.

$E' = 0.26\,E_{-1} - E'_{-1}$ . . . . from equation (17), Table II

$35.8\,l = E' + 35.3\,l_{-1} + 9.5(p_{-1} - p_{-2}) + 1.22\,Z_{-1} - 4.1$ . . . from equation (40), Table III

$Z = 44.4\,l - 43.6\,l_{-1} - 11.8(p_{-1} - p_{-2}) - 1.37\,Z_{-1} - 24.6$ . . . equation (38), Table III

$E = 0.48\,Z + 0.20\,Z_{-1}$ . . . . equation (16), Table II

$p = 3.12\,l - 2.77\,l_{-1} - 0.75(p_{-1} - p_{-2}) - 0.08\,Z_{-1} - 1.65$ . . . equation (25), Table III

Survey of the processes relevant in case O. The several columns are simply calculated successively once the italicized figures are known. These are the data indicated in Table IV as required.

Year	$t-2$	$t-1$	t	$t+1$	$t+2$	$t+3$	$t+4$	$t+5$	$t+6$
$0.26\,E_{-1}'$ for E_{-1} see previous column				− 8	− 7	− 8	− 7	− 7	− 7
$-E'_{-1}$,, E_{-1} ,, ,,				+ 9	− 1	+ 8	0	+ 7	0
E'			− 9	+ 1	− 8	0	− 7	0	− 7
E'			− 9	+ 1	− 8	0	− 7	0	− 7
$35.3\,l_{-1}$ for l_{-1} see previous column			+634	+563	+493	+430	+356	+282	+203
$+9.5(p_{-1} - p_{-2})$,, $p_{-1} - p_{-2}$,, ,,			0	− 4	0	+ 9	− 16	− 20	+ 8
$1.22\,Z_{-1}$,, Z_{-1} ,, ,,			− 49	− 55	− 44	− 55	− 43	− 52	− 44
-4.1			− 4	− 4	− 4	− 4	− 4	− 4	− 4
$35.8\,l$			+572	+501	+437	+362	+286	+205	+140
l		+ 18	+ 16	+ 14	+ 12	+ 10	+ 8	+ 6	+ 4
$44.4\,l$ for l_{-1} see previous column			+709	+620	+541	+449	+355	+255	+173
$-43.6\,l_{-1}$,, l_{-2} ,, ,,			−784	−698	−610	−532	−441	−350	−251
$-11.8(p_{-1} - p_{-2})$,, $p_{-1} - p_{-2}$,, ,,			0	0	0	+ 11	+ 20	+ 25	+ 9
$-1.37\,Z_{-1}$,, Z_{-1} ,, ,,			+ 55	+ 62	+ 49	+ 62	+ 48	+ 59	+ 49
-24.6			− 25	− 25	− 25	− 25	− 25	− 25	− 25

TABLE V (continued)

Year	$t-2$	$t-1$	t	$t+1$	$t+2$	$t+3$	$t+4$	$t+5$	$t+6$
Z		40	45	36	45	35	43	36	45
$0.48\,Z$ — for Z_{-1} see previous column			22	17	22	17	21	17	22
$0.20\,Z_{-1}$			8	9	7	9	7	9	7
E			30	26	29	26	28	26	29
$3.12\,l$			+50.0	+43.6	+38.1	+31.6	+25.0	+18.0	+12.2
$-2.77\,l_{-1}$ — for l_{-1} see previous column			−50.0	−44.3	−38.7	−33.9	−28.0	−22.2	−16.0
$-0.75(p_{-1}-p_{-2})$,, $p_{-1}-p_{-2}$,, ,, ,,			0.0	+0.3	0.0	0.7	1.3	1.6	0.6
$-0.08\,Z_{-1}$,, Z_{-1} ,, ,, ,,			+3.2	+3.6	+2.9	+3.6	+2.8	+3.5	+2.9
-1.65			1.6	1.6	1.6	1.6	1.6	1.6	1.6
p	+2	+2	+1.6	+1.6	+0.7	−1.0	−3.1	−3.9	−3.1
$p-p_{-1}$		0	−0.4	0	−0.9	−1.7	−2.1	−0.8	+0.8

should be made regarding the nature of the movements which have been found. These movements differ for the various variables of the system. They include monotonic movements and cyclical movements of various lengths and degrees of damping, as could be expected on the basis of general theories regarding this subject. All these different kinds of movements jointly form what could be called the mechanism of the "domestic business cycles" of the Netherlands. These "domestic business cycles" are fictitious to a certain extent: they are the cycles which would occur if nothing changed abroad—an assumption used in this report but not supported by experience. Accordingly a direct empirical check is not possible.

Among the most distinctive characteristics of these "domestic business cycles" we find the following:

a) frequent very short fluctuations lasting about two years;

b) the longer movements in general are not periodical, but move toward a new state of equilibrium. The latter could be expressed in a terminology which might sound more familiar to economists, *i.e.* by saying: with regard to the "domestic business cycle of the Netherlands" as found with our imperfect technique (and accordingly to be considered as provisional) a mechanism as assumed by Schumpeter applies. This author also considers a slump as only a period of readjustment leading to a new state of equilibrium after a strong impulse, the depression as the new state of equilibrium from which society emerges only after a new impulse (*e.g.* of a technical nature).

Not too much importance should be attached to this fact however. The structure of the problems we are concerned with here is such that results of this kind (whether a movement develops periodically or in an asymptotic manner, and how long the period may be) are relatively unreliable. The reason for this is that the calculations involved — the advance calculation of the systematic movement over a period covering perhaps 10 years from a given initial point — actually implies a tremendous extrapolation. A slight change in some coefficients is sometimes enough to turn a periodical into an aperiodical movement and *vice-versa*, of which the first parts almost coincide but whose further development increasingly diverges. The most reliable part is, of course, the extrapolation for the first few years, which is sufficient for the problem now being availed. This extrapolation gives us information regarding the direction in which business cycles will develop during the first few years if no disturbing factors arise.

We should like to mention here that the mechanism is most sensitive to changes in the coefficient in the term $Z - Z_{-1}$ in equation (15). When this coefficient is chosen considerably larger than we have now done (this would, through corresponding reduction of the other coefficients, not reduce the correlation of this equation), then very heavy "explosive" fluctuations take place. As the latter are not observed, I have concluded that the coefficient now selected is the right one (compare section 4).

6. THE CONSIDERED ALTERNATIVES OF ECONOMIC POLICY AND THE RESULTS OF THE CALCULATIONS

As stated previously, the formulae developed in the preceding sections may be used, with relatively small alterations, to calculate the developments to be expected in the case of another economic policy. This method is a little rough but, nevertheless, it gives indications of the direction of the effects of a certain policy. Moreover we should remember that this rough method takes into account at least as large a number of factors as can be considered in any line of reasoning.

The economic policies are studied either separately or in combination with each other, in accordance with the suggestion made in section 2.

$P)$ The execution of extra investment projects during a three year period, starting in year $t + 1$, whereby it has been taken for granted, just as in the Labour Plan, that some additional exports (ca. 6%) can be negotiated to pay for the increased imports of raw materials.

$Q)$ The limitation of imports of finished consumer goods.

$R)$ An increase in labour productivity combined with price reduction and without an increase in the production of capital equipment.[13]

$R')$ A reduction of prices without changes in labour efficiency and without wage reductions.[13]

$S)$ A non-recurrent reduction in the wage rate (in year $t + 1$).

---

[13] It has been assumed that this begins at first in the year $t + 3$, in order, in combination with the case P to obtain as true as possible a picture of the complex of measures proposed in the Labour Plan.

T)   Devaluation of the guilder, with reprisals on the part of foreign countries.[14]

These different cases correspond, either alone or in combination, with a number of measures which are recommended to combat the depression. We will have to ascertain here whether they are capable of causing a domestic revival without laying too heavy a burden on the balance of payments. Various of these cases can be effectuated along entirely differing lines. Thus for example, the policy mentioned under *P* can be realized both by the community through public works and by private individuals. The latter case is an automatic result of an increase in productivity as meant under *R* when such an increase is possible only by means of an addition to capital equipment. In the same way the price reduction mentioned under *R'* may be the result of greater efficiency in the management of enterprises (possibly business concentration)—for this reason this case has been mentioned immediately after *R*—but *R'* can be reached just as well by reducing monopolistic prices, *etc.*

In this first summary we have not yet discussed the necessary magnitude of the policy measures or instruments. This cannot always be done in an immediately understandable form. It will be done in Table VI and has also been done in the right half of Table III. By way of introduction it should be mentioned that in general the measures have been assumed to be executed to the maximum degree deemed possible. We have commented on this aspect in section 2.

In the terminology of our equations each of the cases *P* to *T* may be very roughly approximated by additional terms, taken as constant, to some of the elementary equations, and also to the derived equations of Table III. In Table VI these changes in the elementary equations are indicated and briefly explained, while the result, after elimination of irrelevant variables, has been stated in Table III. Making use of the method described in Table V now enables us to calculate the successive movements in each of the economic quantities for each of the cases. A number of these figures has been collected in Table VII; most of these figures are shown graphically in Fig. 20. We see that in Table VII, those shifts in the balance of payments are also given which correspond to the cases under consideration. Thus equipped we are

---

[14] Calculations were made with more and less intense reprisals.

now able to draw a few conclusions regarding the central problem of this report.

O) We find then in the first place that the starting point indicated in Table IV, in the case of a free working of the forces, leads to a (depressive) state of equilibrium which would give 11 to 12 points more employment.

Although the free forces would depress wages further, this would give relatively little gain in employment. The non-labour incomes (in money) also would show little change. The balance of payments will not change its position greatly as far as the current items are concerned.

P) On the basis of such a situation a revival could take place when (as assumed in case *P* and also taken as starting-point of this report section 2), an increase of production for investment starts, either on the part of private persons or on that of public bodies. Case *P* corresponds more to the latter case since no technical improvements in the production process have been assumed. The balance of payments will be influenced somewhat unfavourably during the years of revival; this influence, however, remains within relatively narrow limits (see our commentary in section 2). After the investment period terminates, employment drops again to the initial level. (This is due to the fact that no change in labour productivity has been assumed, and also to the circumstance that the simplifications which we have used, *a priori* eliminate the presence of more than one equilibrium position. This is of lesser importance, however, as far as the reasoning of this report is concerned.)

PR') A more classical revival could take place if a motive for new investment should arise due, for example, to a new invention; or if a technological improvement should come to us from abroad. The development would more or less coincide with the course followed by line *PR'* if there were a particularly strong reason for investment. A similar impulse at a point of time fixed by human will would occur if the combination of measures mentioned in the Labour Plan should be carried out without devaluation. Then a lasting improvement in employment above the previous cases would take place; this improvement would, in the case of a reduction in prices by 5%, be about 3 to 4%. The balance of payments will in this case also be influenced unfavourably but also within restricted limits.

TABLE VI

THE TERMS ADDED TO THE ELEMENTARY EQUATIONS IN THE CASES OF VARIOUS ECONOMIC POLICIES

Case	Nr of the equation	Size of extra term on right-hand side	Brief motivation
P	8	+ 14 (during three years)	Due to this addition the investment volume is about Hfl 250 million larger (guilders of 1923/33) than would be invested on the basis of the previous year's profits.
Q	12	—15	This means that in the competition between the imports of raw materials and that of finished products an "artifical" shift is introduced which causes about 30% of the imports of finished products to be replaced by domestic products.
R	2	—5	Because of these changes, the same quantity of consumer goods could be obtained with about 10% less labour and prices would drop by about 5%. Extra capital formation does not take place (equation 8 does not contain an extra term).
	9	—10	
R'	2	—5	The same price reduction takes place as with R, but no reduction in the quantity of labour in the production of one unit product.
S	1	—5 (during one year)	This implies an extra reduction in wages of 5%, to be applied once.
T			In this case it is simpler to indicate that a number of (external) quantities assume another value e.g. that all prices in foreign markets rise by 30 points. That is to say $p_A = p'_A = q'_A = +25$, $p_w = r'_A = s'_A = +20$. Moreover I goes up 20 points and therefore $I = +10$. At the same time it is assumed that owing to foreign reprisals exports will be 18 points lower than they would have become otherwise. Therefore in equation 6 an extra term of —18 is introduced on the right side.

Q) Restriction of imports of finished products has in itself few consequences as far as employment is concerned. A further analysis of the
calculations shows us that this is due to the fact that rising prices of
products exert a counteracting force: owing to this sales possibilities
are limited. In this case the balance of payments shows a very favourable change, and when used in combination with *P* it is capable of
considerably reducing the unfavourable influence on the balance of
payments.

R) Increasing labour productivity without new production of capital
goods (for brevity's sake we could say efficiency rise) together with the
normal but not completely adequate price reduction has an unfavourable influence on employment. This is to be attributed, in view of
the further analysis of the figures, to the fact that the improvement in
sales possibilities which arises due to the price reduction is more than
offset by the loss of employment due to the rise in efficiency. Here
therefore no compensation theory is applicable. If the increase in
efficiency is coupled to new investments then employment is increased
while those new investments are being made.

In this case the balance of payments shows a slightly more favourable aspect than in case *O* which means that the combination of *P* and
R gives a very slightly more favourable balance of payments than *P*
alone.

R') More favourable in respect of employment is, as was already
mentioned in passing above when discussing the combination *PR'*, a
price reduction which is not the consequence of expanded labour productivity but of either a reduction in monopolistic prices or increased
management efficiency. Actually this depends mainly on the fact that
the smaller remuneration of these groups does not mean a reduction
of equal size in the purchasing power in the consumer goods market;
part of the reduction in these incomes leads to less saving and that is,
in times of depression, no drawback as far as employment is concerned.
From this it follows that we decidedly must think of a reduction in
the income of the well-paid independents; a reduction in the incomes of
the distressed peasants or middle-classers would not have the calculated
effect in this case. The balance of payments is, in this case, again more
unfavourably influenced, although not to a considerable extent and
not beyond the acceptable limits.

TABLE VII

The Course of Development of a Few Important Economic Variables in the Case of Various Economic Policies, as Calculated in the Manner Described in the Text (Assume a Constant Export Position) Employment. (1 point a little less than 1% of the employment assumed as normal)

Policy	year t	$t+1$	$t+2$	$t+3$	$t+4$	$t+5$	$t+6$	$t+7$	Brief indication of the nature of the policy[1]
O	−22	−12	−11	−11	−10	−10	−11	−10	"Free forces"
P	−22	−5	+1	+2	−3	−10	−11	−10	"Public works"
Q	−22	−11	−9	−11	−10	−11	−11		"Protection"
R	−22	−12	−11	−19	−18	−19	−18	−8	"Efficiency rise"
R'	−22	−12	−11	−7	−7	−8	−7	−7	"Business concentration"
PR'	−22	−5	+1	+5	0	−6	−7	−8	"Labour Plan without devaluation"
S	−22	−11	+6	−7	−10	−10	−11		"Wage reduction"
T	−22	+12	+14	+13	−13	+12	+13		"Devaluation with reprisals"
T'	−22	+19	+21	+20	+21				"Devaluation with strong improvement in the Dutch Indies"

[1] The reader is warned not to interpret these brief indications without consulting the text.

Balance of Payments (current items; changes in the initial position; 1 point = $ca.$ Hfl 17.5 mln)

Policy	t	$t+1$	$t+2$	$t+3$	$t+4$	$t+5$	$t+6$	$t+7$
O	−2	−2	−2	−1	−1	−1	0	+2
P	−2	−9	−18	−20	−10	−7	−4	−2
Q	+10	+6	+6	+9	+8	+9		
R	−2	−2	−1	0	+8	+1	+2	+2
R'	−2	−2	−1	−5	−6	−6	+2	−3
S	−2	−3	−28	−22	−13	−2	−4	
T	+24	−17	−19	−21	−21	−18	0	
T'	+44	−8	−11	−14	−14		−19	

S) An average wage reduction across the board of 5% immediately stimulates a strong revival in employment. This is followed, however, after a few years by a drop which leads to the same level as the initial one. It is remarkable that during this revival the balance of payments is influenced most unfavourably.

T) Much more favourable consequences for employment ,as well as for the non-labour incomes, will occur if a devaluation takes place. The difference is striking. It would have been even greater, if we had not assumed severe reprisals on the part of foreign countries at such a strength that in consequence *ca.* 20% of exports, or around 100% of the improvement to be expected in exports without reprisals, is cut off. Our attention is drawn to the fact that in this case the balance of payments, after one very favourable year, then becomes more and more unfavourable. The latter obviously occurs less strongly when, as can be seen in the series of figures *T'* added to the table, it is assumed that the incomes *I* from enterprises working abroad, interest, *etc.* go up more strongly than was assumed in Table VI. For case *T'* it has been assumed that $I = +30$, which is fairly high. The unfavourable result will obviously be less extensive than when the percentage of the devaluation is chosen at a lower figure than the one assumed here (*ca.* 25%). This is not unreasonable either in view of the adaptation already achieved. Here also, a combination with the method of import restriction would have a favourable effect on the balance of payments.

7. RECAPITULATION;
WHAT DOES EXPERIENCE ABROAD TEACH US?

The foregoing has demonstrated that our problem is of a most complicated nature. Even with the great simplification used in the commentary, it was necessary to build up an apparatus for systematizing our thoughts in order to evaluate the various influences which make themselves felt. Only a systematizing of the relations such as is attempted here can, in my opinion, lead to fertile discussion. It is hardly conceivable that mutual understanding and further progress are possible without an accurate localisation of the sources of differences in opinion.

In the meanwhile, nevertheless, a number of phenomena have been neglected in this scheme, such as the influence of the rate of interest on the volume of investments, the influence of stock fluctuations on production, *etc*.

Furthermore there still exists a lamentable lack of the exact information required to do a good job in the analysis outlined here.

Owing to this lack of information, as well as to the parallelism between a number of series, a few of the coefficients in the elementary equations are uncertain. Of some, however, it can be said that, in a first approximation, this does not endanger the conclusions.

A further uncertainty is occasioned by the extrapolation of the calculations into the future. In particular the length of the cycles is an unreliable figure.

Once we take these reservations into account, conclusions can be drawn only with the greatest circumspection. Nevertheless I am of the opinion that these conclusions are considerably more solidly established than many conclusions already published regarding these problems.

The conclusions reached here are that, with a constant demand function and an unchanged price level abroad, a fairly considerable domestic revival of employment can be achieved by means of devaluation. Clearly lesser revivals can be achieved by reducing wages, carrying out public works or by reducing prices without reducing wage rates. A further deterioration of employment is reached if only the productivity of paid labour is increased without producing additional capital goods. Hardly any improvement of employment is attained if our only policy is to apply protection by hampering imports of finished consumer goods.

The balance of payments is most favourably affected by restricting imports of finished consumer goods, most unfavourably by a wage reduction and strong devaluation. In the remaining cases the balance of payments is changed very little. On the basis of the arguments enumerated in section 2, however, a certain deterioration in the balance of payments is acceptable, particularly since the earning-power position of Dutch trade and industry would show less extensive arrears with regard to foreign countries, in the case of devaluation.

The first question put to the readers therefore is answered in the affirmative in this report. A domestic revival is even possible in somewhat differing ways. From the tables various combinations can be compiled which lead to the desired result without taxing overmuch the balance of payments. Among the separate measures moderate devaluation (*e.g.* 20 %) has the most favourable result. The most favourable combination would be a combination of a moderate devaluation, some protection and a number of measures mentioned in the Labour Plan (public works, increase in efficiency through business concentration and cyclical policy).

The second question, which relates to the lesson we should draw from the experience of others, cannot be dealt with exhaustively here due to lack of space. Superficially when reading this report it might be thought that nothing of foreign experience has been used. Indirectly, however, this has partially taken place: a number of the equations which have been utilized has also been investigated with regard to other countries and it has often been found that the result of these investigations made our findings for the Netherlands seem plausible. Thus far, therefore, this experience has proved useful. We have to be careful, however, with comparisons between countries. At the present stage of the investigation it cannot yet be said whether small structural differences might not prove to result in large differences in reaction to certain measures. Striking examples could be given of the great influence which may be exercised by a moderate structural change. For example, a change in the export dependency of a country may greatly affect the results of wage policy.[15] For this reason it is dangerous to use experience gained in one country when judging the policy followed by other countries. For example, because the policy of extensive public works in Sweden has had no unfavourable consequences for the capital market, this policy has been proven possible, but it has not been proven feasible under all circumstances. The balance of payments difficulties due to its policy of creating employment through public works prove nothing about the results of such a policy in the Netherlands and so on. Only a further development of the engineering skill of econometrics will help in this respect in my opinion.

---

[15] This problem has been discussed more extensively in my "*Fondements mathématiques*". There we find that there is a "critical export percentage" with regard to this problem. For a country which has a smaller export percentage, wage rigidity is better during structural depressions, and for a country with a higher export percentage wage flexibility is preferable.

LAG CYCLES AND LIFE CYCLES*

1. In trade cycle theories a distinction is made between exogenous and endogenous movements. An exogenous movement in economic quantities (production, prices, incomes, *etc.*) is caused by changes in the non-economic "data", the natural, technical and institutional circumstances in which economic events take place. An endogenous movement procedes whilst the "data" remain unaltered, emanating from the internal relations which exist between the economic quantities, although this movement must receive its initial impulse from a change in data. In reality smaller and greater changes in data are constantly occurring. Nevertheless most trade cycles investigators are of the opinion, and rightly so I think, that a trade cycle is an endogenous movement which is only disturbed by numerous but small changes in data. This means that the forces issuing from the mutual relationship between the economic quantities are generally stronger than the "disturbing" forces from the outside. A number of important aspects of cyclical theory and policy can accordingly be analysed, leaving the "disturbing" outside forces out of consideration. This course will be followed in this article.

Endogenous movements would not occur at all if the causal relationship between the economic quantities and the "data" were completely simultaneous, that is to say if every economic quantity were only related to the other economic quantities and the "data" of the same moment. In that case what we could call an immediate adaptation of the entire economic system to the natural, technical and institutional conditions of the moment would occur. If we assume that the latter do not change (or, which would lead to the same conclusions regarding business cycle theory, only change slowly and in one direction) there would never be an actual possibility of fluctuations occurring.

---

* "Vertragingsgolven en Levensduurgolven", from *"Strijdenskracht door Wetensmacht, Opstellen aangeboden aan S. de Wolff t.g.v. zijn 60e verjaardag"*. Amsterdam 1938, p. 143–150.

For this reason it is a necessary —although not sufficient—condition that the relationships existing between the several economic quantities should be dynamic *i.e.* that the value taken by one variable at a given moment depends on the values of other variables at previous moments. For example, activity in shipbuilding depends on the profits which have been made in shipping during the previous year; or wages and prices of consumer goods depend on the production attained some time previously. It is true that owing to such a time difference between two or more phenomena which are causally connected a cycle may be caused. The examples which will be discussed later will demonstrate this point.

In the first place we may point out that such a difference in time can occur in several ways, two of which we will examine here. In the first place these time differences may be relatively slight as compared to the length of the cyclical fluctuations; in the second place they may be of the same size. The first kind finds its chief representative in all kinds of lags which occur in economic life as a result of the length of production processes and of numerous "reactions". For example the reaction of entrepreneurs to certain favourable conditions, in the shape of new investments, takes a few months during which the situation has to be watched, plans have to be made or elaborated *etc.* The reaction of wages to altered labour conditions takes some time, *i.a.* due to the contract periods and also to other reasons. The reactions of the cost of living to a changed cyclical situation depends on the period for which stocks have been laid, on the period of hire-purchase transactions and on numerous other conditions which are time-consuming.

The second category of time differences which has been mentioned above—the longer differences in time—is chiefly caused by the life of a number of durable goods. A car has an average useful life of six to seven years and when it is worn out it will be necessary to produce a new one. The latter event then is logically connected with an event pertaining to a number of years previously.

Both the shorter and longer time differences in economic relationships may lead to fluctuations of the same length as cyclical fluctuations but the two kinds of fluctuations show a few differences in character which will be scrutinized further here. For brevity's sake they will be called henceforth "lag fluctuations" and "life fluctuations".

2. An example of a mechanism with lag fluctuations is given by the following model. The following economic variables are under consideration:

L labour income

Z the income not derived from labour, to be called "profit" in short

U the value of the consumer goods sold

V the value of the investment goods sold.

The following relationships are assumed between these variables, all measured as deviations from a moving equilibrium.[1]

(1) The profit equation which shows how "profits" are calculated:

$$(1) \qquad\qquad Z = U + V - L.$$

In this equation $U + V$ is the value of the products sold by all enterprises in the economy. Only wages are deducted as cost elements; the cost of the raw materials used by all enterprises is also converted to wage costs. Besides wages, depreciation should be deducted as a cost but it can be assumed that it changes so gradually that it only shows a trend with no cyclical component. Our equations, however, apply only to the latter category.

(2) It is assumed that the value of the investment goods sold fluctuates with profits. The main reasons are that, on the one hand, investments promise to pay best when profits are generally high and, on the other hand, that the financial possibilities permit investments, both out of own funds and with the aid of outside capital, most easily when profits are high. In this relation we assume a lag of one time unit, which is taken to be four months. Then we get

$$(2) \qquad\qquad V_t = \beta Z_{t-1},$$

whereby β represents a constant coefficient.

(3) Finally it is assumed that the expenditures on consumer goods are related to L and Z in the following way:

In the first place the entire amount of wages is spent on consumer goods immediately.

---

[1] This equilibrium may prove unstable. See: "On the theory of business-cycle control", *Econometrica*, 1938.

In the second place the consumer goods expenditure of independents is determined by both their income Z and by the rise in their capital per time unit. With regard to the latter we assume that it changes proportionally with Z. In these relationships we assume time lags of such a nature that finally we obtain the following formula:

$$(3) \qquad U_t = L_t + \varepsilon_1 Z_{t-1} + \varepsilon_2 (Z_{t-1} - Z_{t-2}).$$

In view of the fact that our first and foremost aim is to give an example, the details of the assumption should not be taken too literally. Nevertheless they correspond fairly well to reality, e.g. in the United States, as an extensive statistical investigation taught me.[2]

If we choose the unit at about 34.000 million dollars, then an estimate of the average value for L and Z over the period 1919–1932, to be indicated by $\overline{L}$ and $\overline{Z}$, reaches 1; $\overline{U} = 1.8$ and $\overline{V} = 0.2$; furthermore we can put $\beta = 0.2$, $\varepsilon_1 = 0.6$ and $\varepsilon_2 = 1$.

The three equations obtained are sufficient to determine the course of Z, V and $U - L$; if we wished to know the course of L and U separately, then a further relationship would be required. This is not essential to achieve our purpose and for this reason we limit ourselves to the above. For example we find that the following movement equation can be applied to Z.

$$(4) \qquad Z_t - (\beta + \varepsilon_1 + \varepsilon_2) Z_{t-1} + \varepsilon_2 Z_{t-2} = 0.$$

The same equation can be found for both other quantities.

The exact significance of this equation is that the value taken by Z during the period $t (Z_t)$ is determined by the values Z_{t-1} and Z_{t-2} which Z has assumed during the periods $t - 1$ and $t - 2$. The distance between two time units, between the first and the last term in this equation, we will call the "interval" of this mechanism. For the values of the coefficients mentioned above we get:

$$(5) \qquad Z_t = 1.8 Z_{t-1} - Z_{t-2}.$$

The Table shown below gives an example; starting from a lowest point where $Z_1 = Z_2 = -0.5$ we find $Z_3 = -0.4$. With the aid of Z_2 and Z_3 it becomes possible to calculate Z_4 and so on. The character

---

[2] A few particulars in this respect are mentioned in my article in *Econometrica*, Jan. 1938 just mentioned and in my *Fondements mathématiques de la stabilisation des affaires*, Paris 1938, where somewhat different definitions were applied.

of the movement can now be clearly seen; moreover it can easily be proven.

$t =$	1	2	3	4	5	6	7	8	9	10
$Z =$	—0.5	—0.5	—0.4	—0.22	0	+0.22	+0.40	+0.50	+0.50	+0.40
$t =$	11	12	13	14	15	16	17	18	19	20
$Z =$	+0.22	0	—0.22	—0.40	—0.50	—0.50	—0.40	—0.22	0	+0.22

The period of the movements depends on the β, ε_1 and ε_2; and it can be shown that the period is increasing if $\frac{1}{4}(\beta + \varepsilon_1 + \varepsilon_2)^2$ approaches ε_2 but does not exceed this value. In our case the period is almost 14 time units or about $4\frac{2}{3}$ year; in any case it is considerably longer than the lags which "cause" it and this is significant with regard to our further argument. Apart from the way as indicated in this model lag cycles can arise in many other ways.

3. The theories which utilize the lifetime of capital goods as a main element in the explanation of the fluctuating level of economic activity, can thus be stylized into a model. We assume that increased production of capital goods leads immediately to increased purchasing power on the part of the producers and accordingly to an increased production of consumption goods; also that the price system alters immediately in conformity with production and for this reason incomes and profits do also. If we indicate the latter by Z, a parallel movement of Z_t with the production y_t of capital goods will exist. If we again measure both quantities in terms of deviations of some equilibrium development, then:

$$(6) \qquad\qquad y_t = \eta Z_t$$

and all other economic quantities also will run parallel to Z_t. The production of capital goods itself can depend on two factors; these are Z_t and the quantity of capital goods which are eligible for replacement after a rigidly determined lifetime. Capital goods with widely varying lifetime T will exist; for simplicity's sake we assume that there is only one kind of production equipment but that of each two there is one with a lifetime of six and one with a lifetime of eight years. In reality the spreading is much greater and numerous intermediate stages exist but, in principle at least, this does not change our considerations in any way that we can detect. If we express the production of capital goods in the year $t - 6$ by y_{t-6} and in the year $t - 8$ by y_{t-8}, then the quantity of production units which are eligible for replacement according to their lifetime is:

$$\tfrac{1}{2}\, y_{t-6} + \tfrac{1}{2}\, y_{t-8}.$$

Our assumption concerning y_t now becomes accordingly:

(7) $y_t = \tfrac{1}{2}\, (y_{t-6} + y_{t-8}) + \zeta\, Z_t,$

and this assumption can now be interpreted in such a way that, depending on Z_t, more or less is replaced than is necessary according to the life of the equipment and secondly that, apart from replacement, new investment still takes place also depending on Z. Combining the equation (6) and (7) we find:

(8) $y_t = \tfrac{1}{2}\, (y_{t-6} + y_{t-8}) + a\, y_t,$

where

(9)
$$a = \frac{\zeta}{\eta}.$$

This therefore is the final equation of a system in which lifetime appears as the only "dynamic factor". As the course followed from year 1 to 8 is given, further developments can also be calculated. During a few of these eight years, owing to factors which we will provisionally consider as accidental, a peak has appeared in the volume of production of production equipment. There will be a propensity for this peak to occur again. This is, in a nutshell, the so-called echo-theory propounded in this country by S. DE WOLFF, not only with respect to the short (about eight-yearly) cyclical fluctuations but also with regard to the long (about forty years) cycle which we will not consider further here.

An objection which has often been made to this theory is that the damping of the cycles would be very considerable in view of the wide variation in the lifetimes of the capital goods. This is true if we leave out the term with Z_t in equation (7) which means that the term $a y_t$ drops out of equation (8). The damping is then even underestimated by this equation since the variation of the lifetimes is greater than we have assumed for simplicity's sake.

The afore mentioned strong damping need not occur, however, if we retain the term which contains Z. For a certain value of a we may get undamped cycles or perhaps cycles which display anti-damping. Indeed it is not difficult to set up examples of this kind. With regard to $a = 0.37$ equation (8) *e.g.* gives a purely periodical solution.[3] In reality, however, the values of a will have to be much greater in order to obtain undamped cycles.

4. We will now make a few comparisons between lag and life cycles. Regrettably lack of space does not allow to back all our statements with a full proof. A few results of investigations will have to suffice.

A first difference springs from the sensitivity of the period to changes in the structural coefficients (such as the figures β and ε with regard to the lag cycles and a to the life cycles). The period of the lag cycles may change very strongly, even when only small changes occur in the structural coefficients. We have to take for granted that such changes take place repeatedly; the comparative invariability in the period of actual business cycles is accordingly somewhat contradictory. The life cycles do not show such sensitivity. Comparatively large changes in a will not exert a strong influence on the period of the cycle.

A second difference is due to the sensitivity to short term disturbances. We chose as an example a country in the middle of a rising phase of the business cycle which normally lasts about five years. Let us assume that owing to an exogenous disturbance the level of economic activity movements is forced downward for one year. If the cyclical mechanism is purely a lag mechanism with an interval of less than a year, business cycles will have entirely and definitely changed their phase: because further movements are entirely determined by the "initial values" during a short period. If, on the other hand, the cyclical mechanism is a lifetime mechanism, then after this disturbance the old course can continue because, for this type of cycle, the present situation is determined by the situation prevailing for a long previous time period. In this case therefore there is a much greater inertia in the cyclical movement. In both cases the precise shape of the smaller fluctuations are determined mainly by the numerous smaller exogenous forces which often occur and which are the main basis for the short-run cyclical diagnoses which appear for example in the newspapers.

It seems to me that both these points of difference, as compared to

---

[3] The function $y = C \sin 2 \pi t/7$, in which C is taken at random, is a solution.

reality, must lead to the view that lag cycles which are founded on relatively short lags are not an adequate explanation of the cyclical movements. But a knowledge of the mechanism of the shorter lags and the connected relationships is vital for problems connected with business cycles. We will once more try to make this plausible by putting the question: if business cycles were caused entirely by the life mechanism of equation (8), would an anti-cyclical policy be effective and if so, what should this policy be? It is clear that an anti-cyclical policy directed at reducing the coefficients $\frac{1}{2}$ in this equation would hardly be suitable. A strong reduction in these coefficients would mean that normally only a small part of the worn production equipment would be replaced, which would be a cure worse than the complaint. A policy which influenced the coefficient a, however, would have an acceptable influence and the cyclical movement would become weaker as $1/1 - a$ decreased. The final equation can be formulated as follows:

$$(10) \qquad\qquad y_t = \frac{\frac{1}{2}(y_{t-6} + y_{t-8})}{1 - a}.$$

This means that a itself must be reduced. However, a is only a symbol representing a number of reactions. In our example they are immediate reactions but in reality they are usually somewhat delayed reactions comprising a "lag mechanism". In order to find out by what policies a can be reduced, further study is required of the relationships characteristic of that mechanism. Although this mechanism is perhaps insufficient to explain the period of the actual movements, it is sufficient to enable us to find the suitable anti-cyclical policy measures.

As a simple example, we will mention "compensating public investments", *i.e.* public investments which move up or down contrary to the cycle of private investments and which are one of the methods of reducing a.

TONNAGE AND FREIGHT*

1. INTRODUCTION

On several occasions attention has already been given in "De Nederlandsche Conjunctuur" to the factors which exercize their influence
on freight rates. A first article[1] drew attention to the significance
which total tonnage seems to have on freight rates, whilst a second
article[2] estimated the relationship between demand and supply factors
for the post-war years. The "Centraal Bureau voor de Statistiek" is
now able to publish the result of similar calculations pertaining to the
pre-war period.

2. ELIMINATING TREND MOVEMENT AND INCIDENTAL FLUCTUATIONS

As has been done previously, the trend movement was eliminated for
the greater part by subtracting the average percentage increase in all
the series (freight rates, supply of tonnage and demand for tonnage).
In order to eliminate at the same time the shorter fluctuations of a
partly incidental nature, the annual increase was calculated for three
successive years, and the average of these annual increases was then
taken. This somewhat cumbersome method leads to five-year
averages of the increase concerned, whereby greater weight is attached
to the middle figure than to the extremes. This is also true, although the
coefficients are more complicated, if we use the theoretically more
exact methods of elimination of ANDERSON.[3] Since the influence of
the weights is not very great, the method indicated was considered to
be sufficiently accurate.

---

* With the cooperation of Mr. B. G. F. BUYS in: *De Nederlandsche Conjunctuur* (1934) March, page 23–35.
[1] *De Nederlandsche Conjunctuur*, March 1931, page 14 *sq.*
[2] *De Nederlandsche Conjunctuur*, March 1933, page 12 *sq.*
[3] *Die Korrelationsrechnung in der Konjunkturforschung*, Bonn, 1929, page
120 *sq.*

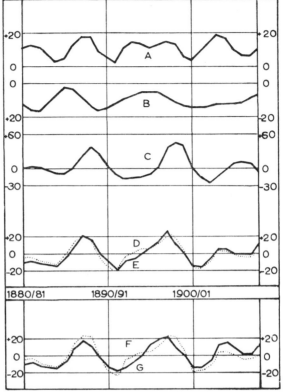

Fig. 1

Percentage increase (5 yearly moving averages) of:
A. demand for tonnage (transport index).
B. total tonnage of the largest countries.
C. coal prices.
D. the calculated ⎫
E. the actual   ⎭ freight index according to Fairplay (homeward freights).
F. the calculated ⎫
G. the actual   ⎭ freight index according to Hobson.

3. FREIGHT RATES

The data used in the correlation calculations are the homeward freights as given in the periodical Fairplay (Year 1916, annex). For comparison, the figures given by HOBSON[4] are reviewed and plotted in Fig. 1. For the period previous to 1885, the figures of Hobson, adapted to the Fairplay figures, were used. For the period 1884–1895 these correspond entirely to the average Fairplay figures.

---

[4] HOBSON, *The Export of Capital.*

4. DEMAND FOR TONNAGE

As we remarked earlier,[5] when the purpose of our analysis is to explain the course followed by prices (in this case freight rates), we should define "demand" as the result of the independent demand factors which together with the freight rate determine the demand which actually occurred. These are the price differences which exist with regard to the main goods transported between the country of origin and the country of destination. Price differences, in their turn, are governed by relative scarcity and are accordingly influenced by variations in harvest or cyclical fluctuations. In this investigation, the quantities actually transported (taking into account the transport distance), although they are also to a certain extent dependent on the freight rate, have been taken as an index of demand. The theoretical consequence of this method is that the regression coefficient of the freight price with respect to actual demand will not be entirely accurate. However, the relation between this coefficient and the supply coefficient is not altered by this. As it can be assumed, as far as the fluctuations of actual demand are concerned, that the fluctuations in the independent demand factors are of much greater significance than the fluctuations in price, it is to be expected that the error in the above-mentioned regression coefficient will prove small. Accordingly a demand index was calculated on the basis of the quantities actually transported and the distance over which transport took place.

Because no figures are available regarding the total weight of all goods shipped and the distance over which these goods have been transported, a demand index had to be set up on the basis of overseas exports of a number of mass products.

Exports of grain from several countries, exports of coal from Great Britain and the United States, exports of oil from the latter country, exports of nitrate of soda from Chile and imports of timber into Great Britain were selected. The export quantities were multiplied by the average distance over which these goods were transported. These distances could be estimated fairly accurately by taking the North Sea ports as the average ultimate destination. The average transport distance of coal from Great Britain could be calculated on the basis of a

---

[5] *De Nederlandsche Conjunctuur*, March 1933, page 25.

statistical survey broken down by country of destination.[6] The average distance for the years 1850, 1860, 1870, 1880, 1890 and 1900 respectively was 2.1, 2.2, 2.2, 2.2, 2.3 and 2.0 thousand nautical miles.

The quantity of product multiplied by distance was expressed in thousands of ton-miles units.

The separate components of the demand index were calculated as follows:

A. GRAIN

a. Exports of grain from the United States of North-America and Canada.

A difficulty occasioned by the fact that the statistical year of American statistics does not coincide with the calendar year. However, since the chief shipments take place in the autumn, the statistical year (July 1st–June 30th) can be compared to the calendar year which precedes it by six months. Although the influence of this shift can be disregarded in the method of the average three-yearly increases, in the case of yearly increases it may have a disturbing influence.

United States' exports of wheat, maize, barley and oats and Canada's exports of all grain were studied. The frontier traffic between Canada and the United States has been taken into account. In studying grain exports from the United States the major ports of export were classified by location into two groups: the Atlantic coast ports (New York, New Orleans) and the Pacific coast ports (San Francisco). This breakdown was significant due to the great difference in transport distance. Such a breakdown, however, could not be applied to Canadian ports. Furthermore, the grain index figures were supplemented with data pertaining to flour transport between the United States and Canada on the one hand, and Great Britain on the other.

b. Grain exports from Argentina did not become sizeable until 1900, which explains the difficulty of obtaining figures for the years previous to 1900. Data regarding wheat exports from 1883 and figures of maize exports from 1901 were included in the index.

c. The extremely important grain exports from Russia are assumed

---

[6] *Journal of the Royal Stat. Soc.*, 1903, page 508.

to originate from the Black Sea ports, an assumption which can be made without the danger of significant error. Up to 1892 exports of wheat, barley, oats and rye were included, after this year exports of all kinds of grain were included.

d. Exports of all grain from Rumania since 1880 were also included in the index.

e. Australia, like Argentina, became important as a grain producer only in later years. Wheat exports from this continent were included in the index.

f. The statistics for India are based on a statistical year other than the calendar year, just as in the North-American countries. Overseas exports of rice (including paddy) and wheat were included. The rice (incl. paddy) exported to Ceylon was deducted.

B. Coal

a. The important series in this case are the exports from Great Britain. Coal bunkered in British ports was deducted. With regard to the calculation of the average transport distance we refer to the introduction given above.

b. Similarly to grain, when reviewing exports of coal from the United States of North America, land traffic (imports into Canada) was taken into consideration.

   Because, in general, coal exports from Germany do not go overseas, they are not included.

C. Oil

a. The only way to convert oil exports from the United States from statistical years to calendar years was to apply the method of two-year averages. Here again exports of oil from the United States to Canada were deducted from the total exports from the United States.

D. Nitrate of Soda

a. Although they are not of decisive influence on price formation, exports of large quantities of nitrate of soda over relatively large distances on tramp steamers could not be left out of consideration.

E. Timber

a. This series was obtained by selecting as starting point the timber imports into Great-Britain. Although accordingly the series is not at all complete, it still gives an rough idea of the volume of timber transport.

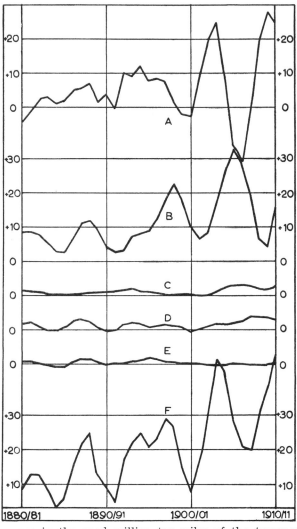

Fig. 2

Absolute increase in thousand million ton-miles of the transport, as far as reviewed, of: A. grain   D. nitrate of soda
                B. coal   E. timber
                C. oil   F. all 5 goods jointly

By summing up the separate series, the total demand index was obtained. Graph 2 illustrates this point. Furthermore it clearly demonstrates the relative unimportance of the series C, D and E. The series B and E are clearly subject to trade cycles; this is not certain with regard to series C and D; but they have been considered subject to cyclical influences in the following.

5. THE SUPPLY ASPECT

The supply picture is determined by two kinds of quantities: in the first place, by the total transport capacity and in the second place by the operating costs. For example when the latter become higher, it is possible that some ships cannot be operated profitably any longer, which might lead to laying them up. Even without reaching this stage the (variable) operating costs influence the freight price because they partly determine the level to which competition is capable of pushing down freight rates. Coal prices (export prices from Great Britain), being the most variable part of operating costs, were included as an independent factor in the calculations.

Just as for demand, when statistically determining transport capacity, the data were restricted to a few important countries i.e. Great Britain, the United States of North-America, Germany and Norway. The appropriateness of this method was shown by the fact that adding Norway to the three countries firstmentioned made no significant difference in the percentage rate of increase. The simple addition of the tonnages is not possible because there is an important difference between the transport capacity of one ton on a steamship and one ton on a sailing ship. The relation between one "steam ton" and one "sail ton" generally being taken in English statistics to be 3:1, this ratio was used in calculating the supply index. Other calculations take the ratio 4:1 as basis. All tonnages were converted into sail tons and subsequently totaled. Apart from the difficulty thus overcome there have also been other factors on the supply side which have brought about a change in the significance of the figures, such as the tremendous improvement of the power plant which has reduced coal consumption to less than half; the improved speed of the vessels; the rise in their tonnage which has contributed to the great reduction in crew per

Crew per ton tonnage on Sl: Sailing ships. St: Steamships on the British fleet

	Sl	St		Sl	St		Sl	St
1870	0.28	0.43	1885	0.21	0.25	1900	0.16	0.23
1871	0.27	0.43	1886	0.20	0.28	1901	0.16	0.22
1872	0.27	0.41	1887	0.19	0.27	1902	0.16	0.22
1873	0.27	0.39	1888	0.20	0.28	1903	0.16	0.22
1874	0.27	0.38	1889	0.20	0.27	1904	0.15	0.21
1875	0.26	0.37	1890	0.19	0.27	1905	0.15	0.21
1876	0.25	0.36	1891	0.19	0.27	1906	0.15	0.20
1877	0.25	0.34	1892	0.18	0.26	1907	0.15	0.20
1878	0.24	0.31	1893	0.18	0.25	1908	0.14	0.20
1879	0.24	0.30	1894	0.17	0.25	1909	0.15	0.20
1880	0.23	0.30	1895	0.17	0.24	1910	0.15	0.20
1881	0.23	0.28	1896	0.17	0.24	1911	0.15	0.20
1882	0.22	0.27	1897	0.17	0.24	1912	0.15	0.20
1883	0.22	0.26	1898	0.16	0.23	1913	0.14	0.20
1884	0.21	0.26	1899	0.16	0.23	1914	0.15	0.20

vessel ton both on steamships and sailing vessels. The figures shown above illustrate this development:

The cost of ship construction declined steadily from £ 18 per ton in 1872 to £ 13 per ton in 1877. In 1885 it was only £ 9 to 10 per ton.

All the latter factors, however, have not been considered in the calculations because their influence has been so gradual that in studying the year-to-year fluctuations they can be ignored for all practical purposes. In an analysis of longer periods these factors would be of decisive importance.

It should also be mentioned that, in the tonnage figures used, the fishing vessels and the American lake vessels have not been included.

6. DISTURBING INFLUENCES

Besides the already mentioned, more normal, economic factors which have their influence on the level of freight prices, we can mention a number of a more abnormal nature. For example, troup transport during war time makes considerable demands on tonnage and in this way influences freight rates. This is shown very clearly in 1900 as a result of the Boer War. An impression of the size of this type of demand for tonnage is given by a note in a report of the Norddeutsche Lloyd

(50 Jahre Norddeutsche Lloyd) from which we see that in order to ship troups to China to put down the Boxer Rebellion, eighteen vessels were required to transport 20.000 men plus ammunition and armament over a distance of 13.000 miles. In 1898 the Spanish Government also called on tonnage to transport troups and supplies to Cuba.

Furthermore it can be surmised that price formation may also be disturbed by partial monopolies. Little historical material can be supplied in this respect. However, this monopoly formation, as known, is limited to the liner trade whilst in the tramp trade it generally has repeatedly failed.[7]

Strikes, also, were often the cause for smaller or larger disturbances of the freight market (e.g. the 1898 strike in the coal mines of South-Wales). Speculations in grain (1898 Wheat corner in the United States) also exercised their influence on the grain prices and on the freight rates.

Although all these influences are levelled off for the greater part by the average five-yearly increases used for the correlation calculation, wherever the yearly differences have been used (graph 6) the particularly high peaks in the years 1898 and 1900 immediately hit the eye.

As a reasonable estimation of the deviations occasioned by all these influences is not feasible, a short explanation with a few notes on the figures in those years where great divergences appear will have to suffice.

7. RESULT OF THE CALCULATIONS

On the basis of the above analysis, an attempt was made, using multiple correlation technique, to estimate as well as possible the fluctuations of the percentage increase in freight rates (based on five-year moving averages). A linear combination of the percentage rise of the following series was made:

a. demand index;
b. total tonnage;
c. coal prices.

The calculations are made for the period 1880–1911; the ten years 1870–1880 show such a rapid structural growth that their inclusion did not seem recommendable. The year 1912 also shows an exceptional

---

[7] Cf. K. GIESE, Das Seefrachttarifwesen, Berlin 1919.

boom in freights for which no reasonable explanation seems to be available; the "Fairplay" records suggest that the cause is psychological; although the tonnage is low (as compared to increased demand) it is far from exceptionally so, while insiders do not give any explanation except the one of low tonnage.

The results of these calculations are shown graphically in Figs.

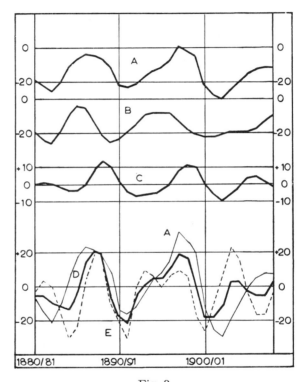

Fig. 3

A. Joint influence on the supply side (tonnage and coal price combined) on the freight change of D.
B. Influence of tonnage.
C. Influence of coal price.
D. Percentage rise (5 year moving average) of the calculated freight index (Fairplay).
E. Influence on D exerted by the demand side.
N.B. The lowest scale applies only to the D line; for A and E the figures of the scale would have to be twice as small.

1 and 3. As can be seen, there is a reasonable correlation with the freight figures of Hobson, and even a good correlation with those of the homeward freights of Fairplay. The formula

$$D = 1.7\,A - 1.6\,B + 0.4\,C$$

demonstrates the relative importance of the three factors: A, the demand index; B, the supply index; and C, the coal price (expressed in 5 year moving averages of the annual percentage increase) on D, the calculated freight rate.

8. COMPARISON WITH THE POST-WAR PERIOD

In the calculations regarding the post-war period, the influence of fuel prices was not yet taken into account. The coefficients found for the influence of the other factors, when the changes in these factors are also measured in percentages, proved to be: for the demand index 0.5 (as compared to 1.7 pre-war) and for the supply index 3.3 (as against 1.6). The significance of these differences will be further elaborated upon in a later article.

9. SIGNIFICANCE WITH REGARD TO TRADE CYCLE RESEARCH

The significance of the results obtained for business cycle research is made clear by determining the relative influence of each of the causes mentioned. For this purpose the breakdown into demand and supply factors is less important than the breakdown (basic to Fig. 4) into:

(*i*) the influence of the harvests and of the tonnage;

(*ii*) the cyclical influences.

The influence of harvests can be called exogenous from a general economic viewpoint. As is generally known, several authors attach considerable importance to harvest fluctuations in explaining cyclical movements. Some (JEVONS Sr. and Jr. and MOORE) even consider the possibility that cycles can be mainly attributed to harvest changes. This opinion is now shared only by a few. Probably the best way of expressing the inter-relation between harvest and trade cycles is to say (as for example is said by FRISCH) that the harvest changes are the *irregular* shocks which continuously disturb the economic mechanism which has its own period, creating thereby not a pure wave but an irregular wave. In this connection it should be noted in passing that the internal mechanism of the cyclical movement can

DESCRIPTION		Units	1870	1871	1872	1873	1874	1
Supply aspect.								
Total tonnage of the fleets of Great Britain, the United States of North-America, Germany and Norway on July 1st		sail-tons × million		11.92	12.51	13.18	13.85	1
Coal price (Aver. export price: Great-Britain)		sh./ton	9.6	9.8	15.8	20.9	17.2	1
Demand aspect.	Quantities transported × distance from:							
1. Grain	United States of North-America and Canada (incl. flour to Great Britain	ton/miles × milliard	4.2	5.8	5.8	9.6	8.7	1
	Argentina	,,						
	Russia	,,	8.4	9.7	6.8	8.5	11.4	
	Roumania	,,						
	India	,,	4.1	4.6	6.1	5.6	4.5	
	Australia	,,						
	Total	,,	16.7	20.1	18.7	23.7	24.6	2
2. Coal	Great Britain	,,	24.6	26.8	27.9	26.6	29.5	3
	United-States of North-America.	,,						
	Total	,,	24.6	26.8	27.9	26.6	29.5	3
3. Oil	United States of North-America.	,,	1.5	1.7	1.6	2.6	2.6	
4. Nitrate of soda		,,	1.5	1.3	1.6	2.3	2.1	
5. Timber	Imports into Great-Britain	,,	5.2	5.4	5.8	6.6	7.5	
	Total demand subject to trade cycles (2 to 5 incl.)	,,	32.8	35.2	36.9	38.1	41.7	4
	Total all demand . . .	,,	49.5	55.3	55.6	61.8	66.3	6
Freight rate.								
1. Index figure Hobson		1900 = 100	185	227	222	248	224	19
2. ,, ,, Fairplay, homeward . . .		,,						
3. ,, ,, ,, , outward		,,						
4. Aver. freight rate grain Montreal, New York to Liverpool		cents/60 liv.	12.8	17.2	15.7	22.0	18.2	1
Fairplay homeward, Procentual increases; weighted five-yearly progr. aver.; deviations from the aver.								
Fairplay homeward, calculated, same . .								
Influence on the calculated freight rate of:								
1. supply (incl. coal price), same . . . . . demand, same								
2. factors not subject to cyclical factors, same factors subject to cyclical factors, same .								

* points to a discontinuity in the series; the figures in brackets have been calculated on

1877	1878	1879	1880	1881	1882	1883	1884	1885	1886	1887	1888	1889	1890	1891
15.38	15.94	16.26	16.59	17.25	18.16	19.39	20.39	20.80	20.59	20.55	20.91	22.15	23.47	24.78
10.2	9.5	8.8	8.9	9.0	9.1	9.3	9.3	8.9	8.4	8.3	8.4	10.2	12.6	12.2
						(12.8)	(15.2)	(14.4)						
14.6	19.9	24,4	22.9	15.0	15,8	*12.9	15.8	1.50	16.2	11.3	12.9	17.5	10.8	26.3
						0.3	0.6	0.5	0.1	1.3	1.0	0.1	1.8	2.4
12.8	17.8	16,5	9.5	9.7	14'1	16.5	15.0	15.8	12.1	17.6	24.5	20.5	18.6	16.8
			2.8	3.4	4,0	3.4	2.7	3.8	3.7	4.1	4.5	5.2	5.1	4.7
6.3	5.6	6,2	9.3	13.6	12,7	13.4	10.5	13.8	13.8	11.5	11,0	11.1	13.6	17.8
			4,4	1.1	1,1	1.1	5.5	3.3	2.2	4.4	4,4	2.2	3.3	1.1
			(41,7)			(47.2)								
33.7	43.3	47,1	*48,9	42,8	47,7	*47.6	50.1	52.3	48.1	50.2	58,3	56.6	53.2	69.1
32.8	33.0	34,5	39.4	41.4	43,8	47.7	49.3	49,9	48.6	51.3	56,3	60.5	63.1	64.9
							1.2	0.9	0.3	0.0	1,2	1.8	1.8	2.4
							(49.3)							
32.8	33.0	34,5	39.4	41.4	43,8	47.7	*50.5	50.8	48.9	51.3	57,5	62.2	64.9	67.3
4.0	3.8	4,6	3.8	5.7	5,5	5.8	6.0	6.1	6.5	6.6	6,2	7.4	7.6	7.5
1.8	2.6	1,2	1.8	2.9	4,0	4.7	4.5	3.5	3.6	5.7	6,2	7.7	8.6	6.9
8.0	6.4	5,6	7.5	6.6	7,5	7.8	7.2	7.4	6.4	6.6	7,6	9.3	8.5	8.0
							(67.0)							
46.6	45.8	45,9	52.5	56,6	80,8	66.0	*68.2	67.8	65.4	70.2	77,5	86.6	89.6	89.7
			(94.2)			(114)	(117)							
80.3	89.1	93.0	*101.4	100	109	*114	*118	120	114	120	136	143	142	150
181	176	158	154	138	135	133	116	104	101	100	111	122	107	100
							120	106	97	95	106	125	103	104
							110	101	105	105	116	118	111	96
14.1	15,2	12.6	11.8	8.3	7,8	9.9	7.0	6.4	6.7	5.0	5.3	7.8	4.8	6.3
			— 10	— 8	— 11	— 13	— 14	— 5	+ 9	+ 22	+ 18	— 1	— 11	— 10
			— 4	— 4	— 8	— 10	— 12	— 2	+ 14	+ 20	+ 18	— 4	— 16	— 28
			— 4	— 7	— 10	— 6	+ 2	+ 8	+ 10	+ 10	+ 8	0		
			0	+ 3	+ 2	— 5	— 13	— 10	+ 3	+ 12	+ 12	— 3	— 7	— 8
			— 15	— 13	— 10	— 3	+ 4	+ 11	+ 14	+ 7	0	— 12	— 8	— 13
													— 12	— 8
			+ 10	+ 9	+ 1	— 8	— 15	— 13	0	+ 15	+ 20	+ 8	— 4	— 14

of the series previously calculated.

TABLE II (continued)

DESCRIPTION		Units	1892	1893	1894	1895	1896	18
Supply aspect								
Total tonnage of the fleets of Great-Britain,		sail-tons						
the United States of North-America, Germany and Norway on July 1st		× million	25.79	26.49	72.12	27.59	27.97	28
Coal price (Aver. export price: Great Britain)		sg./ton	11.0	9.9	10.5	9.3	8.8	8
Demand aspect	Quantities transported × distance from:							
1. Grain	United States of North-America and Canada (incl. flour to Great Britain . .	ton/miles × milliard	20.0	20.6	13.1	19.3	31.7	42
	Argentina	,,	2.5	5.6	8.4	6.1	3.2	0
		,,	(7.9)	(17.8)	(26.7)			
	Russia.		*9.8	20.2	32.0	28.7	25.3	24
	Roumania	,,	4.5	6.8	4.7	4.6	6.1	4
	India	,,	11.6	9.7	11.0	12.0	7.6	7
	Australia	,,	1.1	3.3	3.2	1.6	0.0	0
			(47.6)					
	Total	,,	*49.5	66.2	72.4	72.3	73.9	79
2. Coal	Great Britain.	,,	63.8	60.9	70.0	69.8	72.4	77
	United States of North-America	,,	2.7	2.4	2.4	2.4	1.8	2
	Total	,,	66.5	63.3	72.4	72.1	74.2	80
3. Oil	United States of North-America.	,,	8.1	8.8	9.8	9.7	10.2	10
4. Nitrate of soda		,,	6.5	7.8	8.8	10.8	9.2	0
5. Timber	Imports into Great Britain .	,,	9.1	8.3	9.3	8.8	10.2	11
	Total demand subject to trade cycles (2 to 5 incl.).	,,	90.2	88.2	90.3	101.1	103.8	112
			(138)					
	Total all demand	,,	*140	154	173	173	178	191
Freight rate								
1. Index figure Hobson		1900 = 100	87	84	80	75	79	83
2. ,, ,, Fairplay, outward		,,						
2. ,, ,, Fairplay, homeward		,,	85	86	82	80	76	78
3. ,, ,, ,, , outward		,,	90	82	79	64	85	86
4. Aver. freight rate grain Montreal, New York to Liverpool		cents/60 liv.	5.3	4.8	3.8	5.1	5.8	6
Fairplay homeward, Procentual increases; weighted five-yearly progr. aver.; deviations from the aver.			— 9	— 6	+ 1	+ 8	+ 16	+.
Fairplay homeward, calculated, same. . .			— 4	+ 4	+ 6	+ 6	+ 12	+.
Influence on the calculated freight rate of:								
1. supply (incl. coal price), same.			— 7	— 1	+ 1	+ 3	+ 7	+.
demand, same.			+ 2	+ 7	+ 5	+ 2	+ 5	+.
2. factors not subject to cyclical factors, same			+ 10	+ 12	+ 16	+ 11	+ 11	+.
factors subject to cyclical factors, same . .			— 15	— 6	— 9	— 6	+ 1	+.

* points to a discontinuity in the series; the figures in brackets have been calculated on the basi

898	1899	1900	1901	1902	1903	1904	1905	1906	1907	1908	1909	1910	1911	1912	1913
3.90	30.11	31.29	32.92	34.63	36.20	37.44	38.77	40.54	42.51	43.77	44.17	44.46	45.47	46.98	48.57
).8	10.5	16.5	13.7	12.2	11.6	11.0	10.5	10.8	12.6	12.6	11.2	11.6	11.3	12.6	13.8
4.4	39.0	35.9	23.9	24.0	15.3	12.0	23.4	20.2	19.5	16.5	13.7	13.8	13.2	26.5	23.8
			(5.4)	(3.8)	(10.1)										
3.0	10.8	10.8	*12.1	11.0	22.7	28.6	30.5	29.6	23.8	32.1	28.7	27.2	14.5	44.8	45.7
2.9	17.3	21.0	23.3	29.0	32.6	32.4	34.9	29.5	23.5	20.2	37.9	42.3	41.1	27.5	32.5
5.9	2.3	3.9	5.5	6.8	6.3	3.9	6.5	8.2	8.0	4.4	5.5	8.1	7.5	7.3	7.4
5.6	10.8	7.6	10.6	15.6	19.4	25.9	16.5	14.4	14.7	7.9	16.0	19.7	21.6	24.2	19.5
).4	3.3	3.3	6.1	2.7	0.4	10.0	7.4	9.1	8.6	4.5	9.4	14.3	16.5	9.8	12.9
			(74.8)												
2.2	83.5	82.5	*81,5	89.1	96.7	112.8	119.2	111.0	98.1	85.6	111.2	125.4	114.4	140.1	¡41.8
3.3	90.6	97.0	92.2	95.0	102.5	106.0	108.7	127.2	145.4	143.4	144.5	141.9	148.1	147.4	168.7
2.4	4.2	9.0	9.9	7.2	5.1	6.9	7.5	8.1	11.7	6.9	6.6	10.2	12.3	12.6	15.0
).7	94.8	106.0	102.1	102.2	107.6	112.9	116.2	135.3	157.1	150.3	151.1	152.1			
).8	10.4	10.9	11.6	11.2	10.5	11.3	12.7	13.4	14.4	16.0	16.5	16.6	160.4	160.0	183.7
).9	11.6	11.7	10.2	11.3	11.5	12.0	13.2	13.8	13.2	15.4	17.1	18.7	17.1	19.0	21.4
).4	11.2	11.7	10.9	11.4	12.0	11.0	10.6	11.9	11.4	11.2	11.0	11.6	19.6	19.9	21.9
													11.2	11.5	13.2
2.8	128.0	140.3	134.8	136.1	141.6	147.2	152.7	174.4	196.1	193.9	195.7	199.0	208.3	210.4	240.2
			(210)												
5	211	223	*216	225	238	260	272	285	294	279	307	324	323	350	382
3	88	100	75	71	73	71	76	84	85	73	75	85	95	132	
4	85	100	74	66	71	72	69	68	70	58	64	65	75	105	85
5	79	100	79	58	53	47	55	67	68	65	67	68	77	108	87
5.9	4.8	6.9	2.6	3.0	2.9	2.2	3.5	3.3	3.7	4.0	3.7	3.3	4.1	7.5	7.1
12	+ 1	— 15	— 16	— 6	+ 7	+ 7	+ 1	— 1	— 2	+ 13					
18	+ 2	— 16	— 16	— 10	+ 4	+ 4	— 2	— 4	— 4	+ 4					
13	+ 9	— 7	— 13	— 15	— 10	— 6	— 1	+ 2	+ 3	+ 3					
5	— 7	— 12	— 3	+ 5	+ 13	+ 10	0	— 7	— 7	0					
4	— 11	— 13	— 3	+ 6	+ 10	— 1	— 15	— 15	— 3	+ 13					
23	+ 13	— 6	— 14	— 17	— 7	+ 6	+ 14	+ 10	— 1	— 10					

e series previously calculated.

be somewhat changeable (*e.g.* owing to a changed credit structure). Determining the influence of harvests on the economic system, if it is to be done accurately, will have to be carried out by investigating separately the important branches of trade and industry, such as shipping, for example, and combining the results.[8]

The influence of tonnage is, although on a limited scale, an example of a so-called "internal mechanism". It is an endogenous influence both in its general economic implication and with respect to these

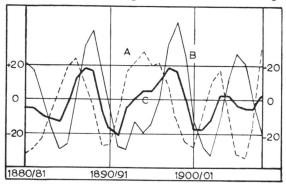

Fig. 4

A. Influence of the factors not subject to cyclical influences (grain transport and size of tonnage) on C.

B. Influence of the factors subject to cyclical influences (coal price and coal transport) on C.

C. Percentage increase (5 year moving averages) of the calculated freight index (Fairplay).

N.B. The scale applies only to the C line.

special branches of trade and industry. The tonnage carried at a certain time reflects the influence of the freight rate itself as it was at a previous time. As explained earlier, a similar relationship can (*cf.* "*A Shipbuilding Cycle*," this volume, p. 139 *sq.*), lead to endogenous fluctuations. Here we find that fluctuations in freight rates have this character in part, but only in part.

The influence of the factors influenced by trade cycles can be considered as an exogenous influence with regard to shipping itself; with

---

[8] Another example is given by the determination of the influence of cotton harvests on the cotton industry; see *De Nederlandsche Conjunctuur*, December 1933, page 26.

regard to the entire economic system it is an endogenous influence. The influence of trade cycles is felt in two ways: (i) through changes in coal prices or, (ii) through changes in the quantities of coal transported. Of particular importance is the fact that the variations both in size of harvests and in tonnage are clearly distinct from the trade cycle fluctuations. Accordingly, there is little doubt regarding the relative influence of each. The history of freight rates can accordingly be told in a much more exact way. For example it can be determined that both in the eighties and in the nineties the first influence which led to a recovery of the freight rate sprang from the tonnage; subsequently we have the influence of harvests and finally, when a certain overproduction in tonnage had already become a fact, a boom caused freights to keep their level or even rise. Freights, however, always reached their turning-point before general trade cycles reached theirs. The recovery of freights after 1903 was due particularly to grain shipments; at that time tonnage was very ample

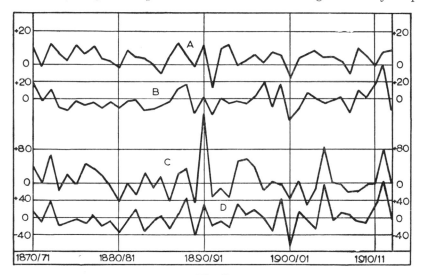

Fig. 5

Percentage increase from year to year of:
A. the general demand index.
B. the general freight index (Fairplay, homeward).
C. grain transport from the United States to Europe.
D. the freight index to the United States.

over a long period. Here again the boom in industry did not come until later. The short recapitulation given here does not imply, as a matter of course, that the mentioned sequence will occur each time; the irregular movement of the harvests creates the chief obstacle in this respect.

10. THE YEARLY FIGURES

Besides the five-year averages already reviewed the annual figures were also studied. Apart from a number of disturbing factors already mentioned and other "incidental" deviations, the harvest fluctuations exert the major influence on these annual figures. The latter is best illustrated when considering Fig. 5, where the annual percentage change in freight rates is compared to the total demand index, to the freights for grain transport from the United States to Europe and to the grain shipments along that route.

11. BREAKDOWN OF THE POST-WAR FIGURES INTO CONTINENTS

Finally Fig. 6 gives the result of a breakdown both of demand and

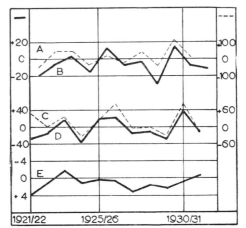

Fig. 6

A. (right-hand scale): Yearly percentage change in the demand for tonnage for Australia (for butter, wool, wheat and flour).
B. (left-hand scale): Yearly percentage change in the freight index to Australia (Statist), the figure for 1926/27 having been corrected in view of the coal strike).
C. (right-hand scale): Yearly percentage change in the demand for tonnage for the Argentine (wheat and maize).
D. (left-hand scale): Yearly percentage change in the freight index to Argentina.
E. Yearly percentage change in total world tonnage.

freight figures by a few continents. We find that good correlation exists between these figures, giving further support to the general correlation discussed in *De Ned. Conjunctuur* of March 1933, page 28.

The freight figures have been corrected in the same way in view of the influence of the coal strike in 1926 as the ones in the March 1933 issue, page 26, pertaining to the general freight index. The figures for Australia are respectively the increases for the harvest year 1922/23 as compared to 1921/22, those of the harvest year 1923/24 as compared to 1922/23, *etc.* The Argentine figures represent the increases from 1921 to 1922, and from 1922 to 1923 (calendar years), *etc.*

TABLE III

VOLUME OF TRANSPORT AND AVERAGE FREIGHT RATES ON CERTAIN ROUTES

DESCRIPTION	Unit	1922	1923	1924	1925	1926	1927	1928	1929	1930	1931	1932	1933
gentina ain transport . . .	1.000 million t/km	79	79	107	71	83	150	140	139	83	162	130	
eight rate: gentina–Great Britain atist.)	1920 = 100	27.1	23.1	27.5	17.6	21.0[1]	25.8	22.6	20.2	14.8	19.2	17.1	
stralia ports of Wheat, Maize, ol and Butter, for rs ending June 30th .	million quintal	79.1	35.8	52.6	78.4	52.3	63.4	49.5	70.0	42.5	91.2	98.9	95.9
eight rate: stralia–Great Britain years ending June 30th	1920 = 100	38.7	31.0	29.2	29.7	25.3	28.8[2]	27.2	26.3	18.7	21.6	20.1	17.9

[1] Figure, corrected for the influence of the coal strike in Great Britain which made freight rates rise during a few months; uncorrected figure: 23.9.

[2] See note 1; uncorrected figure: 31.2.

THE EQUALIZATION OF FACTOR PRICES BETWEEN FREE-TRADE AREAS

1. INTRODUCTORY

Recently, Professor SAMUELSON has shown[1] that, under certain conditions, free trade in final products is sufficient to equalize, in the areas concerned, not only the prices of these products, but also the prices of productive agents or factors. It is the purpose of the present article to give a mathematical proof of his statement for a number of possible constellations, to go into a number of complications that arise for other constellations, and to discuss the limits of its applicability. When speaking of constellations I have in mind:

(i) the number of products, areas and factors considered, and

(ii) the degree to which the production function for the various products differ.

2. TWO COUNTRIES, TWO PRODUCTS AND TWO FACTORS

First of all we may consider the case where the number of products, as well as the number of factors and that of countries, equals two. Let the countries be indicated by subscripts 1 and 2 respectively, the number of workers in the countries by a_1 and a_2, the quantities of the other factor—say land—by n_1 and n_2, and denote by one and two primes respectively the quantities of these factors devoted to the production of food and clothing, which are the two products being considered. This gives rise to the following set of symbols, as shown on the next page.

The quantities produced of both products will depend on the quantities of both factors used in their production and may be indicated by the functions φ for food and ψ for clothing; $\varphi(a_1', n_1')$ representing the quantity of food produced in country 1 and $\varphi(a_2', n_2')$ the quantity

---

[1] P. A. SAMUELSON: "International Trade and the Equalization of Factor Prices", *The Economic Journal*, LVIII, 1948, page 163.

QUANTITIES OF LABOUR AND LAND

Devoted to production of	Labour Country: 1	2	Land 1	2
Food	a_1'	a_2'	n_1'	n_2'
Clothing	a_1''	a_2''	n_1''	n_2''
Total	a_1	a_2	n_1	n_2

of food produced in country 2. *The same production function will be assumed to exist for the same product* in both countries, but for the other product another production function is supposed to exist.

Food will be taken as the standard of value or numéraire. The following prices will then be relevant:

p, the price of one unit of clothing, in terms of food;

l_1 and l_2, the prices of labour in country 1 and 2 respectively and r_1 and r_2, the prices of the use of land (rent) in these countries, all of them in terms of food.

Since we assume *free trade*, prices of products are the same for both countries; prices of factors may be different but it will be proved that, under certain conditions, they will also be equal.

It will further be assumed that there is:

(I) *full utilization of productive resources* and

(II) *free competition between entrepreneurs.*

Condition (I) leads to the following equations:

(1) $$a_1' + a_1'' = a_1$$
(2) $$a_2' + a_2'' = a_2$$
(3) $$n_1' + n_1'' = n_1$$
(4) $$n_1' + n_2'' = n_2$$

Condition (II) yields the following equations:

(5) (6) $$l_1 = \frac{\partial \varphi}{\partial a_1'} = \frac{\partial \psi}{\partial a_1''} p$$

(7) (8)
$$l_2 = \frac{\partial \varphi}{\partial a_2'} = \frac{\partial \psi}{\partial a_2''} p$$

(9) (10)
$$r_1 = \frac{\partial \varphi}{\partial n_1'} = \frac{\partial \psi}{\partial n_1''} p$$

(11) (12)
$$r_2 = \frac{\partial \varphi}{\partial n_2'} = \frac{\partial \psi}{\partial n_2''} p.$$

Finally there will be an equation expressing that p equals the ratio of marginal utilities of the two products, which itself depends on the quantities produced and the incomes. This equation, of which the details need not concern us, will be of this type:

(13)
$$p = f(\varphi_1 + \varphi_2, \psi_1 + \psi_2, l_1, l_2, r_1, r_2).$$

These 13 equations will, as a rule, enable us to determine the 13 unknowns introduced, *viz.* 4 a's, 4 n's, 2 l's, 2 r's and 1 p. Implicitly, however, some further assumptions have been made, *viz.* that *both countries do produce both products*; or, in other words, that all a's and all n's are positive. If one or more of them should prove to be negative, some of the equations would have to be replaced by other ones. We will discuss this later.

3. HOMOGENEOUS LINEAR PRODUCTION FUNCTIONS

In addition to the assumptions already enumerated one further hypothesis will be made, *viz.* that *the production functions are homogeneous linear functions*, *i.e.* that a proportionate increase in the use of both labour and land in the industry concerned will lead to an increase in the same proportion of the quantity produced. This will be the case if the optimum size of the firm is small in comparison with the quantity produced. It can easily be shown that this implies that the marginal productivities in equations (5) to (12) are dependent only on the ratios of the quantities of the factors used, *i.e.*

$$\frac{\partial \varphi}{\partial a_1'} = \varphi_a \left(\frac{a_1'}{n_1'} \right), \quad \frac{\partial \varphi}{\partial a_2'} = \varphi_a \left(\frac{a_2'}{n_2'} \right) \text{ etc.}$$

We may now introduce, as new variables, the ratios:

$$\frac{a_1'}{n_1'} = x_1' \qquad \frac{a_2'}{n_2'} = x_2'$$

$$\frac{a_1''}{n_1''} = x_1'' \qquad \frac{a_2''}{n_2''} = x_2''$$

and rewrite our equations (1) to (12):

(1') $\left\{ \begin{array}{l} x_1' n_1' + x_1'' n_1'' = a_1 \end{array} \right.$

(2') $x_2' n_2' + x_2'' n_2'' = a_2$ I

(3') $n_1' + n_1'' = n_1$

(4') $n_2' + n_2'' = n_2$

(6') $\left\{ \begin{array}{l} \varphi_a (x_1') = p \psi_a (x_1'') \end{array} \right.$

(8') $\varphi_a (x_2') = p \psi_a (x_2'')$ II

(10') $\varphi_n (x_1') = p \psi_n (x_1'')$

(12') $\varphi_n (x_2') = p \psi_n (x_2'')$

(5') $\left\{ \begin{array}{l} l_1 = \varphi_a (x_1') \end{array} \right.$

(7') $l_2 = \varphi_a (x_2')$ III

(9') $r_1 = \varphi_n (x_1')$

(11') $r_2 = \varphi_n (x_2')$

For any value of p chosen provisionally, this system of equations may be used in the following way: equations II may be used to determine the four x's, equations I to find the values of the four n's and equations III will yield the l's and r's. By means of the definitions of the x's we may calculate the a's and from (13) the corresponding p. If this p does not equal the value taken provisionally, we make another choice, until the two coincide. If no such coincidence can be obtained, this is an indication that one of the cases of "specialization" has to be tried. This is to be discussed later (section 5).

4. A PROOF OF PROFESSOR SAMUELSON'S STATEMENT

Equations (6'), (8'), (10') and (12') at once make it clear that $x_1' = x_2'$ and $x_1'' = x_2''$. The equations by means of which x_1' and x_2'' have to be determined, *viz.* (6') and (10'), are identical with (8') and (12') used for calculating x_2' and x_2''. It follows from (5') and (7') that $l_1 = l_2$ and from (9') and (11') that $r_1 = r_2$: *under the conditions enumerated, both wage rate and rent rate are equal in both countries. No transfer of factors is needed to obtain this equality if positive values for all a's are compatible with the data of our problem, i.e.* the given values of total labour and total land supply in both countries and the nature of the production functions. We will now investigate in somewhat more detail the nature of these "boundary conditions".

5. BOUNDARY CONDITIONS; SPECIALIZATION

For each of the countries these may be written in this way:

(14) (15) $n' \geq 0$ $n'' \geq 0$

(16) (17) $x' \geq 0$ $x'' \geq 0.$

It will be necessary to express all of these conditions in terms of x' and x'', in order to find out as quickly as possible whether a solution is or is not acceptable. Conditions (16) and (17) have a simple meaning, which can also easily be translated into geometrical terms: the point $(x'; x'')$ shall be situated above the horizontal and to the right of the vertical axis. Conditions (14) and (15) may be expressed as follows: since $n'' = n - n'$ we have $x'n' + x''(n - n') = a$, the total labour supply.

Solving for n' we have:

(18)
$$n' = \frac{a - nx''}{x' - x''} \geq 0.$$

Similarly we have

(19)
$$n'' = \frac{a - nx'}{x'' - x'} \geq 0.$$

These conditions may be interpreted in the following way.

(18′)
$$\begin{cases} \text{If } x' > x'', \text{ we must have } x'' \leqslant \dfrac{a}{n} \\[2mm] \text{if } x' < x'', \text{ we must have } x'' \geqslant \dfrac{a}{n}. \end{cases}$$

(19′)
$$\begin{cases} \text{Similarly, if } x'' > x', \quad x' \leqslant \dfrac{a}{n} \\[2mm] \text{if } x'' < x', \quad x' \geqslant \dfrac{a}{n}. \end{cases}$$

These conditions may be summarized by saying that one of the x must be smaller and the other greater than a/n, i.e.

(20)
$$x' \geqq \frac{a}{n} \geqq x'' \quad \text{or} \quad x' \leqq \frac{a}{n} \leqq x''.$$

In geometrical terms, the point (x', x'') is not permitted to enter the areas I and II (cf. Fig. 1). It may be shown that the borderlines L and M correspond to the cases of *specialization*, i.e. the cases where one

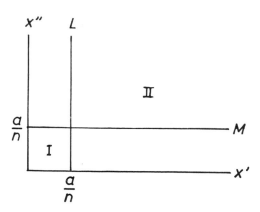

Fig. 1.

of the countries or both are producing only one of the two commodities.

Suppose that the solutions of our equations (1) to (13) inclusive do not obey these conditions and that both x's are either $< a/n$ or both are $> a/n$. In such cases the number of workers and the area of land devoted to one of the industries will be found to be negative. Since this is an impossible proposition, we have to choose these quantities equal to zero; and these equations have to be substituted for the corresponding equations among (6'), (8'), (10') and (12'). Three cases may be distinguished:

(1) only country 1 specializes;

(2) only country 2 specializes; and

(3) both countries specialize.

It may, of course, be proved that specialization in the industry requiring comparatively more labour will occur in the country where a/n is larger than in the other country, and specialization on the "land-intensive" industry in the other country. If the values of a_1' and n_1' are negative and those for a_2'' and n_2'' are not, only country 1 will specialize and it will specialize on clothing. *It will be clear that as soon as specialization enters into the picture, the equality of wage rates is no longer necessary.*

6. DENSITY OF POPULATION AND WAGE LEVEL

In the foregoing analysis we have considered the total labour and land supplies of the countries as given, and inquired into the influence of varying price conditions, and varying production functions. In fact, the results will be different according to the technical properties of the industries considered. With a great difference between the degrees of "labour intensity" (no matter in what way defined) of the two industries there will be a greater probability of non-specialization than with a small difference. We will now consider another aspect of the mechanism described, by asking *what influence on a country's wage level will be exerted* (given a "world market" price ratio between the two products) *by a changing ratio between the supplies of labour and land, i.e.* a changing density of population. Fresh interest in this way of formulating the population problem has recently been aroused by the stimulating investigations by E. WAGEMANN.[2] Our analysis will make it clear that the curve representing (*cf.* Fig. 2) the functional relationship between a/n as the independent variable and l as the

---

[2] E. WAGEMANN: *Menschenzahl und Völkerschicksal*, Hamburg, 1948.

dependent one will consist of three parts. For low values of a/n there will be specialization on the land-intensive industry (say food); and l will be the higher, the smaller a/n; for high values, on the other hand, there will be specialization on the labour-intensive industry (clothing), l being lower, the larger a/n. In between there will be co-existence of

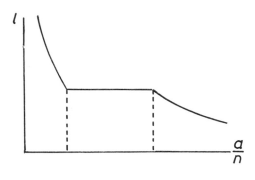

Fig. 2.

the two industries and for this whole range l will be constant, since, according to equations (4') to (12') inclusive, it does not depend on a and n as long as there is co-existence of the two industries. This middle part of the curve will therefore be horizontal.[3]

7. INCREASING THE NUMBER OF COUNTRIES

We may summarize our findings in the previous sections by saying that specialization is possible, but not necessary in the case of two countries, two products and two factors. It will be worth while studying other constellations with regard to these numbers; and we will find that for some of them specialization is always a necessity.

Let us therefore ask what happens if any of these numbers increases. *Increasing the number of countries* is a simple matter. Our system of equations already consisted of an equal number of equations for each

---

[3] The interesting analogy of this curve with the graphical representation of Van der Waals' Law in physics may be pointed out. In this law the connection between pressure (vertical axis) and density (horizontal axis) for a substance is expressed; the horizontal part representing the range of the co-existence of the fluid and the gas phase.

of the two countries together with one equation for the price ratio p:
the equations for country 1 *e.g.* being characterized by the subscripts 1.
Similar groups of equations may be added for any number of new
countries and their discussion would then proceed along the same lines
as given above. Evidently the equalization of factor prices will exist
only as long as none of the countries is forced—by its data in connection with those of the production functions and the price ratio—to
specialize. Of course this becomes increasingly improbable as the
number of countries increases and in particular as the range of their
population density widens.

8. INCREASING THE NUMBER OF FACTORS

Next we consider an *increase in the number of factors*. We shall assume
three: labour, land and capital, the quantities of the latter factor
applied in the two industries being k', and k'', respectively. Omitting
the subscript for the country we have the following equations for each
country (where m represents the interest rate, $u' = k'/n'$ and $u'' = k''/n''$:

$$(21) \qquad (l =)\ \varphi_a(x'\,,u') = p\psi_a\,(x''\,,u'')$$

$$(22) \qquad (r =)\ \varphi_n(x'\,,u') = p\psi_n\,(x''\,,u'')$$

$$(23) \qquad (m =)\ \varphi_k(x'\,,u') = p\psi_k\,(x''\,,u'')$$

$$(24) \qquad \qquad x'n' + x''n'' = a$$

$$(25) \qquad \qquad n' + \quad n'' = n$$

$$(26) \qquad \qquad u'n' + u''n'' = k$$

These six equations must be satisfied by the values of the six unknowns x', x'', u', u'' and n', n''. The interesting difference with
the case of two factors is that no longer the ratios x and u, now four
in number, can be determined by means of the equations (21), (22)
and (23). *Our proof on the equalization of factor prices is no longer valid*:
the equations by which x', x'', u' and u'' are found are no longer identical for all countries. And it may easily be seen that, if a certain set
of values x', u', x'', u'' satisfies these six equations, it will no longer
satisfy them if the value of one of the data a, n and k is changed. Only
a proportionate change in these data will not affect the values of x',

u', x'' and u''. Hence our conclusion: *Samuelson's statement is not correct if the number of factors is three while the number of products is two.*[4]

9. INCREASING THE NUMBER OF PRODUCTS

Let us now increase the number of products to three while leaving the number of factors equal to two. Indicating by x''' the ratio a'''/n''' for the third industry by χ the corresponding production function and by q the price ratio between the third and the first product, our system of equations now becomes, for each country:

(27) (28)
$$[l =]\, \varphi_a(x') = p\psi_a\,(x'') = q\chi_a\,(x''')$$

(29) (30)
$$[r =]\, \varphi_n(x') = p\psi_n\,(x'') = q\chi_n\,(x''')$$

(31)
$$x'\,n' + x''\,n'' + x'''\,n''' = a$$

(32)
$$n' + \quad n'' + \quad n''' = n$$

Disregarding the expressions in square brackets, we have six equations for six unknowns (three x's and three n's). Upon closer inspection, however, we see that in the first four equations (27) to (30) inclusive only three unknowns appear, whereas in the last two equations three more unknowns are introduced. This means that generally the system is partly overdetermined and partly underdetermined. Generally speaking, therefore, there will be no solution; a closer study reveals that in this case *as a rule specialization will be necessary.* This closer study may be based upon the introduction of hypotheses on the dynamics of the system from which the development of production in the three industries may be derived. It may be shown, under rather general assumptions, that this development ends with the elimination of one of the industries—except for the trivial case that the production functions of two industries are the same.

10. AN EQUAL NUMBER OF FACTORS AND PRODUCTS

The difficulties dealt with will not present themselves if we increase at the same time the number of commodities and the number of factors in such a way that their numbers remain equal; say n. Indicating by

---

[4] It can easily be proved that the same is true whatever be the numbers of factors and products if only there are more factors than products.

superscripts the industries and by subscripts the factors, our unknowns are now a_k^i being the quantity of factor k applied in the production of commodity i. Indicating by x_k^i the proportion a_k^i/a_1^i, we have $n(n-1)$ unknowns x; in addition we are left with the unknowns a_1^i $(i = 1 \,.\, .\, n)$. Using a corresponding system of notation for the production functions and their derivatives, we indicate by φ_k^i the derivative with respect to factor k of the production function for commodity i. Finally the prices of the factors may be written as l_k and the price ratio of commodity i with respect to 1 as p_i. Our equations are:

$$(33) \qquad [l_k =] \; \varphi_k^1 \, (x_2^1 \ldots x_n^1) = p^2 \varphi_k^2 \, (x_2^2 \ldots x_n^2) = \ldots p^n \; \varphi_k^n \, (x_2^n \ldots x_n^n)$$
$$(k = 1 \ldots n)$$

$$(34) \qquad\qquad \Sigma_i \, x_k^i \, a_1^i = a_k \quad (k = 2 \ldots n)$$

$$(35) \qquad\qquad \Sigma_i \, a_n^i = a_1.$$

This system of n^2 equations (omitting the expressions in square brackets) determines the n^2 unknowns, viz., $n(n-1)$ values x and n values a_1^i). It again appears that the equations (33), whose number amounts to $n(n-1)$ are identical for all countries. They are sufficient to determine the $n(n-1)$ quantities $(i = 1 \,.\, .\, n, k = 2 \,.\, .\, n)$. It follows that *in this case too there is an equalization of factor prices.*

11. SUMMARY

We will briefly summarize our findings. It appears that in an international economy, under certain conditions, viz.:

(I) free trade;
(II) free competition between entrepreneurs;
(III) full utilization of productive resources;
(IV) identical production functions in all countries for the same product;
(V) optimum units small in comparison with markets and
(VI) certain numerical conditions are fulfilled by the data, making specialization undesirable,

there will be an equalization of factor prices, even if factors cannot move from one country to another.

The proposition holds good for an equal number of factors and products, independently of the number of countries. It may be proved by showing that factor prices within any country are independent of the relative abundance of the various factors, being the only data differing from one country to another. It is not correct, however, except in borderline cases, if the number of factors is unequal to the number of products. If the number of factors is smaller than the number of products, specialization is always necessary and this no longer warrants the equality of factor prices. If, on the other hand, the number of factors exceeds the number of products, factor prices will no longer be independent of the relative abundance of the factors for each individual country and hence will not be equal for all countries. Finally, specialization may also occur if the number of factors equals the number of products. This depends on the divergencies in the relative abundance of factors in the various countries, together with the differences in production functions or, in simple but somewhat vague words, the differences in "land intensity" or "labour intensity" between industries.

LONG-TERM FOREIGN TRADE ELASTICITIES*

1. IMPORTANCE OF LONG-TERM ELASTICITIES OF IMPORTS AND EXPORTS

The elasticity of the volume of imports or exports of any one country with respect to its price level may be either conceived of as a short-run elasticity or as a long-run elasticity. In the first case we think of the reaction of that volume which materializes within some short period, say one year; in the second case we think of the total reaction during a long period. From this it follows, however, that these concepts can be exact only if we indicate the periods. And this aspect of the phenomenon is fully dealt with only if we conceive of the volume x_t in question (imports or exports) during time unit t as a function of price levels during a whole range of preceding time units t, $t—1$, $t—2$, $t—3$, etc. In principle this range should be infinitely long:

$$(1) \qquad x_t = \varepsilon_0\, p_t + \varepsilon_1\, p_{t-1} + \varepsilon_2\, p_{t-2} + \ldots\ldots = \sum_0^\infty{}_i\, \varepsilon_i\, p_{t-i}.$$

In this case, the short-run elasticity could be defined as:

$$\varepsilon_s = \varepsilon_0\, \frac{\bar{p}}{\bar{x}}$$

if if $\bar{x}$ and $\bar{p}$ are the particular values of x and p for which we want to know the elasticity; and the long-run elasticity as:

$$\varepsilon_L = \frac{\bar{p}}{\bar{x}} \sum_0^\infty{}_i\, \varepsilon_i.$$

The reasons for the lagged reactions included in our equation (1) may be e.g. that a certain change in price level induces a change in some production process, but only after certain machines now in operation are worn out. Or it may take some time before a switch in imports or exports is effectuated, since every switch involves certain costs which one is only prepared to incur if the change in price level is considered to be a lasting one, not just a temporary one.

---

* Published in Metroeconomica, December 1949, pp. 174-185.

It will be remembered that our equation (1) represents a case of what IRVING FISHER introduced as a *distributed lag*.

It seems useful to distinguish between short-term (however defined) and long-term elasticities of foreign trade. It may be useful in many other instances also: our special interest in foreign trade elasticities may be made clear by reminding the reader of some present-day problems for which they are of especial importance. The main problem for Western European countries nowadays is how to balance their foreign accounts. One of the methods used recently has been devaluation; other ones may be wage reductions or increases in productivity. In all these cases the degree of success will depend on the reaction of imports and exports of the country concerned to the price change. It is a well-known fact that success may even be completely absent if the sum of the elasticities of imports and exports is approximately equal to one. Recent statistical investigations[1] indicate that these elasticities are in fact in many cases as low as that. The consequence is that not very much can be expected from these methods to equilibrate the balance of payments. The implications of this consequence are far-reaching. They might mean that only by permanent quantitative import restrictions may equilibrium be maintained. Before drawing this conclusion we must however ask whether the elasticities as found by the statisticians just quoted are only short-run elasticities and whether long-run elasticities are not higher. To this question this paper is devoted.

2. LONG-TERM vs SHORT-TERM ELASTICITIES

The measurement of elasticities as performed by the authors just mentioned is based on multiple correlation analysis of the year-to-

---

[1] R. HINSHAW: "American Prosperity and the British Balance of Payments Problem", *The Review of Economic Statistics*, XXVII, 1945; J. TINBERGEN: "Some Measurements of Elasticities of Substitution", *The Review of Economic Statistics*, XXVIII, 1946; TSE CHUN CHANG, "International Comparison of Demand for Imports", *The Review of Economic Studies*, XIII, 1945-46; "The British Demand for Imports in the Inter-War Period", *The Economic Journal* LVI, 1946; "The British balance of Payments 1924-1938", *The Economic Journal*, LVII, 1947; "A Statistical Note on World Demand for Exports", *The Review of Economics and Statistics*", XXX, 1948.

year fluctuations in imports or exports as dependent variables. The independent variables used in the explanation of these fluctuations include, in most cases, some index of home prices (or export prices), some index of foreign prices and some index of national income of the importing country. Sometimes more variables are included, one of them being an indicator of the quantitative restrictions applied. No attempt has so far been made, however, to include lagged values of the price series and hence the measurements are essentially attempts to measure the short-run value of elasticities. In some cases, where the correlation is very strong—as for a number of separate, well-defined commodities such as wheat, cotton or pig iron—it may be seen from the graphs, that the short-term influence explains the fluctuations to a great extent and that influences with small lags, say up to three years, cannot be very large. If they had been so, the correlation would have been a lagged one, easy to detect from the graphs. Much longer lags should evidently be introduced here, in order to get total elasticities much in excess of the figures reported by the authors.

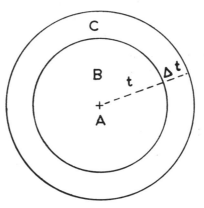

Fig. 1

Nevertheless it is probable that the long-run elasticities are higher, and perhaps much higher, than the short-run elasticities. There are various reasons for believing this. A number of the factors making for a relatively low elasticity work only temporarily. Existing contracts may prevent an immediate shift of demand to the cheapest supplier; after the contracts have expired this factor no longer works. Ties of a psychological or political character may hinder the shift. But after some psychological inertia has been overcome, this may change also. The shift may—as we already stated—require the introduction of new machinery; this will therefore last until the old machinery has been sufficiently written off. A switch always incurs costs of information, *etc.* It will not be undertaken therefore, as has been already observed, if the price change is considered a temporary one. But as time proceeds and the price change happens to be a lasting one, there will come a moment where even this cost of switching will no longer work as an obstacle.

Hence there are many reasons for expecting a lagged reaction, surpassing the immediate reaction. There remain, however, factors which are also working in the long run to prevent a complete shift to the cheapest supplier. And it may sometimes be possible to make *a-priori* estimates of the long-term elasticity based on the nature of these factors. The simplest example is that of *distances*, causing differences in *transport costs*.

The existence of distances puts a maximum to the increase in demand caused by a given decrease in prices. Only the customers for whom, under the new circumstances, extra transport costs will be lower than the price reduction effectuated will be attracted. This may be illustrated by Fig. 1. Assume that the customers of a small country A are evenly spread over the circle B. Potential new customers are supposed to be spread with the same density outside that circle. If now a price reduction Δp is applied, the customers in a ring C, of width Δt, will be attracted if transport costs over that distance are equal to Δp. What is the resulting elasticity of demand? Evidently it is equal to

$$\varepsilon = \frac{\Delta x}{\Delta p} \frac{p}{x},$$

where

$$\frac{\Delta x}{x} = \frac{\text{surface of ring}}{\text{surface of circle}} = \frac{2\pi t \Delta t}{\pi t^2} = \frac{2\Delta t}{t} = \frac{2\Delta p}{t}$$

Hence

$$\varepsilon = 2\frac{p}{t}.$$

Now if we know something about t/p, *i.e.* the ratio of transport costs to total price, we are able to estimate the elasticity under the simplified conditions assumed. For such bulk goods as wheat and pig iron transport costs between *e.g.* South America and the European coast are of the order of magnitude of 10% of the price. In such a case we would have $\varepsilon = 20$. For piece goods the ratio of transport costs to price will probably be lower, leading to even higher elasticities.

There are, however, other factors making for inelasticity even in the long run. One may be *differences in qualities* due to inherent differences in soil, climate or technical skill of the population. These differences are not only important for separate commodities but even much more so for the whole of a country's "export basket". Its composition can be changed only gradually and within certain limits, and this is probably the most powerful reason for long-term elasticities lower than the figure just quoted as an example. The differences in quality may take the special form of technical risks, *i.e.* the risk of quality divergencies or the risk of interruption of supply.

Another major class of factors is that of *political factors*. Regardless of distances or other purely technical and economic reasons for cheapness a country's exports may be in demand or not in demand if that country is or is not a part of a political group. The most outstanding examples one meets when studying the structure of international trade are those of the ties between a country and its overseas territories; the most important case being that of the British Empire. Whereas Germany's and America's customers are mainly the countries in their immediate neighbourhood, Britain's customers are often the Empire members.

3. MEASUREMENT FROM LONG TIME SERIES

From these *a-priori* considerations it appears to be of much interest to measure long-term elasticities of imports or exports. What ways are open to us? There seem to be several, although each of them is beset with special difficulties. The first possibility would seem to use time series over a long period. A formula of type (1), when the necessary other explanatory variables are added, could be tested by the usual methods of multiple correlation only if we have long series of figures at our disposal. Even then it may prove to be a very risky procedure. There may exist, on closer theoretical examination, a number of factors influencing the observed movements which are hardly accessible to measurement. In the long run, various factors may be variable which are not so in the short run, especially such factors as quality, technical uses made of the commodity in question, *etc.* Not all of them will be relevant to our problem, *i.e.* to the relative competitive position of the countries considered. This can only be judged by insiders. As an example which, at first sight, appears to have a good chance of success, we will take the demand for British pig iron by the United States during the period 1879–1914. As variables we take:

Q_t quantity of pig iron imported into the United States as a percentage of total American consumption;

P_t import price (including duties) as a percentage of home price in the United States;

v_t an index representing the cyclical situation, *viz.* production of pig iron as a percentage of its trend value.

It was attempted to explain the fluctuations in log Q_t in two ways, *viz.* once by the fluctuations in log P_t and log v_t and once by those in log P_t with a distributed lag and in log v_t. In order to account for the distributed lag the following variables were added to log P_t and log v_t: log P_{t-1}, log P_{t-2}, log $\bar{P}_{t-3/6}$ and log $\bar{P}_{t-7/10}$, where $\bar{P}_{t-3/6}$ indicates the average price for the years $t-3$ to $t-6$ inclusive and $\bar{P}_{t-7/10}$ the average price for the years $t-7$ to $t-10$ inclusive.

TABLE I

REGRESSION COEFFICIENTS AND $1 - R^2$
in the Explanations of log Q_t

Explanatory variables	log P_t	log P_{t-1}	log P_{t-2}	log $\bar{P}_{t-3/6}$	log $\bar{P}_{t-7/10}$	log v_t	$1-R^2$
	Regression coefficients						
Case I	—3.6	*	*	*	*	—1.6	0.106
Case II	—3.1	—0.2	—0.1	—0.4	—0.7	—1.1	0.044

* *Not included.*

The results of the calculations are shown in graphs 2 and 3 and in Table I, where R represents the multiple correlation coefficient.

It appears that the correlation, although already high in case I, is considerably increased by the introduction of the lagged terms, all of which appear with the correct sign. The long-term elasticity as estimated by case II would amount to $-(3.1 + 0.2 + 0.1 + 0.4 + 0.7) = -4.5$ as against -3.1 when measured by the first member in

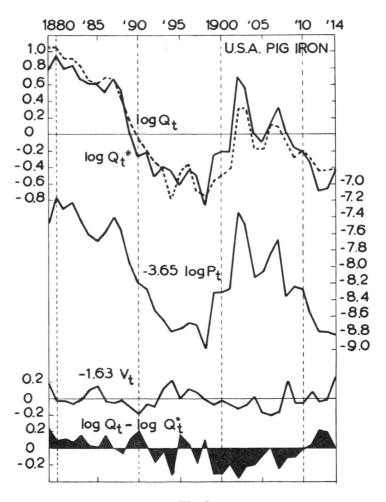

Fig. 2

the same equation or —3.6 when measured by case I. The difference between short-term and long-term elasticity (assuming that no lags longer than 10 years would exist) would be only moderate.

The same procedure was used in an analysis of the imports of raw cotton into the United Kingdom, comparing imports of American and Indian cotton. Here it appeared impossible to obtain a satisfactory explanation of the fluctuations in the ratio between these two imports.

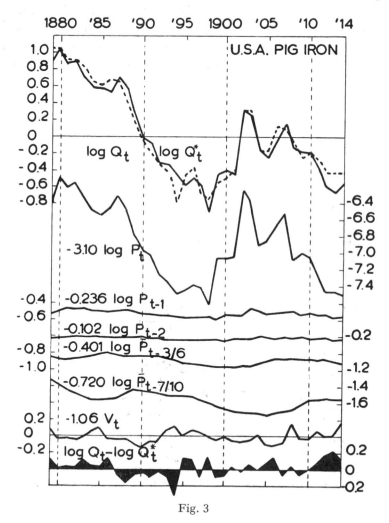

Fig. 3

An even cruder procedure would consist of a simple comparison of two rather distant time units. This was done for total exports of manufactured articles for a number of countries. These exports, expressed as a ratio to world exports of manufactures (volume figures) were compared with relative prices of these products (price index for exporting country divided by world price index) and a scatter diagram constructed (*cf.* chart 4). Three periods were compared, *viz.* 1881–1890, indicated by (1), 1901–1913 (2) and 1926–1935 (3). The scatter is not very well organized; for such a country as the U.S.A. the slope of the regression line is positive. Of the negative slopes, the one with the lowest elasticity shows an elasticity of about 4; the

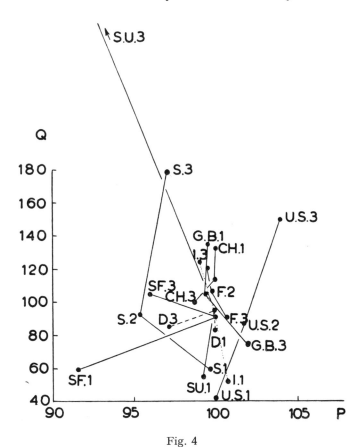

Fig. 4

next lowest is about 12, and many are considerably higher. These measurements are of little value, however, as long as it is impossible to
explain the deviations in the scatter. It seems probable that the price
index-numbers are none too adequate and can hardly take into account
the changes in quality that the products under review must have
shown.[2]

4. MEASUREMENTS FROM CROSS-SECTION STUDIES

The other way to measure long-term elasticities is by using cross-
section figures, *i.e.* by comparing different cases observed at the
same moment, just as we do *e.g.* when deriving long-term income
elasticities of consumer demand from family budget statistics. In
our case it comes to comparing different countries whose products
for some reason or another are different in price. This we may still
do in various ways. First we may compare products which for the
supplying countries have a different price ratio. This was done by
MAC DOUGALL, who compared products of the United Kingdom and
the United States, the relative costs of which diverge widely because
of differences in relative efficiency. The figures suggest a fairly
high elasticity, although exact price figures are lacking.

Another possibility consists in comparing relative prices and
quantities of the same commodity sold in different markets, price
differences varying from one market to another because of distances
and perhaps for other reasons as well. This has been attempted by
the present writer for a number of commodities, one of which is pig
iron. The relative shares in the imports into various countries were
calculated (*i.e.* ratio of imports from the United Kingdom to total
imports from U.K., U.S.A. and Germany) and the resulting percentages classified and represented by the intensity of the shade in three
maps of which Fig. 5 is an example. From these maps it can be
seen that the market shares vary from almost 0 to almost 100%
and are greatly dependent on the relative distances from the three
supplying countries considered.[3] For our purpose is it of particular

---

[2] Most of the figures have been taken from: *Industrialization and Foreign
Trade, League of Nations,* 1945.

[3] With the political exceptions already mentioned, in particular for
Britain.

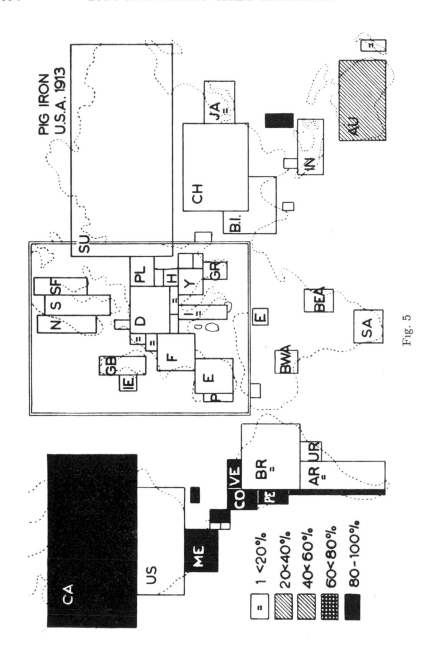

Fig. 5

interest to note that, starting from a market supplied mainly by one of the big three, we have to go only a relatively small distance in order to arrive at a market supplied mainly by one of the others. The distance is small in the sense that the freight difference corresponding with this distance is only about 5–10% of the price. This means that the market share may move by about 80% because of a price change of about 8%, corresponding with an elasticity of the order of magnitude of 10.

A more direct and more accurate attempt was finally made by collecting figures on imports and import prices of pig iron into a number of importing countries and comparing, for the pairs Germany/U.K. and U.S.A./U.K. the relative quantities imported into and the relative import prices charged to the buying countries. The results are shown in diagrams 6 and 7 and in Table II.[4] In order to eliminate the possible political ties existing between the supplying and the buying countries, two calculations of elasticities were made in each case, the second excluding British territories from the customers.

TABLE II

CROSS-SECTION ELASTICITIES FOR RELATIVE IMPORTS OF PIG IRON IN A NUMBER OF COUNTRIES

(First elementary regression; diagonal regression coefficients in brackets)

| | | Supplying countries compared | |
		Germany/U.K.	U.S.A./U.K.
Including British territories[a]	1913	−3.9 (− 8.3)	−2.0 (−14.6)
	1929	−9.5 (−15.3)	−6.2 (−11.2)
	1932	−1.6 (− 5.0)	−3.4 (− 5.3)
Excluding British territories[a]	1913	−1.9 (− 7.5)	−1.3 (−15.9)
	1929	−6.5 (−14.4)	−0.1 (−16.0)
	1932	−1.6 (− 5.0)	−3.1 (− 5.2)

[a] Australia, Canada and Union of South-Africa.

It is interesting to note that the exclusion of British territories among the buyers, does not, as one might have expected, increase

[4] The full statistical material will be supplied by the author on request.

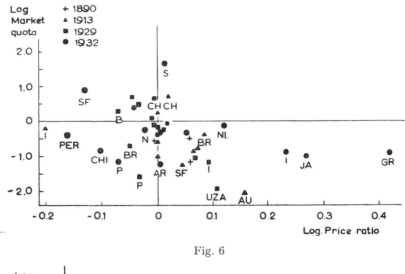

Fig. 6

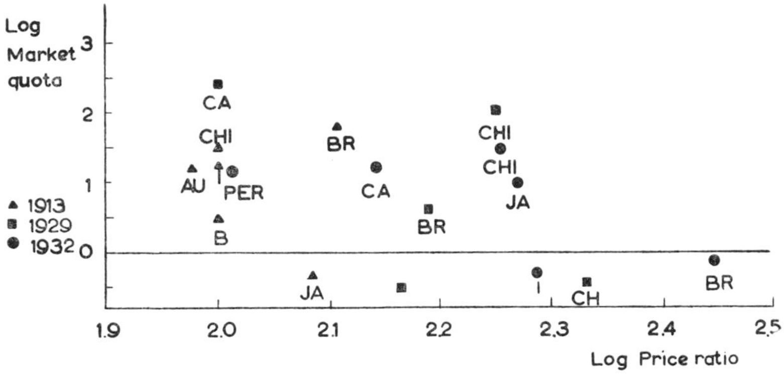

Fig. 7

the elasticity. It is still more interesting, however, that the elasticities found here are not as high as our *a-priori* considerations (based on distances alone) would suggest; the average value being—3.4 for the first elementary regressions and—10 for the diagonal regressions; and their median values—2.6 and—9.8 respectively. When considering these figures it should not be forgotten that they refer to a specific commodity, for which the short-run elasticity is necessarily greater than the figures for export baskets as a whole.

5. CONCLUDING REMARKS

In this paper in honour of Costantino Bresciani-Turroni, whose work on the measurement of elasticities has been generally admired, an attempt has been made to measure long-term substitution elasticities of imports as distinguished from short-term elasticities. Two methods are tried, *viz.* one using long time series and "distributed lags", and one using "cross-sections". Their application to the case of pig iron leads to figures of — 4.5 and of — 3.6 to — 10, respectively. From the first method as well as from previous measurements of short-term elasticities it seems probable that these higher elasticities refer to reactions that require at least a few years.

ON THE THEORY OF ECONOMIC INTEGRATION*

CONTENTS

1. SETTING OF THE PROBLEM; DATA AND UNKNOWNS

The integration of a number of countries is a complicated process of policy and development, which can be adequately described and studied only if we introduce into our study the behaviour of a large number of variables (production, prices, import duties, *etc.*) for a considerable number of consecutive time units. In this essay only the economic aspect of integration will be considered; the purely political and cultural aspects, although very important, will be left out entirely.

As in any problem of no matter what kind, we will have to indicate, first of all, the *data* and the *unknowns*. The data may provisionally be said to be the present situation of the countries considered, with their populations, land and capital resources, technical abilities, tastes and institutions. Among these institutions are their *economic policies*. The unknowns of the problem are the changes to be effectuated in these policies. Our problem being a problem of economic policy, it will be particularly useful to distinguish between *targets* and *instruments* of policy. Among the data of our problem the targets have to be included also; the unknowns are, more precisely, the changes in instruments of economic policy.

---

* Published in *Les Cahiers de Bruges (Bruges Quarterly,)* 1952, p. 290.

We will not try to indicate in any detail the data describing the present situation. May it suffice to remind the reader of the differences (between the countries of Western Europe for example) in land and capital per head, and consequently in productivity which is reflected in differences in real income per head; and to remind him of differences in *taxes* and of the existence of import barriers in the double form of *import duties* and *quantitative restrictions*, leading to differences in price level.

We will go into some more detail, however, as to the description of the target, *i.e. the final situation aimed at.* In a more general way this may be said to be the situation of maximum welfare of the given block of countries which, if sufficient time be given to overcome temporary difficulties, can be obtained with the technical and psychological data, but allowing variations in the institutional data, particularly the instruments of economic policy. By this rather general formulation of our target we want to stress that a maximum of welfare should be aimed at without interference from any arbitrary institutions of a national character, such as, in particular, trade restrictions. Provisionally however, we will assume that transfer of capital and of population is impossible; accordingly we distinguish between *three phases of integration:* (I) without capital and population transfers; (II) with only capital transfers permitted; (III) with both capital and population transfers permitted. Our general formula does not imply that all import restrictions should be removed; it is left to the analysis to find out whether or not this is desirable. The formula does not pay attention, moreover, to a fundamental difficulty in the theory of economic policy, *i.e.* that it is not certain that a consistent definition of "welfare" and "maximum welfare" can be given. We come back to this question in section 2.

First, however, we want to add to the data of our problem the rather general condition that the target shall be reached with a minimum of shocks or setbacks; it may be called *the condition of continuity* and implies the avoidance of unnecessary jumps (sudden changes) and unnecessary temporary reductions in welfare. The condition will prove to be important for certain questions of the consecutive order of the measures to be taken or of the "correct moment" for certain measures.

As already said, the unknowns of the problem are the measures of economic policy to be taken; they may be subdivided into negative and positive measures: the elimination of certain existing institutions, as well as the establishment of new ones. The discussions on European integration have so far emphasized the negative part of the program; however we should not overlook the positive part.

Our problem cannot be separated from the *general problem of economic policy*, which is also relevant to the internal affairs of each country; a problem that for certain purposes may be usefully formulated as the choise between planning and freedom. This is a choice, not in the sense that only one of these two possibilities should be chosen for the whole field of economic policy, but in the sense that for each element of economic life such a choice has to be made. The most desirable degree of centralization of economic decisions should be determined for each sector and each activity. In the description of the negative and the positive part of the program of integration the reader will find concrete examples as we see them.

2. THE MEANING OF "MAXIMUM WELFARE"

It is a well-known statement in modern economic theory that maximum welfare cannot be quantitatively defined. The welfare of a group of people is dependent on the welfare of each of the individuals; and there are no quantitative means to compare individual welfare feelings. Given a certain initial state of affairs, only certain classes of changes can unambiguously be said to be improvements, or to bring increases in welfare, namely, those changes where everybody is experiencing an increase in or at least no decline of welfare. Such changes where the situation of some individuals improves and that of others deteriorates, cannot be classified objectively as either improvements or deteriorations in welfare. No general solution acceptable to all economists has so far been formulated; and there remains room, therefore, for differences of opinion.

The approach chosen in this essay is the following. A situation II in a certain country will be considered better than an initial situation I if total consumption in that country has increased. Total consumption in this context means total consumption of consumer goods as well as investment goods. The various goods are valued, further, according to their prices "on the world market". A hypothesis implicit in this approach is that distribution is such as to make everybody share in the increase in consumption. This is not, of course, guaranteed without special measures.

3. ELIMINATION OF IMPEDIMENTS TO TRADE AND PAYMENTS
(1) UNDER "CONSTANT RETURNS"

A central part of integration programs for the first phase, where capital and population are not yet permitted to move, is formed by the removal of all barriers to free trade and multilateral payments. The target aimed at is the *"single market"* (*marché unique*), where only total demand and total supply, taken for all countries together, have to be equal and only one price prevails for each commodity, at least for each "international commodity", *i.e.* commodity whose transport cost may be neglected in comparison to its price. For all trade taken together, it is no longer necessary, in this final situation of equilibrium, that bilateral trade between any two countries should be in equilibrium, but only total imports and total exports (goods and services taken together) should be equal to each other (apart from possible capital transfers).

The thesis that the elimination of trade barriers contributes to maximizing welfare is taken from the theory of international trade. It is not in all circumstances correct; we shall have to discuss to what extent and in what conditions it is so.

There is general agreement among economists that under certain general conditions, to be discussed below, the statement is correct in a world of "constant returns". By this phrase economists indicate conditions of production where the production of each consecutive unit of a certain good requires the same quantity of productive effort. Assuming for the sake of simplicity that there is only one productive agent or factor of production, say, labour, then this state of production may be described by one single figure or coefficient telling us how much labour one unit of the product requires. And this will hold good for any quantity produced. Let us call this coefficient the labour intensity of the product in a given country. The existence of fixed labour intensity coefficients for all goods in all countries concerned would mean that we can, once for all, indicate the *"comparative cost"* for all commodities in a given country and in all countries. Suppose we choose the units in which we measure the various goods so as to have the same value—say $1—on the world market. If then, country A can produce one unit of wheat in one hour and one unit of iron in 1,1 hour, the comparative cost of wheat in that country is lower than that of iron. If, in another country B, one unit of wheat can be produced in 2 hours and one unit of iron in 1,8 hours, country B has a lower comparative cost for iron than for wheat. In the case of free trade it is more advantageous for country A to produce wheat and for country B to produce iron. For country A can, even if it did not want any more wheat, produce in one hour a unit of wheat and exchange it, on the world market, for one unit of iron. But if it had to produce that unit of iron itself, it would cost 1.1 hours. Similarly it is more profitable for country B to produce iron and no wheat. With fixed prices and fixed labour intensities, each country would concentrate on the production of that one commodity which it produces at the lowest comparative cost. This would be the optimum economic situation; given the fact that each country can consume only what it earns with its own production, maximum production would mean maximum consumption. And any other use of its labour would leave each of the countries with a lower production.

This is particularly true for the other uses to which labour would be put if *import duties* were imposed. If for historical reasons, it is thought that other industries with lower comparative cost advantage, are justified by the possible occurrence of either higher transport costs or of military insecurity, these industries can exist only behind the wall of a protective tariff. In our example, country A could produce iron just as well as wheat only if an import duty of 10% could keep the internal iron price at $1.1. And country B, too, could produce wheat only if a duty existed bringing its price in B at 2/1.8 or about $1.11. In these conditions, however, the total world market value of both A's and B's production would be lower than without tariffs and abolition of these would, therefore, raise welfare.

Our model may be refined by assuming that there is a *limit* to the *"capacity"* of each industry in each country. This means that no more than, say 2/3 of all workers in country A, can produce wheat; all arable land—supposed of equal quality—would then be in use. On the other hand let us assume that no more than 3/4 of B's workers can be engaged in iron making, since the capacity of blast furnaces is then fully used. The consequence will be that in both countries there will not be complete specialization. Part of the workers will be employed in other, less productive industries. Among these, those will be most attractive that rank second in the series of comparative cost figures; if their capacity is fully used, the third industry will be taken. If all workers are to be employed, their wage rate must be such that even the least productive industry needed for full employment does not incur losses.

4. ELIMINATION OF TRADE BARRIERS:
(2) UNDER DECREASING OR INCREASING RETURNS

We have explored above the consequences of the basic assumption of a world producing at constant unit cost or "constant returns". These consequences are exaggerated if, instead of this structure of production, we assume another one, namely production at increasing marginal cost or "decreasing returns". This state of affairs may be most easily understood by considering each industry as a combination of different industries, each of them with a limited capacity. Just as in the preceding model, production will again be concentrated; in the more attractive sections, until with decreasing productivity a limit is reached where marginal productivity coincides with the wage level.

Certain complications arise if we introduce the phenomenon of "increasing returns" or decreasing marginal cost, *i.e.* the fact that, in many manufacturing industries, it is cheaper to produce large quantities than to produce small quantities. In many such cases the cost of producing one more unit (the marginal cost) is lower than the average cost of production. This means that prices cannot be equal to marginal cost, for then nobody would be prepared to produce. Free trade will not, in such circumstances, lead to the optimal use of productive resources in a country. This optimal use of resources might involve the production of a certain quantity of iron also, if the marginal cost of such production would be below the world market price. Entrepreneurs will not be prepared, however, to do so as long as they do not receive a price covering their average cost, which is higher than marginal cost. They could only be induced to do so if they got a higher price. This argument is frequently used against free trade and hence against integration. Its importance should, however, not be over-estimated.

It is true that under the conditions assumed, free trade would not lead to the optimum situation. The underlying reason is that the correct productive reaction of entrepreneurs cannot be induced by free pricing and production generally, but only by a complicated system of subsidies or taxes or both. The simplest example in this case would be subsidizing according to fixed cost; however, we shall not go into the implications of such a system. The introduction of an import duty could make the entrepreneurs consent to the correct production program; but, as shown by a closer examination, the reaction of consumers would then lead to an erroneous pattern of income spending. Therefore protection is not the correct remedy.

Apart from this conclusion, the point can be made that probably the extent to which the assumed technical conditions apply is not of much importance. Indeed the field in which decreasing costs apply is restricted and may be said to be almost entirely of a micro-character. The easiest way of making this clear is perhaps to point to the large number of plants that exist in most industries. If decreasing costs prevailed to an appreciable extent, the number of plants would be small. Evidently the optimum size of a plant in most industries is small in comparison to the total production of the industry; meaning that increasing returns apply only over a limited interval of production (including transport of products). If this is so, the industry may, for purposes of macro-economic problems, be considered as one of constant marginal cost. The smallest unit of production may then, without much loss of accuracy, be taken to be equal to one optimal-size plant. This argument is reinforced by the large number of industries; it means that the production of an optimum-size plant, even if it should approach the total output of one product, will still be small in comparison to the production of a country as a whole.

One last argument may also be of constructive value in this controversy: even if further technical developments should in many industries lead to optimum-size plants which are large in comparison to the production in the type of industry considered, the optimal position for a group of countries will be one with free trade, namely, a position where each country has specialized on a certain number of industries and the products are freely exchanged. Although this optimal situation will be one of free-trade, it is not probable that it will be reached by free competition only. Deliberate regulation of industries along these lines—as suggested *e.g.* by the Petsche Plan—will be a more effective approach (*cf.* section 8).

5. ELIMINATION OF TRADE BARRIERS: (3) FINAL REMARKS

There are other reasons why the mere elimination of trade barriers may not lead to a position of maximum welfare. A most important assumption made in the proof of the central thesis of free trade is that all the productive resources available are actually used in production. In the particular case of labour this is equivalent to the assumption of full employment, or at least high and stable employment—accepting the fact that for various reasons it is not always possible to employ 100% of the number of workers.

Further assumptions are implicit, as already indicated, in the welfare definition which we have accepted for the sake of convenience. They may be that income distribution is not too far removed from the optimal one—whatever that may mean—or that desirable corrections will be possible without affecting the advocated policies of international trade. This is not necessarily always so.

It is important to notice that in the optimum position for the first phase of integration now discussed there will be equality of prices of international commodities, but *not necessarily equality of "factor prices" i.e.* of the wage rate, the interest rate or the rent level. As long as immigration is not free, such large differences may remain between countries, in capital and land per head of the population, that the marginal productivity of *e.g.* labour will not be equal and hence real wages will differ. It would not be in the interest of the countries with fewer resources than the others to increase their wage rates to a common level: they would not be able to compete and their level of unemployment would increase.

On the other hand it is not necessary that capital per head should be completely equalized in order to make wages uniform. Wages can be equal even if one country has fewer resources than the others; the condition being that such a country is permitted and able to specialize on the less capital-intensive industries.

6. CONTINUITY CONDITIONS

As we have already stated, certain conditions will have to be fulfilled if shocks in the development or unnecessary set-backs are to be avoided. In order *e.g.* that restrictions in the imports of any country be eliminated, it is necessary that *no internal restrictions* should be left, such as rationing or price regulations as a consequence of, say, war scarcity. This means that equilibrium between demand and supply at the price desired must be possible, at least for supply and demand of all goods together, defined in some way or another. As long as certain general lags in either productivity or in financial stability have not been overcome, free trade may lead to too great disturbances. These lags need not be absent for all commodities, for the very reason for free trade may be to eliminate partial scarcities; but on the other hand the country concerned should then be able to export other commodities.

A condition that must be fulfilled if *multilateral payments* are to be realized is that these payments be roughly in equilibrium. If they are confined to "current payments", *i.e.* payments for current imports and exports of goods and services, there will have to be equilibrium in this part of the balance of payments. If complete freedom of payments is discussed, including capital transfers, equilibrium in the balance of payments as a whole will be required—a condition hardly fulfilled in most Western European countries nowadays.[1]

If the *convertibility of monies*—which is implicit in the establishment of multilateral payments just discussed—is not proposed for all currencies, but for a group of them only, then the condition to be fulfilled will be less stringent: equilibrium will be needed in the supply and demand of the sector of the balance of payments referring to the currencies considered. Such was the case *e.g.* at the moment of the creation of the European Payments Union: at that time equilibrium in the dollar sector did not yet exist, and it does not yet, but equilibrium in the European sector was possible.

The problem of convertibility may be worked out a little further in the following way. It arises only in a world of disequilibria, as do the problems of continuity previously discussed. Here it is disequilibria in

---

[1] Integration of the "second phase" does not require this much, since it implies only free capital transfers to the other countries of the group.

the balances of payments which create the problem. A set of currencies may be said to be of different strength according to the devaluations that would be necessary to restore equilibrium in the corresponding balances of payments. As long as there are certain gold reserves available to every country, convertibility can be introduced by decree. But it cannot be maintained if the currencies are of unequal strength. With regard to the stronger of two currencies, convertibility will not create difficulties, but for the weaker one it will. The regulation of convertibility will have to cope with these difficulties. It will also have to be mutually consistent: if currency A is declared to be convertible into B and *vice versa*, and the same for A and C, then also B and C have to be considered convertible. There must therefore be groups of mutually convertible currencies. The condition that a group can be maintained evidently implies the existence of balance-of-payments equilibrium for the sectors, in each national balance of payments, of the group considered.

We have discussed some conditions concerning the state of affairs at the moment when certain measures of integration are introduced. Other conditions originating from *the velocity of the process of adaptation*, may be added. This process will imply the shift of workers and capital from one industry to another, a transition which requires time and energy. This again means that too rapid an integration will create considerable difficulties and losses. The minimum loss connected with migration of capital will be obtained if only that portion should be shifted that is worn out each year and has to be replaced. Similarly the minimum of loss involved in a transfer of workers would be obtained if all young workers entered the new industry and the number of workers in the old industry diminished through the natural process of retirement of the oldest workers. If this—very low—speed of transition were chosen, the disadvantage of the erroneous division of labour under protection would continue for quite some time. An optimum speed will have to be found where the increased transition losses are compensated for by the decreased protection losses.

Finally something should be added about the correct scheduling of the various steps towards integration. As we stated in section 1, the condition of continuity also requires that a minimum of setbacks is involved. Now, a number of different paths towards integration are conceivable, such as the temporary creation of *partial areas of integration*, which are afterwards, integrated completely. Here the important question arises whether the partial integration is really a step in the correct direction. Sometimes this is decidedly not so, since a partial integration may create new protection which will not persist with complete integration.

7. THE SECOND AND THIRD PHASES OF INTEGRATION

If in addition to permitting goods and services to move freely from one country to another, we also permit capital to do so in the "second phase of integration", a new and better optimum can be obtained. This follows from the fact that the marginal productivity of capital is different in the various countries and that new investments will therefore be more productive in the relatively under-capitalized countries. These will probably be the overpopulated countries. The same thing is true if, in the third phase, people are permitted to move. Only then will it, in principle, be possible to have the optimal distribution of both capital and labour over the given—and immovable—natural resources. In the second phase equality of interest rates, and in the third phase equality of wage rates will be realized—if we omit such factors as the preference to live in a certain country, a factor which is not unimportant in real life! From this last remark it will be evident the integration will be less complete in the third phase than may be assumed for the first and second phases; it will also be clear that a host of problems of an extra-economic character will be involved in this last phase. The particular economic difficulty with the second and (even more so) with the third phase is the opposition of interests involved. It is not in the interest—at least not in the direct interest—of the present populations of the "richer" countries to have the populations of the "poorer" areas move in. It is only of a certain indirect interest to them, which |it is not easy to evaluate: the interest of reducing the antagonism between richer and poorer countries and thus the possibility of conflicts.

The fact that it is not in the direct interest of the richer countries to eliminate barriers to immigration combined with the "continuity condition" (section 1) leads us to the suggestion that the influx of immigrants be such as to avoid serious setbacks in prosperity in the richer countries. This is equivalent to advocating a process of gradual convergency in welfare between richer and poorer areas by keeping welfare in the richer countries at a lower rate of increase and raising the rate of increase in welfare in the poorer countries.

Still another aspect of the third phase is the possibility of *regulating the growth of population*. Looked at from the economic viewpoint of the integration area it will be in the common interest of all countries in the area that the speed of increase in population be mitigated. This side of the problem needs to be studied more intensively than it is at present.

8. POSITIVE MEASURES OF INTEGRATION

As we have already observed it is a mistake to suppose that economic integration could be achieved by the mere elimination of existing instruments of economic policy. Those who hold this opinion overestimate the power of free competition as well as the preparedness of the present-day world to play the game of free competition in all circumstances. A number of positive measures will be necessary, and they may be summarized under four headings:

(*a*) automatic consequences of the elimination of trade barriers;
(*b*) measures of supervision;
(*c*) measures to maintain the conditions under which free competition works favourably;
(*d*) measures to supplement the forces of free competition.

The elimination of trade barriers and the creation, thereby, of the single market, implies certain *automatic consequences*. In order to make that market work in the correct way it will be necessary *e.g.* to make import duties of the integrated territory *vis-à-vis* third countries uniform in all the integrated countries; to have indirect taxes the same everywhere within the integrated area and to cause the rules according to which scarce currencies (in particular dollars) are made available, to be the same in these countries. Perhaps we should add the warning, referring to section 5, that the equalization of wages and of social insurance premiums, does not necessarily follow as a desirable measure.

Further it will be necessary to organize a certain *supervision* of both the negative measures and their automatic consequences just described. Otherwise it is by no means certain that these measures would be executed completely and in the best way; the temptations felt by certain groups or governments to neglect certain elements may be too great.

As we have previously pointed out, free trade, as a special form of free enterprise, will influence general welfare favourably only if certain conditions are fulfilled, of which the most important is the condition of *high and stable employment*. Experience has shown, however, that high and stable employment cannot be obtained by laissez-faire. Certain forms of employment policy will be necessary complements of any integration. To a certain extent such a policy can and should be pursued on a world-wide basis and should therefore be the task of the United Nations, apart from the duties which the national governments have in this field. But to a certain extent these tasks could be supplemented and made easier if the integrated area itself has a distinct policy and applies the corresponding instruments and organs. Part of such a policy could be the co-ordination of financial policies of the co-operating countries to effect the maintenance of financial stability or, in the scientific phrase, "monetary equilibrium".

Finally there is an important field of *supplementary action* in order to bring about, by direct endeavours, certain of the wholesome consequences of the single market. It is in particular in the field of specialization and interplant co-operation that direct steps seem to promise more than the indirect forces of competition might, in the end, perform. In order to obtain the most efficient concentration of the production, say of certain spare parts or semi-finished goods, in a few plants, making long production runs possible, deliberate schemes of co-operation and direct conversations probably will be the quickest way. Such conversations and the final co-operation will be necessary not only in order to avoid duplication in this world of complicated technical problems, but also for the elimination of the existing feelings of distrust among many competitors, both in the same country and among different countries. It seems to be the most effective way in which many industrialists could contribute to the integration.

9. CONCLUDING REMARKS: THE NEED FOR QUANTITATIVE RESEARCH

These theoretical considerations about integration are almost entirely qualitative in character. They should be supplemented with actual measurements in order to determine the order of magnitude of the phenomena discussed and their relative importance. A further development of the theory seems fruitful only on the basis of such quantitative knowledge: too often one may misjudge the relative importance of the various aspects of a problem if one does not know their relative influence. Unfortunately our statistical knowledge of the data pertinent to economic integration is very restricted. Figures concerning the level of production costs are very scarce and in numerous cases are completely unavailable. A vast bulk of rather elementary documentation is lacking and should first be built up. Improvement of production statistics as well as special investigations into individual industries will be necessary. As long as these data are not available much of our discussion on economic integration will lack the precision needed to permit far-reaching conclusions, or to enable us to draw up a program of integration for the next decade.[2]

---

[2] A bold piece of pioneering work has been undertaken by my colleague P. J. VERDOORN in a Report for the Dutch Economic Society (autumn-1952 meeting).

CUSTOMS UNIONS:
INFLUENCE OF THEIR SIZE ON THEIR EFFECT*

1. MODEL USED

In this note we propose to focus on only one aspect of the effects of customs unions, namely how these effects change with an increasing number of members and how they are distributed over members and non-members. The nature of the problem implies that we are not primarily interested in the qualitative differences between various types of unions, or even between the goods produced in the countries concerned. We will therefore use a model which in these respects is as simple as possible, and in which attention is concentrated on the countries as entities and the number of them. The model is a macro-model with regard to each country, using the concepts known from such models. Each country is assumed to produce one product, its national product, which it sells both at home and abroad. Each country imports the products of all the other countries, the prices of which, via the cost of living, influence the cost of production. The prices of the national products influence the relative demand for them, and total demand exerted by any one country is equal to its income. Customs unions, by influencing the prices at which consumers and producers can buy, influence the relative demand for the various nations' products.

The countries will be supposed to be of "equal importance", meaning that demand for their products (at a given income and price level), will be assumed equal and the supply functions of their products will be taken to depend in an identical way on the relevant variables (*cf.* section 2). This makes it unimportant in which country a customs union originates. The restriction that the countries must be of equal importance is not a real one, since countries may be combined into larger units. The number of countries will be taken to be N.

A process will be studied which starts with a state I, characterized by

* Published in *Zeitschrift für die gesamte Staatswissenschaft* 113 (1957), pp. 404-414.

equal import duties levied by all countries on all other countries' imports. Then a union between two members is established which eliminates duties between them. The union is expanded by letting the number of members, n, grow until all nations are included and a state of completely free trade exists. At any stage in the process, the production and real income of each country can be calculated and so their level of economic development can be ascertained.

2. SPECIFICATION OF DEMAND AND SUPPLY FUNCTIONS

Individual countries will be indicated by one subscript and commodity flows between them by two subscripts whose order indicates the direction of movement. Thus V_{ki} represents the value of exports from country k to country i, and is the mathematical product of the quantity v_{ki} and the price p_k of k's economic output.

$$(2.1) \qquad V_{ki} = v_{ki}\, p_k.$$

Zeros indicate summation over the subscript concerned; *i.e.* v_{k0} is the total volume of product k shipped to consumers in all countries and is assumed to be equal to the quantity supplied. Similarly, V_{k0} is the total value of this product, representing at the same time country k's national income.

Duties are assumed to be *ad valorem* duties of level t, and the price paid by a consumer in a country levying an import duty on k's product will be $p_k (1 + t)$.

Demand is taken to be of similar structure in all countries. Demand for product k by country i is given by the equation:

$$(2.2) \qquad V_{ki} = \frac{1}{N}\, V_{i0} - \frac{\varphi}{N^2}\left(p_k T_{ki} - \frac{1}{N}\sum_h p_h T_{hi}\right).$$

This may be interpreted in the following way:

Basically a fixed proportion $1/N$ of income V_{i0} is spent on commodity k. This amount is adjusted, however, if the price level at which the commodity is available to the consumer, $p_k T_{ki}$, diverges from the average price level at which all commodities are made available $1/N \sum_h p_h T_{hi}$. In these two expressions T_{ki} or T_{hi} stands for $1 + t$ if import duties are levied on commodities k or h, and for 1, if no duties are imposed. The coefficient φ is indicative of the degree of this adjustment, or this substitution between goods. If quantities of goods and of money are so measured as to make all prices and total money income in the free-trade situation equal to 1, φ represents the *elasticity with which the value of product k varies in response to relative price changes.* The demand function (2.2) satisfies the condition that total income is completely spent on all commodities, a fact easily verified by adding up (2.2) for all values of k from 1 to N.

Supply is assumed to satisfy the relation:

$$(2.3) \qquad v_{k0} = \frac{1}{N}\,\bar{\sigma} - \sigma\,\frac{\sum\limits_{h} p_h\,T_{hk}}{N^2 p_k}.$$

This equation may be interpreted to mean that supply is equal to a fixed quantity $\bar{\sigma}/N$, to be called productive capacity (and assumed equal for all countries), minus a correction which varies directly with the ratio of "costs" $1/N \sum_h p_h\,T_{hk}$ to price received p_k. Costs are taken equal to an unweighted average of the prices to be paid for all goods consumed by country k, and therefore roughly represent "costs of living", as observed in section 1, for that country. As long as all changes in relative prices are small—an assumption we make throughout—the corrections which must be made in the weights because of unequal consumption of different goods are second-order corrections.

The shape of the supply curve may be said to represent the producers' willingness to expand production if a higher real price can be obtained for the product. At the same time it reflects the existence of decreasing returns and the possibility of expanded production, both of which are essential for a realistic setting of our problem.

A few words may be said about the most probable values of the coefficients used in the equations. Assuming that we choose the units of the commodities and of money in such a way as to make all prices and total money demand in the free-trade position equal to one, we will later find [(cf. equation (5.3)] that this implies that $\bar{\sigma} - \sigma = 1$. It also implies that all supply elasticities are equal to σ (in that free-trade position). Since under conditions of full employment supply the elasticity is very small, it follows that then also σ should be small, implying that $\bar{\sigma}$ is only a little greater than 1. However, under conditions of overcapacity, σ and $\bar{\sigma}$ may both be higher.

Our coefficient φ, as was already observed, represents the elasticity of substitution for the value of, or expenditure on, each commodity. With regard to volume, such elasticities have often been found to be in the neighbourhood of 2, implying that φ may be about 1. Deviations to both sides seem possible. Perhaps in the short run the lower, and in the long run the higher figures may prevail.

3. WELFARE CONCEPTS TO BE USED

In order to appraise the effects of customs unions of different size, we shall have to use welfare concepts. We propose to use as the main concept one usually applied in questions of international trade, namely total production (for all countries together) and real income (for each separate country). Real income represents the value of national product divided by the price level of goods consumed, taking into account any changes in the terms-of-trade. In addition to the main concept, we shall pay some attention to the distribution among countries (already implied if we calculate real incomes for the separate countries) and among commodities. It has to be assumed that a more evenly distributed consumption basket represents a higher satisfaction than a more unevenly distributed one. In our case of symmetry between goods, this is a reasonable and simple assumption, which in other cases however would have to be replaced by references to utility functions.

From the symbols introduced in section 2, it follows that our main welfare concepts satisfy the following formulae:

Total production:

$$(3.1) \qquad v_{00} = \bar{\sigma} - \frac{\sigma}{N^2} \sum_k \frac{\sum_h p_h T_{hk}}{p_k}.$$

Real income of country k:

$$(3.2) \qquad w_k = \frac{v_{k0}\, p_k}{\sum_h p_h} = \frac{\bar{\sigma}\, p_k}{\sum_h p_k} - \sigma \frac{\sum_h p_h T_{hk}}{N \sum_h p_h}.$$

These expressions will be given more specific and simpler forms for the various states we are going to deal with in section 4. The essence is that there are two average price levels appearing in (3.2): the average *after duty* [also appearing in (3.1)], representing costs to producers and determining supply (together with p_k), and the average *before duty*, appearing in the denominator of real income, being the price paid by the country at large.

4. EQUILIBRIUM BEFORE AND AFTER UNION BETWEEN n OF N COUNTRIES

Our task will now be to solve the system of equations described in section 2 for different sets of data. The first set, corresponding with state I, would be one where between any two countries $T_{hk} = 1 + t$, whereas for $h = k$, $T_{hk} = 1$. With the establishment of the union, the values of T_{hk} between members of the customs union have to be taken equal to 1 also, and the number of members has to be gradually increased, in order to end up with a state III of free trade in which all $T_{hk} = 1$. We can obtain all these results at once by considering a state II in which n countries are united in a customs union; taking these as the countries 1, 2 . . . n, and indicating by m the number of countries outside the union, we have the following matrix of T_{hk}:

k＼h	1	2	...	n	$n+1$	......	$n+m$
1	1	1	...	1	$1+t$	......	$1+t$
2	1	1	...	1	$1+t$	......	$1+t$
...	...	...	...	...	...	......	...
n	1	1	...	1	$1+t$	......	$1+t$
$n+1$	$1+t$	$1+t$	...	$1+t$	1	......	$1+t$
...	...	...	...	...	...	......	...
$n+m$	$1+t$	$1+t$	...	$1+t$	$1+t$	......	1

It can be shown in a general way that the variables p_k of our system of equations of section 2 have to satisfy the following set of equations which express equilibrium between supply (2.3) and demand [derived from (2.2)]:

(4.1)
$$(\bar{\sigma} + \varphi T_k) p_k - \frac{1}{N} \Sigma_h p_h (\sigma T_{hk} + \varphi T_h) = V_{00}$$

where

(4.2)
$$T_k = \frac{1}{N} \Sigma_i T_{ki}$$

and

(4.3)
$$V_{00} = \sum_i V_{i0}.$$

Because of the symmetry assumed in section 3 between our countries, we can expect that there will be only two different duty-free price levels, namely p_u for the custom union member countries and p_s for the separate countries. Hence, there are two equations (4.1) only, one where k is a member country and one where k is a non-member country. In each, the index h will, in succession, indicate member and non-member countries. Keeping in mind the number of each type, we will find:

k a member:

$$\left\{\bar{\sigma} + \varphi\left(1 + \frac{m}{N}t\right)\right\}p_u - \frac{1}{N}\left[np_u\left\{\sigma + \varphi\left(1 + \frac{m}{N}t\right)\right\}\right.$$
$$\left. + mp_s\left\{\sigma(1+t) + \varphi\left(1 + \frac{N-1}{N}t\right)\right\}\right] = V_{00}$$

k a non-member:

$$\left\{\bar{\sigma} + \varphi\left(1 + \frac{N-1}{N}t\right)\right\}p_s - \frac{1}{N}\left[np_u\left\{\sigma(1+t) + \varphi\left(1 + \frac{m}{N}t\right)\right\}\right.$$
$$\left. + mp_s\left\{\sigma\left(1 + \frac{m-1}{mN}t\right) + \varphi\left(1 + \frac{N-1}{N}t\right)\right\}\right] = V_{00}.$$

From these equations we deduce:

(4.4)
$$\frac{p_s}{p_u} = \pi = \frac{\bar{\sigma} + \varphi\left(1 + \frac{m}{N}t\right) + \sigma\frac{n}{N}t}{\bar{\sigma} + \varphi\left(1 + \frac{N-1}{N}t\right) + \sigma\frac{t}{N}} = 1 - a$$

where

$$a = \frac{n-1}{N}\frac{\varphi - \sigma}{\bar{\sigma} + \varphi}t.$$

We now proceed to the calculation of our welfare concepts. Here it will be useful to introduce two other symbols, namely $p_{(u)}$, the price level of goods inside a union member country, and $p_{(s)}$, the price level inside a non-member country. Disregarding, as before, the second-order terms in the weights, we have

$$(4.5) \qquad p_{(u)} = \frac{1}{N} \left\{ np_u + mp_s \left(1 + t \right) \right\}$$

$$(4.6) \qquad p_{(s)} = \frac{1}{N} \left\{ np_u \left(1 + t \right) + \left(m - 1 \right) p_s \left(1 + t \right) + p_s \right\}.$$

The first of these equations expresses the fact that a member country gets the products of all member countries duty-free, whereas the second states that a non-member gets only its own product in that way.

Calculating total production, we may also use the concepts p_u, p_s, $p_{(u)}$ and $p_{(s)}$ to write it as follows (*cf.* 2.3):

$$v_{00} = \frac{1}{N} \sum_k \left(\bar{\sigma} - \sigma \frac{p_{(k)}}{p_k} \right) = \frac{1}{N} \left(N\bar{\sigma} - n\sigma \frac{p_{(u)}}{p_u} - m\sigma \frac{p_{(s)}}{p_s} \right) =$$

$$= \bar{\sigma} - \frac{\sigma}{N^2} \left\{ n \frac{np_u + mp_s(1+t)}{p_u} + m \frac{np_u(1+t) + (m-1)p_s(1+t) + p_s}{p_s} \right\}$$

$$= \bar{\sigma} - \frac{\sigma}{N^2} \left\{ n^2 + mn \left(1 + t \right) \left(\pi + \frac{1}{\pi} \right) + m \left(m - 1 \right) \left(1 + t \right) + m \right\}.$$

Since, according to (4.4), $\pi = 1 - a$, and, approximately $1/\pi = 1 + a$, the a-terms vanish and we obtain:

$$(4.7) \qquad v_{00} = \bar{\sigma} - \sigma - \frac{\sigma t}{N^2} \left(N + n - 1 \right) \left(N - n \right).$$

Real income of a union member is:

$$w_u = \frac{1}{N} \frac{\bar{\sigma} p_u - \sigma p_{(u)}}{p} = \frac{\bar{\sigma} - \frac{\sigma}{N} \left(N + mt - ma \right)}{N - ma},$$

where p stands for the duty-free average of prices. For small values of t and a we may approximate this by

$$\frac{1}{N} \left(\bar{\sigma} - \sigma - \frac{\dot{\sigma}m}{N} t + \frac{\dot{\sigma}m}{N} a \right) \text{ or:}$$

$$(4.8) \qquad w_u = \frac{1}{N} \left\{ \bar{\sigma} - \sigma - \frac{\dot{\sigma}m}{N} t + \frac{m \left(n - 1 \right)}{N^2} \frac{\bar{\sigma}t}{\bar{\sigma} + \varphi} \left(\varphi - \dot{\sigma} \right) \right\}.$$

Similarly, we obtain for non-members:

$$(4.9) \quad w_s = \frac{1}{N} \left\{ \bar{\sigma} - \sigma - \frac{\dot{\sigma}(N-1)}{N} t - \frac{n(n-1)}{N^2} \frac{\bar{\sigma} t}{\bar{\sigma} + \psi} (\varphi - \dot{\sigma}) \right\}.$$

5. SOME CONCLUSIONS

The process can now be summarized as follows. Writing for (4.7):

$$(5.1) \quad v_{00} = \bar{\sigma} - \sigma + \dot{\sigma} t \left\{ -1 + \frac{1}{N} + \frac{n(n-1)}{N^2} \right\}$$

we observe that in the initial state I, without union, production is at the level (taking $n = 1$):

$$\overset{I}{v_{00}} = \bar{\sigma} - \sigma + \sigma t \left(-1 + \frac{1}{N} \right)$$

and that in the final state III of free trade (where either $t = 0$ or $n = N$)

$$(5.3) \quad \overset{III}{v_{00}} = \bar{\sigma} - \sigma$$

representing a total gain of $\sigma t (1 - 1/N)$, which for large N is practically σt.

The *process of change from I to III* is expressed by the last term in (5.1): $\sigma t [n(n-1)/N^2]$ and appears to be accelerated. For $N = 6$ the consecutive values are (after multiplication by 36):

$$2 \qquad 6 \qquad 12 \qquad 20 \qquad 30,$$

implying that the progress achieved with each additional member of the union, is:

$$2 \qquad 4 \qquad 6 \qquad 8 \qquad 10.$$

It is interesting to note that *these figures are equal* to the number of elements in the T-matrix (in which, with each new member the value of $1 + t$ is reduced to 1) or, *to the number of tariff walls eliminated.*

This economic gain is *not equally shared between members and non-members.* The exact distribution depends on the value of $\varphi - \sigma$ in particular. If $\varphi > \sigma$ we see from (4.8) and (4.9) that members are in a more advantageous situation than if $\varphi < \sigma$, and the reverse is true for the non-members. Assuming, at first, that $\varphi = \sigma$, we find that non-members are not affected at all by the process of integration: they remain at what was the pre-integration income level for all countries.

Accordingly, the advantages, in comparison to the pre-union stage, are shared equally by the members. This implies that late-comers experience a substantial welfare increase upon entering the union.

If $\varphi > \sigma$, that is, *if the substitution elasticity in demand values (cf.* section 2), *is relatively large with regard to supply elasticity, non-members may even suffer losses from the integration process.* Inversely, if $\varphi < \sigma$, the non-members will share somewhat in the advantages; and consequently the members will then have smaller advantages. *The members will, however, never suffer a setback below the pre-union state,* as is shown by the following transformation for w_u:

$$(5.4)\quad Nw_u = \bar{\sigma} - \dot{\sigma} - \frac{N-1}{N}\,\frac{\bar{\sigma}}{\bar{\sigma}+\varphi}\,\sigma t + \frac{m\{(n-1)\,\bar{\sigma}-\sigma\}}{N^2\,(\bar{\sigma}+\varphi)}\,\varphi t$$
$$+ \frac{n\,(n-1)}{N^2}\,\frac{\bar{\sigma}}{\bar{\sigma}+\varphi}\,\sigma t.$$

Here the third (negative) term is still a little bit less than $-(N-1/N)\,\sigma t$: meaning that the first three terms are a little bit higher than pre-

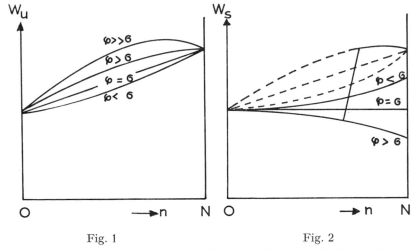

Fig. 1   Fig. 2

Fig. 1: Real income w_u of union members as a function of the number n of union members.

Fig. 2: Real income w_s of non-members of the union as a function of the number n of members (———), compared with real income (– – –) of members. Heavy line represents real income of any single country, jump indicates transition to union.

union total production. And the last two terms are positive. The fourth term is positive because we have to assume that $\bar{\sigma} > \sigma$; otherwise there would not be a positive production level under any circumstances. Consequently, the real income of a member country never falls below the initial level.

This does not mean, however, that each step of the integration process, will always improve the situation of the member countries. As is shown by the third term of (5.4), as well as by the last term in (4.8), there are forces tending to diminish a member country's real income, since m appears as a factor in an otherwise positive term. *If member countries have gained substantially in the earlier phases of integration, there may be reductions in real income in the later stages of integration if the value of φ is high.* As an illustration we may take the following numerical values:

$$\bar{\sigma} = 1\tfrac{1}{3} \qquad \sigma = \tfrac{1}{3} \qquad \varphi = 2.$$

The development of real income of a member country is now (multiplied by 3240):

$n = 1$	$w_u = 525$
2	532
3	538
4	540
5	541
6	540

It can also be shown that a *member's real income is always higher than a non-member's*. From (4.8) and (4.9) it follows that $N(w_u - w_s)$ $= \dfrac{n-1}{N} \dfrac{\bar{\sigma} + \sigma}{\bar{\sigma} + \varphi} \varphi t$ and this is positive irrespective of the value of $\varphi - \sigma$.

The situation may be described in a general way by Figs. 1 and 2, which represent the development over time—due to a regular increase of the size of the union—of the real income of a member country and of a non-member country respectively. The former's real income develops along a straight line for $\varphi = \sigma$ and along a parabolic curve for other relative values of φ and σ. From Fig. 1, it will be clear that retrogressive movements may occur for $\varphi \gg \sigma$ (much larger than σ) in the latter phases of integration. Real income of a non-member country develops along a horizontal line for $\varphi = \sigma$ and along the parabolae indicated in Fig. 2 for other values. Since in the process considered every non-member country is bound to become a member country at some time, the development will first occur along one of the light, fulldrawn curves and then jump to one of the dotted lines (which are a replica of the curves of Fig. 1). Especially for the higher values of φ the jump will be considerable (see heavy line).

For those readers who prefer to have some further explanation of the occurrence of the retrogressive movements in real income (which are true also for member countries), it seems useful to calculate the relative price and production levels for each phase of integration.

With regard to relative prices, equation (4.4) discloses that producers' (duty-free) prices of non-member countries in comparison to the same prices for members, are either gradually falling (when $\varphi > \sigma$) or gradually rising (when $\varphi < \sigma$) up to the point where only one non-member is left. With the inclusion of the last country in the union, price levels again become equal. The price ratio will be falling if demand elasticity (as defined above) surpasses supply elasticity, because then duties are affecting demand more than supply. In other words, *union members experience, from the extension of the union, a price-raising demand influence for $\varphi > \sigma$, which surpasses the cost-reducing supply influence.* When, on the other hand, $\varphi < \sigma$, price-reducing influences surpass price-raising influences.

The influences exerted by these relative price changes on each country's real income are the following:

(1) With each increase in the number of members of the union n, the quantity produced

$$\frac{\bar{\sigma}}{N} - \frac{\sigma \{np_u + m(1+t)p_s\}}{N^2 p_u} = \frac{\sigma}{N} - \frac{\bar{\sigma}}{N^2}\left\{n + m(1+t)\frac{p_s}{p_u}\right\}$$

changes because, first of all, in the expression {} (the cost-to-price-ratio), one term $(1+t)p_s/p_u$ is replaced by a term 1. Goods previously imported from an outside country are now obtained from the new member country.

(II) The quantity produced is, in addition, influenced by the change in p_s/p_u as a consequence of the increase in union membership.

(III) Similarly, the "terms of trade" factor in real income

$$\frac{Np_u}{np_u + mp_s} = \frac{N}{n + m\frac{p_s}{p_u}}$$

is affected, first, because a term p_s/p_u is replaced by a term 1 and second, because p_s/p_u changes in value.

Closer consideration shows that the nature of the changes depends in the following way on the size of σ:

Influences	$\sigma > \varphi$	$\sigma = \varphi$	$\varphi > \sigma > \varphi - (\bar{\sigma} + \varphi)\frac{N}{n-1}$
(I)	rise	rise	rise
(III)	rise	0	fall
(II) and (IV)	rise	0	fall

From this Table it appears that an increase in union membership always raises the members' real income when $\sigma \geq \varphi$, but may reduce it when $\sigma < \varphi$, because of influences (II), (III) and (IV). Values for σ below $\varphi - (\bar{\sigma} + \varphi) N/(n-1)$ are very improbable, since for $\varphi > 0$ they are negative.

Since, as we saw, in the somewhat longer run φ surpasses σ in most cases, the possibility that member countries will suffer a reduction in real income in the later phases of integration, is not merely theoretical. This is not the only example of somewhat unexpected consequences of changes in the terms-of-trade.

It seems useful, at this moment, to remember that real income is a rather rough measure of welfare. The distribution of consumption among the various goods becomes more equal in the later phases of integration and this, as a rule, is a favourable element in welfare. Our present model does not permit us to estimate its influence.

6. SUMMARY

A set of countries is considered, each of which produces one commodity, with identical supply functions showing elasticities σ. Demand functions are identical for these countries and symmetrical with regard to the various goods. Expenditure on each commodity shows a price elasticity of substitution of $-\varphi$. Initially all countries levy import duties t on all imports. Then a customs union is formed between two countries and gradually expanded until all countries are members. Total production appears to increase in an accelerated way, in proportion to the number of tariff walls eliminated. For $\varphi = \sigma$, the real income of member countries rises according to a straight line, while the real income of non-member countries remains constant as long as they do not join the union. For $\varphi \neq \sigma$, the time path is parabolic (*cf.* Figs. 1 and 2), implying that real incomes may sometimes even fall: if $\varphi > \sigma$, income falls continuously in the non-member countries; in the later phases, in the member countries as well. Each country except the pioneers of the union will at a certain moment make the jump from the "non-member curve" to the "member curve". (Heavy line in Fig. 2.)

A SIMPLIFIED MODEL OF THE CAUSATION OF TECHNOLOGICAL UNEMPLOYMENT*

1. INTRODUCTORY

The purpose of the present paper is to find the influence on employment of some of the outstanding "data" (extra-economic determining factors). For this purpose, a simplified model has been constructed in which these data and the chief economic variables find their places. Since it is not intended to picture cyclic variations and causations, the model may be called a "long-run model". It excludes some of the most typical cyclical phenomena such as stock-exchange speculation and the existence of small lags of all kinds which are of importance to the explanation of cycles but do not seem to be so for long-run developments.

Since the investigators were interested chiefly in studying the consequences of technological development for employment and the consequences of some of the best-known devices to improve employment, special attention was given to the corresponding sections of economic life.

The calculations have been made for the United States prewar structure (using figures for 1910) and for the postwar pre-Roosevelt structure (using averages for 1919–1932).

2. VARIABLES AND DATA INCLUDED IN THE ANALYSIS

Variables: a = total employment,
b = employment in investment-goods industries,
c = employment in consumer-goods industries,
u = volume of production of consumer goods,
$\bar{u}$ = "normal" volume of production of consumer goods[1]

---

* Written with P. DE WOLFF, *Econometrica* 7 (1939) p. 193.
[1] For explanation, *cf.* section 2

v = volume of production of investment goods,

v_{-T} = ditto, T units of time before,

v_e = volume of production of investment goods for expansion of plant,

p = consumer-goods price level,

q = investment-goods price level,

$\bar{n}$ = "normal"[1] non-labour remuneration contained in p,

n' = non-labour remuneration contained in q,

L = labour income (total wages),

E = non-labour income,

E' = non-labour consumption outlay,

E'' = non-labour savings.

Data: $\bar{g}$ = "normal" labour quota in unit of consumer goods,[1]

γ = increase in labour contribution in such unit for increase in production by one unit,

g' = labour quota in unit of investment goods,

h = deflated depreciation allowance per unit of product

T = lifetime of investment goods,

l = wage rate,

μ = "transition period",

ΔM = credit creation per time unit,

$\bar{E}$ = "normal" income of non-workers,

$\bar{E}'$ = "normal" expenditure of non-workers on consumption,

ε = non-workers' marginal propensity to consume,

t = time.

Some of the terms have to be further explained and so has the choice of the data. This may best be done by discussing, one by one, the relations constituting our "model".

3. THE RELATIONS ASSUMED IN THE MODEL

(1) Starting with total employment a, this may be split up into two parts b and c:

(1) $$a = b + c.$$

---

[1] For explanation, *cf*. section 3.

(2) Employment b in investment-goods industries will be dependent on the volume v of production of these goods by:

(2) $$b = g'v,$$

where $1/g'$ is labour productivity in this branch. The latter is assumed to be a given quantity, determined by technological development, but independent of v and of the wage rate l. These simplifying hypotheses have not been made for consumer-goods industries, but since investment-goods industries are far less important it was thought useful not to go into these details here.

(3) For consumer-goods industries, the relation between employment c and volume of production u is taken as:

(3) $$c = \{\bar{g} + \tfrac{1}{2}\gamma\,(u - \bar{u})\}u.$$

This comes to assuming that the inverted labour productivity or the labour quota per unit of product is a linear function of the volume of production itself; $\bar{u}$ is a reference value of the latter, which may be called the "normal" production. For $u = \bar{u}$, the quantity of labour required per unit equals $\bar{g}$, which is given by technical development. It will be assumed also to depend on wage rates, but since wage rates are also considered as data—for reasons to be set out afterwards—this dependency may be considered later (section 6, B). There is no serious restriction in the linearity of the function if we consider only small variations in volume of production. The chief reason why inverted productivity depends on the volume of production will be that for a larger production less efficient plants, or parts of plants, or methods, will be necessary.

(4) The volume of investment-goods production v may be split up into two parts, production for replacement and production for expansion of plant; the former is assumed to be equal to total production of investment goods, T time units before, where T is the lifetime of investment goods (including, apart from machines, also buildings and even houses).

We therefore get:

(4) $$v = v_{-T} + v_e.$$

(5) The volume of production of consumer goods u will be determined, in the first instance, by incomes spent and price level. It is assumed that wages are spent wholly; this leads to:

(5) $$up = L + E'.$$

(6) In a sense this is only a tautology, which has to be completed by an equation telling how consumption outlay E' by non-workers depends on their incomes; this is assumed to satisfy the relation:

(6)
$$E' = \bar{E}' + \varepsilon(E - \bar{E}).$$

The relation is linear, which again is no serious restriction if small variations are considered. The coefficients $\bar{E}$, $\bar{E}'$, and ε may be called "normal" income, "normal" expenditure, and marginal propensity to consume, respectively.

(7) The two income categories included in the foregoing analysis both depend on economic activity. Total wages L are simply the product of employment a and wage rate l:

(7)
$$L = al.$$

Non-labour income will be discussed later.

(8) The formation of prices may reasonably be treated first. Since long-run relations are considered, prices may be said to equal marginal cost. Marginal cost for consumer goods will consist of:

(I) Marginal remuneration of non-workers: $\bar{n}$;

(II) Marginal labour cost. Since total labour cost equals $cl = \{\bar{g} + \frac{1}{2}\gamma (u - \bar{u})\} ul$, marginal labour cost will be found by differentiation with respect to u and be equal to:

$$\{\bar{g} + \gamma(u - \tfrac{1}{2}\bar{u})\}l;$$

(III) Depreciation allowances. For simplicity and since they are only a small proportion of total costs these are assumed to be independent of the volume of production, but proportional only to prices of investment goods; they will be indicated by hq.

Adding up, we get:

(8)
$$p = \bar{n} + \{\bar{g} + \gamma(u - \tfrac{1}{2}\bar{u})\}l + hq.$$

(9) Since investment goods play a less important role than consumer goods, their prices q are not considered in so much detail. Depreciation allowances will for the prewar case be neglected, and, as before, g' is considered to be independent of v.

(9')
$$q = g'l + n'.$$

For the postwar case, calculations including depreciation allowances have also been made, using the formula:

(9)
$$q = g'l + n' + qh.$$

For simplicity, h has been taken equal for both groups of industries. The resulting errors are small.

(10) We are now able to calculate non-labour income, by subtracting, from the total value of production $pu + qv$, depreciation allowances huq (for postwar calculations $huq + hvq$), and wages

(10)
$$al = [\{\bar{g} + \tfrac{1}{2}\gamma(u - \bar{u})\}u + g'v]l;$$

the result being:
$$E = u\bar{n} + \tfrac{1}{2}u^2 l + vn'.$$

(11) One self-evident relation may be added here:

(11)
$$E' + E'' = E.$$

(12) Turning to the sphere of capital formation we have to ask: What funds are available and how are they spent? The funds are:

(I) the stream of savings, E'' per time unit;

(II) newly created credits, M (provisional notation) per time unit;

(III) a money stream coming into existence since the accumulated depreciation allowances are not fully used for replacement—replacement being equal to investment-goods production T time units ago and depreciation allowances being based on plant existing at this moment. These funds yield a stream of $(uh + vh - v_{-T})q$ [in the prewar case $(uh - v_{-T})q$].

This total is spent for two purposes:

(I) the purchase of durable capital goods, as far as they represent new investment; their value is $v_e q$; and

(II) wage and other income payments connected with an expansion of business. These sums have to be paid for a transition period only; after this period the receipts from increased production will enable the entrepreneurs to pay increased incomes. Indicating the rate of increase in total wages by $\dot{L}$, that in other incomes by $\dot{E}$, and the length of the transition period by μ, the necessary amount—sometimes referred to as increase in circulating capital—will be $\mu(\dot{L} + \dot{E})$. The period μ may be estimated roughly by putting it equal to the circulation period of income, i.e., total money in circulation M, divided by income $L + E$.

The foregoing leads to the equation:
$$E'' + \dot{M} + (uh + vh - v_{-T})q = v_e q + \mu(\dot{L} + \dot{E}),$$

which, since $v = v_{-T} + v_e$, may be written:

(12)
$$E'' + \dot{M} + (uh + vh - v)q = \mu(\dot{L} + \dot{E}).$$

In some calculations this will be simplified into:

(12′) $$E'' + \dot{M} + (uh - v)q = \mu(\dot{L} + \dot{E}).$$

Of course, this equation does not tell anything about the motives of investment activity. This question will be considered later (section 4).

(13) There remains one further equation to be discussed, *viz.*, the one between accumulated investment (in the physical sense) and the normal capacity to produce. Since v represents the volume of production of investment goods per unit of time, and T the lifetime of these goods, there will, at any moment t, be in existence a quantity of $\int_{t-T}^{t} v_\tau\, d\tau$ of them. Per unit of time, $1/T$ of this quantity will normally be "consumed" in the production process. This consumption represents the "contribution," $h(\bar{u} + \bar{v})$, to the normal production $\bar{u}$ and $\bar{v}$ of consumer and investment goods, respectively, h being the factor introduced as "deflated depreciation allowance".

Thus we get:

$$h(\bar{u} + \bar{v})T = \int_{t-T}^{t} v_\tau\, d\tau.$$

Since we will find T to be equal to about $2\frac{1}{2}$ units of 10 years, we may replace the integral by:

$$\int_{t-1}^{t} v_\tau\, d\tau + \int_{t-2}^{t-1} v_\tau\, d\tau + \int_{t-2\frac{1}{2}}^{t-2} v_\tau\, d\tau.$$

and since v_t will, in what follows, indicate the volume of production of investment goods in a finite period of which t is the centre, this sum equals, approximately:

$$\tfrac{1}{2}(v_t + v_{t-1}) + \tfrac{1}{2}(v_{t-1} + v_{t-2}) + \tfrac{1}{4}(v_{t-2} + v_{t-3}).$$

Our equation becomes, therefore:

(13) $$h(\bar{u} + \bar{v})T = \tfrac{1}{2}v_t + v_{t-1} + \tfrac{3}{4}v_{t-2} + \tfrac{1}{4}v_{t-3}.$$

Since, in our prewar calculation and in one of the postwar calculations, we neglect depreciation allowances in investment-goods industries, in these cases equation (13) will be replaced by:

(13′) $$h\bar{u}T = \tfrac{1}{2}v_t + v_{t-1} + \tfrac{3}{4}v_{t-2} + \tfrac{1}{4}v_{t-3}.$$

4. DATA, UNKNOWNS, AND CONSTANTS

The equations (1) to (13) will be used for the description of long-term movements of employment and other economic phenomena. In this description some of the phenomena introduced will be considered as data, others as "phenomena to be explained". Our distinction will not quite coincide with that of usual theory. A few words may therefore be added to defend our choice. We shall consider as data:

(I) The technical coefficients $\bar{g}$, g', h, T, and γ, determining, to some extent, the production function of our model society;

(II) The psychological coefficients $\bar{E}'$ and ε, determining the behaviour of consumers (non-workers);

(III) The institutional coefficient μ, intimately connected with the velocity of circulation of money;

(IV) The wage rate l and the rate of increase in circulation $\dot{M}$. These will, in general, be considered as economic phenomena, to be explained by theory. Both of them are, however, in present circumstances, highly subject to policy. Our procedure will be to consider them as independent variables and to find out how the choice of their magnitude influences employment and other economic phenomena. If then a certain change in l, say $\varDelta'l$, is found to be the most favourable change for a given purpose, it may quite well be that "natural developments", *i.e.*, normal economic forces, lead already to a change $\varDelta''l$; the task of policy then being to complement this $\varDelta''l$ until the total value $\varDelta'l$ is reached. For the solution of such problems it is not necessary to know the "natural development" $\varDelta''l$. Similar remarks may be made with respect to $\dot{M}$. The "regular" motives to investment are no longer of importance to its determination as soon as complementary government investments (public works and deficit financing) are included as a possibility.

(v) The remuneration per unit of product $\dot{n}$ of the marginal non-worker in consumer-goods industries and n' of non-workers in investment-goods industries. These are considered as constants—and therefore as given—since:

(a) In most literature about technological unemployment not much attention is given to their movements;

(b) Many elements in them will in fact be very sticky, such as interest, rent and "the adequate income" of an independent entrepreneur. Interest and rent are often fixed for very long times and "the adequate income" is something largely determined by tradition and past experience.

In order to be quite sure that the hypothesis of constant $\dot{n}$ and n'

is not a dangerous one, additional calculations have been made where instead of $\dot{n}$, total non-workers' income was considered constant—meaning that the remuneration per unit of product varies inversely with production volume u—and the deviations with our case appeared to be small.

Not all data have been supposed to be constant. Apart from $\dot{n}$ and n', just mentioned, this has been assumed to be so for γ, T, $\bar{E}'$, ε, and μ. On the other hand, l, $\bar{g}$, g', h, and $\dot{M}$ have been considered as (independently) variable. And the problem solved is that of the change in employment, prices, incomes, and production occurring as a consequence of given changes in the independent variables.

In order to solve this problem it is convenient to combine some of the equations and to differentiate them with respect to time. This latter device is not carried out for equation (12), which already contains differential coefficients. In order to simplify concrete calculations, finite (but small) rates of increase are substituted for differential coefficients. These do not relate, strictly speaking, to time period t, but to the moment between t and $t + 1$. For uniformity's sake, equation (12) is also brought into the form relating to that moment, which comes to adding to any term like E'' a term $\frac{1}{2}\Delta E''$. All these operations combined lead us to the following system of equations:

(14) $\quad \Delta a = \{\bar{g} + \frac{1}{2}\gamma(u - \bar{u})\}\Delta u + u\{\Delta\bar{g} + \frac{1}{2}\gamma(\Delta u - \Delta\bar{u})\} + v\Delta g' + g'\Delta v,$

(15) $\quad \Delta v = \Delta v_{-T} + \Delta v_e,$

(16) $\quad \Delta p = \{\bar{g} + \gamma(u - \frac{1}{2}\bar{u})\}\Delta l + l\{\Delta\bar{g} + \gamma(\Delta u - \frac{1}{2}\Delta\bar{u})\} + h\Delta q + q\Delta h,$

(17) $\quad (1 - h)\Delta q = g'\Delta l + l\Delta g' + q\Delta h,$

(18) $\quad l\Delta a + a\Delta l + \varepsilon\Delta E = u\Delta p + p\Delta u,$

(19) $\quad E'' + \frac{1}{2}(1 - \varepsilon)\Delta E + (hu + hv - v)q + \frac{1}{2}(hu + hv - v)\Delta q$
$\quad\quad + \frac{1}{2}q(h\Delta u + h\Delta v - \Delta v) + \frac{1}{2}qu\Delta h + \frac{1}{2}qv\Delta h + \Delta M$
$\quad\quad\quad = \mu(\Delta E + a\Delta l + l\Delta a),$

(20) $\quad\quad \Delta E = \bar{n}\Delta u + n'\Delta v + \gamma lu\Delta u + \frac{1}{2}\gamma u^2\Delta l,$

(21) $\quad \dfrac{\bar{u} + \bar{v}}{\bar{v}}\Delta\bar{u} = \dfrac{\frac{1}{2}\Delta v_{-3} + 1\frac{1}{2}\Delta v_{-2} + 2\Delta v_{-1} + \Delta v}{2hT}$
$\quad\quad\quad\quad\quad - \dfrac{\frac{1}{2}v_{-3} + 1\frac{1}{2}v_{-2} + 2v_{-1} + v}{2h^2T}\Delta h.$

In the establishment of the last of these equations a further hypothesis has been made, in order to avoid consideration of some unimportant details: it has been assumed that $\Delta \bar{u}$ and $\Delta \bar{v}$ show the same proportion as $\bar{u}$ and $\bar{v}$.

As has already been stated in the discussion of the separate equations, several cases have been considered. The above system of equations relates to one (the most complete) postwar calculation. A simpler calculation has been made with postwar and with prewar figures. In these latter calculations depreciation allowances for investment-goods industries have been neglected; this leads to the equations indicated with a prime and gives the following equations instead of (17), (19), and (21):

(17') $$\Delta q = g' \Delta l + l \Delta g',$$

(19') $$E'' + \tfrac{1}{2}(1 - \varepsilon)\Delta E + (hu - v)q + \tfrac{1}{2}(hu - v)\Delta q + \tfrac{1}{2}q(h\Delta u - \Delta v)$$
$$+ \tfrac{1}{2}qu\Delta h + \Delta M = \mu(\Delta E + a\Delta l + l\Delta a),$$

(21') $$\Delta \bar{u} = \frac{\tfrac{1}{2}\Delta v_{-3} + 1\tfrac{1}{2}\Delta v_{-2} + 2\Delta v_{-1} + \Delta v}{2hT}$$
$$- \frac{1}{2h^2 T}\,\Delta h(\tfrac{1}{2}v_{-3} + 1\tfrac{1}{2}v_{-2} + 2v_{-1} + v).$$

The unknowns of this system are Δa, Δu, Δv, Δv_e, ΔE, Δp, Δq, and $\Delta \bar{u}$; the independent variables: Δl, $\Delta \bar{g}$, $\Delta g'$, Δh, ΔM. The coefficients in these equations are all magnitudes relating to the actual situation and to some extent represent the economic structure as far as it seems to be important for long-run changes.

5. STATISTICAL INFORMATION

We have attempted to measure approximately the values of the coefficients in equations (14) to (21) and (17'), (19'), and (21'). This required a considerable amount of statistical work, the details of which would take far too much space to be given here. Of course great accuracy cannot be claimed for the results obtained. Some further trials have shown, however, that the character of most of the results obtained does not change very much if the statistical values taken are replaced by different values based on uncertainty margins esti-

mated. All this must, however, be preserved for a subsequent mono-
graph.

Before mentioning the figures used something must be said on the

TABLE I

SUMMARY OF STATISTICAL INFORMATION USED

Sym-bol	Description	Value 1910	Average value 1919–1932§
$\bar{g}$	Mean labour quota in consumer-goods industries for normal production	0.40	0.54
γ	Increase of marginal labour quota in consumer-goods industries per unit of increase in output	0.11	0.13
u	Volume of production of consumer goods	1.83	1.51
$\bar{u}$	"Normal" volume of production of consumer goods	1.83	1.51
g'	Labour quota in investment-goods industries	0.75	0.70
v	Volume of production of investment goods	0.34	0.37
h	Deflated* depreciation allowance per unit of output	0.07	0.10
ε	Marginal propensity to consume for non-workers	0.70	0.70
E''	Amount of total savings	0.22	0.21
μ	Transition period[†] (unit: 10 years)	0.05	0.07
$\bar{n}$	"Normal" remuneration of non-workers per unit of output of consumer goods§	0.43	0.26
n'	Remuneration of non-workers per unit of output of investment goods	0.25	0.20
T	Lifetime of investment goods (unit: 10 years)	2.5	2.5
v_{-3}	Volume of production of investment goods in time period —3	0.07	0.10
v_{-2}	Volume of production of investment goods in time period —2	0.12	0.24
v_{-1}	Volume of production of investment goods in time period —1	0.18	0.36

*$I.e.$, deprecation allowance if prices of consumer goods and of investment goods are taken equal to one.
§For explanation of term, see text.
[†]The principle underlying the choise of units invalidates, in some respects, the comparability of the last column with the last but one.

system of units used. For both time points considered the following principles for the choice of units have been applied:

(I) All prices have been taken equal to one;

(II) All money amounts have been measured in total wages bill as unit.

From (I) it follows that—at the moment considered—each quantity figure (a, u, v, etc.) is equal to the corresponding value figure (L, up, vq, etc.). From (II) it follows that—at that same moment—$a = 1$, since $L = 1$ and $l = 1$. Of course this is not necessarily the case for any later moment, since all variables considered may change.

Given this system of units, certain comparisons between the 1910 and the 1919–1932 figures are not possible. The values $u = 1.83$ for 1910 and $u = 1.51$ for 1919–1932 do not mean, *e.g.*, that the volume of production fell. They mean that the value of production of consumer goods fell in proportion to total wages.

The figures used are given in Table I. The reader will easily find all he wants for substituting in the equations (14)–(21). An exception must be made for the values Δv_{-3}, Δv_{-2}, and Δv_{-1}. These are, however, only contributing to the nonvariable terms in the equations which do not interest us for our problem and which have, therefore, not even been calculated.

One general remark may be added. The aim of statistical measurement has not been to test the equations (1) to (12). On the contrary, these have been considered as generally accepted and a number of the structural coefficients have been calculated with their help. Only equation (13) will be found not to be satisfied; the values found for the right-hand member and the left-hand member are rather divergent. There may be good reasons for this. Anyhow, the consequences of this discrepancy for our results have been calculated and were found to be unimportant.

6. RESULTS OF CALCULATIONS

Putting in the figures and solving for the unknowns yields the results given in Table II.

The first line of Table II means:

Case 1: $\Delta a = -0.55\Delta l + 0.97\Delta \bar{g} + 0.11\Delta g' + 2.18\Delta h + 9.42\Delta M$ + constant, and so on.

The application of these results to concrete problems requires some caution in that often changes in one of the independent variables may entail changes in others. This must be considered carefully for each case treated.

TABLE II

RESULTS OF CALCULATIONS

Coefficients obtained in solution for left-hand variable.

Case		Δl	$\Delta \bar{g}$	$\Delta g'$	Δh	ΔM
1	$\Delta a =$	− 0.55	+ 0.97	+ 0.11	+ 2.18	+ 9.42
2		− 0.92	+ 0.59	+ 0.29	+ 1.08	+ 8.72
3		− 1.03	+ 0.59	+ 0.13	+ 1.49	+ 8.72
1	$\Delta u =$	− 0.79	− 1.37	− 0.20	− 3.94	+14.96
2		− 1.13	− 1.17	+ 0.078	− 2.87	+11.04
3		− 1.29	− 1.17	− 0.13	− 4.46	+11.04
1	$\Delta v =$	− 0.35	− 0.38	− 0.28	+ 0.89	+ 4.20
2		− 0.36	− 0.33	− 0.24	+ 0.99	+ 3.10
3		− 0.39	− 0.33	− 0.28	+ 2.54	+ 3.10
1	$\Delta E =$	− 0.40	− 0.96	− 0.20	− 2.26	+10.48
2		− 0.44	− 0.60	− 0.012	− 1.12	+ 5.70
3		− 0.52	− 0.60	− 0.12	− 1.55	+ 5.70
1	$\Delta p =$	+ 0.52	+ 0.91	+ 0.093	+ 2.48	+ 0.99
2		+ 0.60	+ 0.88	+ 0.14	+ 2.10	+ 1.11
3		+ 0.59	+ 0.88	+ 0.12	+ 3.23	+ 1.11
1	$\Delta q =$	+ 0.75	—	+ 1.00	—	—
2		+ 0.70	—	+ 1.00	—	—
3		+ 0.78	—	+ 1.11	+ 1.11	—
1	$\Delta v_e =$	− 0.35	− 0.38	− 0.28	+ 0.89	+ 4.20
2		− 0.36	− 0.33	− 0.24	+ 0.99	+ 3.10
3		− 0.39	− 0.33	− 0.28	+ 2.54	+ 3.10
1	$\Delta \bar{u} =$	− 1.00	− 1.11	− 0.82	−34.82	+12.14
2		− 0.58	− 0.53	− 0.38	−22.60	+ 5.01
3		− 0.62	− 0.53	− 0.45	−26.23	+ 5.01

1. Prewar case [equations (14)–(21) with primes where they exist].
2, Comparable postwar case (same equations, but postwar figures).
3. Complete postwar case (equations without primes).

A. TECHNICAL PROGRESS AND EMPLOYMENT

Technical progress may be taken to mean any change in technical coefficients yielding lower costs per unit of product than before. Disregarding for a moment g', the reduction may be the result of:

(I) a reduction in $\bar{g}$, with an accompanying (but smaller) increase in h(l and q are supposed to be one); commonly known as *mechanisation*;

(II) a reduction $\bar{g}$ without a change in h mostly known as *rationalisation*; and

(III) a reduction in h with or without a (smaller) increase in $\bar{g}$. Such cases will frequently represent what Schumpeter called *"new combinations"*.

The remarkable result obtained by our calculations is that reductions in $\bar{g}$ (increases in labour productivity) are unfavourable to employment. This stands in contrast to what is known as the compensation theory. Let us go into some more detail here.

Since $a = gu + g'v$, where g is the amount of labour per unit of consumer-goods output, the direct consequence of a change in g may be taken to mean $\Delta a = u\Delta g$, the change in a for constant u, which, under these circumstances, is equal to $u\Delta\bar{g}$ or $1.83\Delta\bar{g}$ in the prewar case and $1.51\Delta\bar{g}$ in the postwar case. The compensation theory (whatever form it be given) holds that this direct, unfavourable, influence is offset by indirect consequences, which evidently result in changes in production. A number of these indirect consequences are taken account of in our calculations, as, *e.g.*, price change, influence of change in incomes, etc. Our results show that these repercussions are not able to compensate for more than about 50 per cent of the direct influence.

Our results do not include repercussions *via* the other independent variables. But they could be made to do so if we knew how much l, M, *etc.*, change for a given change in $\bar{g}$. There is little reason to include changes in l. Most authors are interested in knowing whether there will be compensation without wage changes.

Changes in h and in M may, however, be included. But it is not easy to see what relation exists between a given change $\Delta\bar{g}$ in $\bar{g}$, and the changes in h and M that accompany them.

As to changes in h only a certain limit can be indicated: it is in the nature of technical progress that $\Delta\bar{g} + \Delta h < 0$, since the left-hand side represents the increase in cost of production per unit. This does not, however, in our case give very narrow limits as to the results of changes in h. If $\Delta h = - \Delta \bar{g}$ (one extreme) we find that full compensation would be obtained since in Δa the coefficient for $\Delta h >$ that for $\Delta \bar{g}$. If, on the other hand, $\Delta h = 0$, which is certainly within the limit of possibilities, our previous conclusion still holds. From this it seems that the consequences of technical progress on employment are widely divergent for various types of technical changes. It may therefore be useful to know something on the actual changes in $\bar{g}$ and h. Our—admittedly very rough—estimates for the United States as a whole over the period 1850–1910 suggest that there is not a very close relation between $-\Delta \bar{g}$ and Δh, and, as far as such a relation exists, $-\Delta \bar{g}$ is about ten times as large as Δh. This would be somewhat reassuring, since it would mean that the influence of changes in h on employment is not so large.[2]

There remains the question of the repercussion on M. It is equally difficult to see of what nature and extent this repercussion is. It could be argued that an increase in labour productivity stimulates new investment activity and therefore ΔM. This connection is not, however, necessarily very intimate. It depends on the character of the technical change. An increase in labour productivity may, but need not, be accompanied by an increase in real investment. Therefore it seems better to hold separated the two phenomena and to state explicitly that *our conclusions concerning partial compensation bear on the case where no additional investment occurs as a consequence of the change in g.*

B. WAGES AND EMPLOYMENT: THE ELASTICITY OF THE DEMAND FOR LABOUR

Our formulae enable us to find, as a by-product, what influence on employment is exerted by a change in wage rates. By the choice of our units the coefficients for Δl found in the equations for Δa are equal to the elasticity of demand for labour. This elasticity would be somewhat more than one-half for 1910 and about unity for the postwar period.

[2] Similar calculations were made for the Netherlands. The coefficient found for $\Delta \bar{g}$ was very near to that found for the U. S., but the coefficient found for Δh was much smaller. The difficulty just dealt with did not exist therefore for that country.

Some qualifications must, however, be kept in mind. First, that we are dealing with long-run elasticities and that our figures do not take account of such cyclic phenomena as hoarding in depression. Secondly, that they have been made under the hypotheses enumerated, of which the most important one is that no changes in the other independent variables occur as a consequence of the wage-rate change. This means in particular that labour productivity would not be affected by a change in wages. It seems more realistic, at least for the very long run (after a couple of years, *e.g.*), to assume that the technical constants $\bar{g}$, g', h are functions of the wage rate. It is not easy to get accurate information on these functions which, by the way, must depend on the production function. A very rough estimate, based on a study by Professor GUSTAV ÅKERMAN[3] may be made in the following way. Professor ÅKERMAN found that, out of 19 cases of rationalisation which he studied, $12\frac{1}{2}$ were due to increases in real wages (cases which were described as only partly due to increases in real wages being counted for one-half), whereas out of these $12\frac{1}{2}$ cases, $6\frac{1}{2}$ would in the case of a wage reduction, be undone again. There is, therefore, a clear indication of "hysteresis": a different reaction for $\Delta l > 0$ and $\Delta l < 0$. We may summarize the situation by saying that 0.5 ± 0.2 of the cases of rationalisation were due to wage changes, where the upper sign relates to wage rises and the lower to wage falls. Now $\Delta\bar{g}$ was, between 1921 and 1931, in our units, equal to -0.14, whereas $\Delta(l - p)$, representing the change in real wage rate, amounted to $+0.22$. If, since we have to do with a rise in wage rates, $7/10$ of the fall in $\bar{g}$ or -0.10 is to be attributed to the change $+0.22$ in $l - p$, then the relation between $\Delta\bar{g}$ and $\Delta(l - p)$ must be

$$\Delta\bar{g} = -\frac{0.10}{0.22}\Delta(l - p) + \Delta\bar{\bar{g}}$$

for wage rises, where $\bar{\bar{g}}$ is the part of $\bar{g}$ which is to be attributed to other factors than wages. For wage falls the coefficient has to be changed in the proportion 0.7 to 0.3. We therefore get:

$$\bar{g} = -0.45\Delta(l - p) + \Delta\bar{\bar{g}} \text{ for } \Delta(l - p) > 0\text{,}$$
$$\bar{g} = -0.19\Delta(l - p) + \Delta\bar{\bar{g}} \text{ for } \Delta(l - p) < 0\text{,}$$

---

[3] "Om den industriella rationaliseringen och dess verkningar", *Arbetslöshets-utredningens betänkande I*, Bilagor, Band 2, Stockholm 1931.

or summarized:

$$\Delta \bar{g} = - (0.32 \pm 0.13) \Delta(l - p) + \Delta \bar{\bar{g}}.$$

This may now be combined with our results for case 3: $\Delta a = -1.03\Delta l + 0.59\Delta \bar{g}$, neglecting further terms, and $\Delta p = 0.59\Delta l + 0.88\Delta \bar{g}$, neglecting further terms.

It follows that

or
$$\Delta \bar{g} = - (0.32 \pm 0.13)[\Delta l - 0.59\Delta l - 0.88\Delta \bar{g}] + \Delta \bar{\bar{g}},$$
$$\Delta \bar{g} = - (0.17 \pm 0.04) \Delta l + (1.4 \pm 0.2) \Delta \bar{\bar{g}}.$$

Finally,

$$\Delta a = - 1.03\Delta l - (0.10 \pm 0.02) \Delta l + (0.83 \mp 0.12) \Delta \bar{\bar{g}}.$$

The elasticity of demand for labour would, according to this rough evaluation, not be changed considerably by the reaction on $\bar{g}$ which is exerted by l. And in this correction the influence on h, which will generally be of the opposite sign, has even been neglected.

C. Hours and Employment: the Influence of a 40-Hour Week on Employment

We are also able to find the influence of a change in working hours from, say, 48 to 40. Taking a week as the unit of labour, this means that $\bar{g}$ and g' will rise in the proportion $5:6$; thus $\Delta \bar{g} = 0.11$ and $\Delta g' = 0.14$. The effect on h is not certain; if depreciation were proportional to production, no change in h would be involved; if it were proportional to time, a maximum change in h of $1/5$ or 0.02 would be the effect of the change in hours; therefore $\Delta h = 0.01 \pm 0.01$. As to wages, two different cases may be considered; first, no change in weekly wages which means that $\Delta l = 0$; secondly, a proportionate reduction in weekly wages, meaning that $\Delta l = -0.17$. Using formula (3) we find:

Δa, for:	$\Delta h = 0$	$\Delta h = 0.02$
$\Delta l = 0$	0.08	0.10
$\Delta l = -0.17$	0.26	0.28

It must again be emphasized that these changes represent long-run changes, disregarding cyclic influences. They seem to be very favourable for the case of shorter hours: an increase of 8 to 10 per cent of employment would result when weekly wages are kept constant and one of 26 to 28 per cent if hourly wages are kept constant.

It will be clear that the effect on total consumption is less favourable. Using the formula for u (case 3) we find:

Δu, for:	$\Delta h = 0$	$\Delta h = 0.02$
$\Delta l = 0$	$-0.15 \; (-10\%)$	$-0.23 \; (-15\%)$
$\Delta l = -0.17$	$+0.07 \; (+ \; 5\%)$	$-0.02 \; (- \; 1\%)$

The percentage changes have been given in brackets ($u = 1.51$).

D. CONCLUDING REMARKS

We have not yet exhausted our formulae. They enable us, in principle, to calculate consequences of other structural changes and also to calculate the effects on the other variables such as p, q, E, etc. Part of this may be left to the reader and to later publications. As an example, one further problem may be considered, viz., to find the increase in total incomes $al + E$ or $\Delta a + \Delta E$ for a given increase in M, obtained by additional investments ΔM financed by credit creation. Evidently this is the problem of the multiplier, but under conditions somewhat different from those assumed by KAHN and KEYNES. A reserve capacity has been assumed to exist in this sense that less and less "good" investment goods are available for increase in production [cf. equations (3) and (8)]. No dole has been supposed to exist and the community considered is a closed one. From Table v we find: $\Delta a + \Delta E = (8.72 + 5.70)\Delta M$, which means a multiplier of about 14.

Similar calculations[4] have been made for Holland; they show, in many respects, similar results; but the multiplier is found—as it should be—to be much lower, viz., of the order of magnitude of 2.

Central Statistical Office
The Hague, Netherlands

---

[4] These will be published in a Report made by the Netherlands Central Statistical Office on the request of the High Labour Council.

ON THE THEORY OF TREND MOVEMENTS*

CONTENTS

1. INTRODUCTION

The purpose of the present paper is to make a contribution to the theory of trend movements or, to state it differently, to the dynamics of long-term economic movements. The object of this particular field of economics may first be characterized by clearly defining its position among related fields. These are statics on the one hand, and the dynamics of short-term movements on the other. The object of statics is to find the equilibrium position of an economy whose population, stock of capital goods, state of technology *etc.* are given and in most cases are assumed to be constant. The dynamics of short-term movements deals with the explanation of "fast" movements, such as trade cycles, or else of speculative special movements such as those

---

* "Zur Theorie der langfristigen Wirtschaftsentwicklung", *Weltwirtschaftliches Archiv*, 55 Band (1942 I), p. 511–549.

caused by fluctuations in crops, *etc*. In these dynamic models also, the assumption of a constant population, stock of capital goods, and state of technology is frequently utilized.

The purpose of a theory of trend movements is to investigate economic movements extending over decades or even centuries. Such a theory must not overlook the development of population, capital *etc.*, in fact it must make these the special subject of its analysis. Its central problem may be briefly expressed in the following question: how do production, employment, living standards and other factors change under the influence of population growth, technical development and capital formation? A more exact definition of this problem will be given later, yet this question is sufficient to suggest the scope of the subject.

It must be borne in mind that the theory of trend movements does not concern itself with the short-term fluctuations which show the actual movements. The study of the components of such movements is left to the analysis of the dynamics of these short-term movements. This limitation in scope must be made in order that the analysis does not become too complex and difficult. Whether or not such dissociation from the actual movements is generally permissible will be discussed later (see section 4).

In this paper even more restrictions will be made. Such restrictions, however, are not of vital importance for the contents of our theory and could be eliminated in a complete elaboration. Furthermore we will not take the trouble to explain the so-called long cycles. Their effect appears primarily in price movements; their influence on production, employment, and capital formation as well as the fluctuations of real wages is secondary. This does not mean, however, that we shall consider them to be irrelevant. The basic problem of trend movements, above all that of the deflated variables of the economy, is of a different nature and consists in discovering the basic causes of continuous increases in these series. Our analysis will be aimed particulary at the decisive determinants of economic growth and the extent to which it can be influenced.

This approach is perhaps even more justified with regard to the third restriction to be introduced, that of an elimination of monetary phenomena from our model of economic development. Monetary aspects are especially important for short-term movements and most of all for explaining fluctuations in prices, wages and rates of interest. In the case of long-term movements the determination of the fluctuations of these latter variables may be separated almost entirely from those of the real quantities in the economy, as will be shown later. We will therefore omit them for the most part and perhaps publish in another article an investigation into these problems.

Finally—and this is the end of our definition of the subject—we will not discuss individual goods and markets but will always consider the economy as a whole.

2. FIRST STEPS IN PUBLISHED LITERATURE

As is often the case in economics, the literature on long-term trends is classified into two distinctly separate fields between which there exists a vacuum. On the one hand, we have the statistical literature describing the outward appearances of the trend movement; this literature gives rather detailed numerical illustrations of the phenomena but states the economic interrelations only in a more or less superficial manner, as we shall show later. On the other hand, there is the theoretical literature which, apart from a very few exceptions, presents a qualitative analysis and for this reason excludes *a priori* the possibility of formulating numerical conclusions. This is why econometrics in this field as well appears to be the most adequate method of investigation. Econometrics is defined as the combination of a mathematical-economic treatment with a statistical analysis.

The greater part of the statistical literature has been published by Harvard University. Harvard's research in the field of trade cycles has led to the publication of a wealth of statistical data on which most of the published series of trend components are based. It will be remembered that there are two methods of defining trends: the non-mathematical and the mathematical. The non-mathematical method uses either free-hand curves—which can hardly be called scientific—or moving averages which cannot have any significance for the theory of trends. The mathematical method first assumes a definite type of curve—a straight line, a parabola, or an exponential curve—and defines the constants of this curve by the method of least squares. This method, it must definitely be granted, has significance for the

Please send me descriptive folders of new publications in the series "Contributions to Economic Analysis".

Name ....

Address ....

City, Zone, State ....

NORTH-HOLLAND PUBLISHING COMPANY

P.O. Box 103

AMSTERDAM-Netherlands

theory of trends. This is because a connection with this theory is possible if the choice of the type of curve is based on a theory. Here we should like to add immediately that only in exceptional cases has this ever happened in an entirely satisfactory manner. But there are a few such cases.

The most common types of curves are those mentioned above. The use of the straight line may generally be explained by the fact that, for short intervals, it can be considered to be the first approximation to any other curve; the parabolas of several powers can be explained as approximations of higher order. The exponential curve (whose points describe a geometrical series of ordinate values for equidistant abscissæ) may be visualized in the first place as a linear development of logarithms; or, in the second place,—and this is theoretically clearer— as the result of a simple law of growth, whereby the annual increase in the variables under review is proportional to the magnitude of these variables already reached. Here we recognize the first signs of a theory, of a certain interlinkage of causes. It is true that a linear equation for development may be just as easily constructed, yet for most economic processes the latter will be less natural than the formula for the exponential curve. The simple formula mentioned above can sometimes be applied to the growth of population and to the formation of capital. However, this is true only for especially uncomplicated conditions which hardly ever occur in reality.

Others may be added to the three simplest types of curves we discussed above. First to be mentioned is the logistic curve expressed in the equation

$$x = \frac{a}{1 + e^{-bt+c}},$$

where t is time and a, b, and c are the constants. The corresponding growth curve is obtained if the increase of one variable is proportional:
   a. to the quantity x already reached of this variable and
   b. to the remaining space of development $a-x$; therefore a plays the part of an absolute limit which is drawn for variable x.

The validity of this law of growth has been established to a degree for certain kinds of bacteria colonies which were supplied with a given quantity of food per unit of time. There have also been attempts to explain the growth rate of human populations by this formula. Under certain circumstances reliable approximations are obtained.

In some respects the investigation of long-term trends at Harvard culminates in the work of KUZNETS and SNYDER. In his "Secular Movements in Production and Prices"[1], KUZNETS investigated a large number of production and price series, whereby he defined, among other things, the "primary trend".

In doing so he made use of two types of curves, namely the logistic curve mentioned above and the Gompertz-curve expressed in the formula:

$$x = ae^{-bc^t}$$

Both have a common characteristic: growth saturation. In his book KUZNETS tries first of all to explain these saturation phenomena. These are correlated chiefly with the "penetration" of certain new products into the economy and are therefore more characteristic of individual markets than of an entire economy. On the other hand, KUZNETS uses qualitative methods and what he gives—although very interesting—is more an enumeration of the relevant symptoms than a formulation of an economic theory. Since he dealt only with data for individual markets, this would indeed have been a difficult task.

In his small German volume, "Wesen und Bedeutung des Trends"[2] he gives a brief summary of the results he obtained. In the appendix he promises to present "a brief historical survey of the treatment of the problem in economics",[3] yet for the most part he gives only a very interesting discussion of the statistical treatment of the problem. An economic theory of the trend, however, is nowhere to be found.

The works of SNYDER[4] are more important for our purpose in as far as they deal with the economy as a whole. As a trend curve SNYDER frequently uses an exponential curve or at least suggests it by implying

[1] S. S. KUZNETS, *Secular movements in production and prices. Their nature and their bearing upon cyclical fluctuations.* (Hart, Schaffner & Marx Price Essays, 46). Boston and New York 1930.

[2] S. S. KUZNETS, Wesen und Bedeutung des Trends. Zur Theorie der säkularen Bewegung. *Veröffentlichungen der Frankfurter Gesellschaft für Konjunkturforschung*, H.7., Bonn 1930.

[3] *Idem*, note from the editor.

[4] C. SNYDER, *Business cycles and business measurements. Studies in quantitative economics*, New York 1927.

logarithmic methods. Unfortunately, one looks in vain for a quantitative theory of the trend.

In Germany, WAGEMANN published important material containing extremely interesting ideas about long waves of various kinds.[5] Other material has been published by a number of other authors, especially HOFFMANN.[6] However, a theory as we conceive it is not offered.

To my recollection, the beginnings of such a theory are found only in CASSEL's "Theoretische Sozialökonomie".[7] In paragraph 6 of chapter I he deals with the "uniformly progressing economy". With a truly exact theory he demonstrates that the magnitudes assumed by its variables correspond to exponential curves. All the same, such a uniformly progressing economy postulates a constant technology and is also in other respects very simplified in nature.

As far as I can see, all the other theoretical literature is purely qualitative. All one has to do is to open a few textbooks on economics or a few manuals of business cycle theory to confirm this opinion. As must be expected with a qualitative analysis, there is considerable difference of opinion about the significance of the individual factors. Some authors exaggerate the importance of population growth,[8] others overemphasize technical development, and still others the formation of capital.[9] An added difficulty is the diverging conceptions of the term technical development. We shall come back to this later (see section 5).

3. THE PURPOSE OF A TREND THEORY

It may be useful before tackling the subject itself to ask ourselves what is the purpose of trying to find a theory of long-term movements.

[5] E. WAGEMANN, *Struktur und Rhythmus der Weltwirtschaft. Grundlagen einer weltwirtschaftlichen Konjunkturlehre*, Berlin 1931. To my knowledge, WAGEMANN has so far given his views on long waves only in lectures.

[6] W. HOFFMANN, "Wachstum und Wachstumsformen der englischen Industriewirtschaft von 1700 bis zur Gegenwart", *Probleme der Weltwirtschaft*, 63, Jena 1940.

[7] G. CASSEL, "Theoretische Sozialökonomie", *Lehrbuch der Allgemeinen Volkswirtschaftslehre*, Abt. 2, Leipzig 1918.

[8] So H. VON BECKERATH, "Der moderne Industrialismus. Gewerbepolitik". *Grundrisse zum Studium der Nationalökonomie*, Bd. 11, 1, Jena 1930, p. 13.

[9] To an extent, this is the case with P. H. DOUGLAS, *The Theory of Wages* (New York 1934), insofar as he attributes technical development to an increase in capital intensity in production.

One can differentiate between direct and indirect purposes. The direct purpose is first to explain the rising movement of the abovementioned economic variables; second to find a mathematical formula for the curves in question, and finally, to determine the influence of such factors as population growth, technical development, wage demands, capital formation and the rate of growth. An explanation of the growth curve has sometimes been attempted by previous authors with a more or less pronounced secondary objective of propaganda. The intention was either to demonstrate the advantages of a liberal economic policy (*e.g.* for raising national prosperity) or else its disadvantages (the development of certain disproportions). The purpose we have in mind, however, can only be to become more familiar with the process of development and hence to ascertain its degree of susceptibility to control.

The indirect purpose of our attempt is found in the following:

a. A theory of trends makes it possible to give a better foundation to the treatment of the problems of statics. It will be agreed that in some cases it is unsatisfactory to try to solve important problems of economic analysis and policy under the assumption of a constant capital quantity or a constant population. In particular, the investigation of measures which have different effects over short and long periods of time is rendered more difficult by this assumption. In statics there is only one level of equilibrium of the economic variables; this level is either raised or lowered by the measure concerned. In reality, however, there is a continuous movement which may, for instance, have a downward direction in the beginning and move upward with time, in contrast to the uni-directional development which would have occurred had no such measure been taken. Differentiations of this kind, however, are obscured by the static analysis of the problem.

b. A theory of trends also creates a better foundation for the analysis of the dynamics of short-term movements. Here the same applies *mutatis mutandis* as for statics. A particularly important problem is illustrated by the question of the influence of certain trade policies on the long-term movement. The treatment of such questions requires a theory which represents both long-term and short-term movements simultaneously. It is true that this makes it basically very complicated. The construction of such a theory, however, is facilitated by a preceding theory regarding the long-term movement itself.

4. DOES A THEORY OF LONG-TERM MOVEMENTS DISREGARDING SHORT-TERM MOVEMENTS HAVE ANY SIGNIFICANCE?

This question can be discussed only briefly within the scope of this article. Since it is of elementary importance, however, we cannot omit it entirely. In order to give an answer let us assume that we already have a complete theory explaining both long-term and short-term movements. In accordance with such a theory the economic system under review will follow different movements which can be classified into periodic components and aperiodic components.[10] The sum of the aperiodic components determines the trend movement of the system. The periodic components show different degrees of damping. Thus there are two types of economic systems, *viz.* such where all periodic components are damped, *i.e.* where the amplitudes of oscillation are decreasing and such where one or more of these components show ever-increasing amplitudes. The movements of the first type of system will deviate only temporarily from the trend movement, whereas the movement of the second type of system will generally show considerable fluctuations along the trend. For such systems a study of the trend has no point because it does not form the "center of gravity" of the short-term components. In the case of systems of the first type the trend actually constitutes the "general tendency" (la tendence générale) of the total movement. In our eyes this is the justification of a theory of the long-term movements. Therefore, such a theory exists only for systems of the first type. This justification applies at the same time to statics. For a certain number of economic systems, but only for them, statics has a meaning. This group, like the "first type of systems" is characterized by the damping of its periodic movements. It differs from the latter systems insofar that its trend runs only horizontally so that there is no progressive movement or in other words no trend component.

---

[10] The assumptions on which these conclusions are based and their proofs can be found in my paper: "Einige Grundfragen der mathematischen Konjunkturtheorie", *Archiv für mathematische Wirtschafts- und Sozialforschung*, Leipzig, Bd. 3 (1937), p. 1 *sq.*, 83 *sq.*

The approximation of the actual movement by the trend depends upon the amplitude of short-term movements (which depend in turn upon the accidental disturbances to which the system is exposed). Under certain circumstances it can be a very close approximation. However, a theory of trends as we give it will probably be too inaccurate for questions of economic policy, *e.g.* the problem of full employment. We shall come back to this subject later.

Now we should like to discuss shortly a mathematical question closely connected to the previous one. All movements of a dynamic system, as we have shown[11] can be perceived as solutions of the so-called final equation of the system, that is, each solution of this equation corresponds to a component of the total movement. The question now arises whether —with a given final equation—we can find the trend components without first solving them completely. Only then we can speak of a special theory of the trend movement. Under certain circumstances, the detailed discussion of which is outside the scope of this article, we can show that we can reach this aim if we neglect the small lags in the final equation. This simplifies the equation; it has fewer solutions, is easier to solve and the remaining solutions yield exactly the same trend components. This procedure, which is also valid for static analysis, might be justified as follows (although we do not know the exact conditions to which it is subject) : a trend movement is always a slow movement. Therefore, the difference between two subsequent values of a variable is very small. We may therefore treat it as of no importance.

5. THE ELEMENTS OF THE THEORY

5.1. THE PRODUCTION FUNCTION

It was already pointed out that for the time being we shall discuss the real variables of the economy, relating to goods and services, but not deal with individual markets. We shall therefore deal with only one type of goods (which can be used for both consumption and investment purposes) and call its volume of production u. Apart from that we shall introduce two factors of production, labour and capital. The third factor, land, will not be considered here because its volume

---

[11] TINBERGEN, *loc. cit.*

is assumed to be constant. For most countries this will be correct. The volume of labour applied will be expressed as a, the volume of capital applied, in which we will assume land to be included, as K.[12] The quantity for any given moment may be measured either by the volume of goods incorporated therein or by the market value of the productive property corrected for price fluctuations. We understand by this the market values divided by a general price index such as the cost of living or the index of capital good prices. Actually this involves a number of other problems which we do not intend to discuss here.

Between the volume of production u and the volumes of applied production factors a and K there exists a technical relation which changes in the course of time and which we call the production function or production equation; that is, u is a function of a and K:

$$u = \varphi (a,K).$$

There is little knowledge of the exact shape of the production function. As far as we know, only DOUGLAS[13] tried to examine the function statistically. DOUGLAS is occupied with the production of the entire industry which he considers as a whole. He does not go as far as we do, since we consider the total production of all industries and trades of a country as a whole. He forms the following function:

$$u = ca^\lambda K^\mu,$$

[12] As far as possible, our symbols are the same as in other publications.

[13] DOUGLAS gives a summary of the first series of investigations on this point in his book *The Theory of Wages*. Later the following articles appeared: M. L. HANDSAKER AND P. H. DOUGLAS, "The theory of marginal productivity tested by data for manufacturing in Victoria", *The Quarterly Journal of Economics*, Cambridge, Mass., Vol. 52 (1937/38), p. 1 *sq.*, p. 215 *sq.* – G.T. GUNN AND P. H. DOUGLAS, "Further measurements of marginal productivity", *Ibidem*, Vol. 54 (1939/40), p. 399 *sq.* – M. BRONFENBRENNER AND P. H. DOUGLAS, "Cross-section studies in the Cobb-Douglas function", *The Journal of Political Economy*, Chicago, Ill., Vol. 47 (1939), p. 761 *sq.* – G. T. GUNN AND P. H. DOUGLAS, "The production function for American manufacturing in 1919, *The American Economic Review*, Evanston, Ill., Vol. 31 (1941), p. 67 *sq.* – For critical remarks on the works of DOUGLAS see a.o.: J. M. CLARK, "Inductive evidence on marginal productivity, *Idem*, Vol. 18 (1928), p. 449 *sq.* – D. DURAND, "Some thoughts on marginal productivity, with special reference to Professor Douglas' analysis", *The Journal of Political Economy*, Vol. 55 (1937), p. 740 *sq.* – H. MENDERSHAUSEN, "On the significance of Professor Douglas' production function", *Econometrica*, Menasha, Wis., Vol. 6 (1938), p. 143 *sq.*

where c, λ and μ are constants. By suitable selection of the units for u, a, and K we can make $c = 1$. We shall proceed in the same manner. Douglas' function is therefore an exponential formula of the simplest imaginable type. Still, it should be preferred to the even more simple additive linear formula $u = c_1 a + c_2 K$ because the latter shows differential quotients which are independent of a and K. This would mean that the optimal productivity of labour and capital respectively is independent of the volume of the applied factors of production. Such an assumption is clearly too special. Douglas' selection of the former formula therefore is understandable.

DOUGLAS is furthermore of the opinion that the values λ and μ must satisfy the relation

$$\lambda + \mu = 1$$

that is, that the formula must be linear homogenous. This means that a proportional increase of a and K, $i.e.$ of the applied volumes of labour and capital, must result in a proportional increase of the volume of production. In general this applies only within the limits of constant returns. This condition exists if all enterprises have their optimal size and if their number is large. In such a case a small change of production can take place by increasing the number of such optimal enterprises. For an analysis of slow movements which do not deviate much from the state of equilibrium, and for a whole country in which the individual enterprises are small, this assumption seems justified.

This formula has been generalized by EDELBERG[14] for the case where three production factors are used. If the volume of land used is n, the formula reads

$$U = a^\lambda K^\mu n^\nu,$$

where

$$\lambda + \mu + \nu = 1.$$

As mentioned before, we shall combine capital and land in the following and express the total volume of the two production factors as K. Moreover, we shall use DOUGLAS' formula of the linear homogenous

---

[14] V. EDELBERG, "An econometric model of production and distribution", *Econometrica*, Vol. 4 (1936), p. 210 *sq.*

type. In one respect we will generalize it by attaching a factor increasing with time ε^t; we therefore write:

$$(1.1) \qquad\qquad u = \varepsilon^t a^\lambda K^{1-\lambda}.$$

Thus we take into account the possibility of an increasing (perhaps also decreasing) effectiveness of the production process in time and we have the possibility of including the element of technical development in our model.

The term "technical development" warrants some explanation. It is used by several authors with contradictory meanings. Those who think along statistical lines generally conceive it as the increase in the (statistical) labour productivity, *i.e.* the relation between the volume of production and the volume of labour, probably because it is the easiest to be determined. It is obvious, however, that every reduction of the real costs, whether through reduction of the capital costs per production unit or labour costs per unit, must also be considered as a technical development. It is also possible that labour costs will rise if capital costs decrease more than proportionally.

An increase in labour productivity may be obtained by two different means. Firstly, the production function can remain unchanged and the capital intensity of production can be increased. Secondly, we can also change the production function, in other words obtain a higher volume of production with the same volume of labour and capital. DOUGLAS assumed that in the periods he studied the production function of the industry remained unchanged and that the increase in labour productivity is due exclusively to the increased capital intensity of industrial production. He points out that this process also deserves the name of technical development, in any case in outward appearance, insofar as it is linked with the introduction of new capital goods and working methods. It must not be forgotten in this connection that these methods of higher capital intensity — although belonging to the same production function — may have been previously unknown. This is true particularly for the country with the highest capital intensity in the world.

Such an increase in labour productivity will, however, always be accompanied by a corresponding decrease of capital productivity; we have here the process of mechanization, the replacement of labour by capital. In addition we have the simultaneous increase of both labour productivity and capital productivity, which may be called rise in efficiency. The latter will occur if ε^t in our formula (1.1) increases. We should like to emphasize once more that we understand and define the terms labour productivity and capital productivity in their strictly statistical meaning, *viz.* as simple quotients; hence they have nothing in common with the economic terms marginal productivity of labour and capital respectively.

For the logic of our analysis another problem is of interest, namely whether we may consider labour productivity as a datum or not. This obviously depends on the production function. If we use DOUGLAS' production function as a basis for our analysis, labour productivity is apparently no datum but a function of some variables of the problem, the quantities a and K. We shall soon come across another production function where labour productivity constitutes an independent datum.

DOUGLAS has also tried his best to determine the value of the exponent λ statistically. Not all the methods of determination he quotes are convincing, as I pointed out in another publication[15]; nevertheless his results should be fairly close to the real values. What he found was $\lambda = 3/4$; λ specifying, as we shall see later, what fraction of the national income goes to labour as income, and for most countries this fraction is actually around 3/4. In the following we shall therefore use DOUGLAS' linear-homogenous formula, and take $\lambda = 3/4$.

The main point we should remember is that DOUGLAS' function is based on the hypothesis that labour and capital are completely substitutable. We are not certain that this complies with the facts. In order to get an idea of the consequences of such a hypothesis we have made some computations on the basis of a different production function,[16] a function which presupposes that labour and capital are entirely complementary, *i.e.* exactly the contrary. Obviously this assumption goes much too far. A certain degree of substitutability no doubt exists. The second production function may best be expressed

---

15 J. TINBERGEN, "Professor DOUGLAS' Production Function", *Revue de l'Institut international de statistique*, 1942, 1/2.

16 In: "Het streven naar efficiency en de werkgelegenheid", *Nederlandsch Instituut voor Efficiency, Publicatie Nr. 199*, Purmerend 1941.

in a formula which differs slightly from the above. If the volume of production is stated as u and the two production factors are entirely complementary, this means that both a and K are strictly defined by u; we therefore write

$$(1.2, 2.2) \qquad a = gu \qquad K = hu,$$

where g represents the quantity of labour per production unit and h the quantity of capital per production unit. The values g and h need not be constants; in any case g will show a decreasing trend in the course of time. As can easily be seen, g is the reciprocal of labour productivity; in this production function, labour productivity is therefore a datum, *i.e.* a non-economic, pre-determined quantity.

5.2. DEMAND AND SUPPLY OF LABOUR AND CAPITAL

We shall further assume that production is in the hands of enterprises competing with one another, paying both workers and capital owners for their cooperation according to the prevailing market prices. These market prices—the real wage rate l' and the real interest rate m'—are therefore considered by the individual enterprises as fixed quantities. For every entrepreneur it is therefore a question of achieving the maximum profit according to the formula

$$u_i - l'a_i - m'K_i,$$

where u_i, a_i and K_i represent the production obtained by an entrepreneur and the volumes of labour and capital respectively applied. Hence it follows that

$$\frac{\partial u_i}{\partial a_i} = l' \quad \text{and} \quad \frac{\partial u_i}{\partial K_i} = m',$$

i.e. every entrepreneur will expand production to a point where the value of the output of the last worker is just equal to his wages, in other words where the law of marginal productivity of wages is applicable. Much the same is true for the interest rate: the employment of capital is expanded to a point where marginal productivity is equal to the interest rate. Substituting the expression of the DOUGLAS function for u_i we get:

$$\tfrac{3}{4}\left(\frac{K_i}{a_i}\right)^{\frac14} \varepsilon^t = l' \qquad \tfrac{1}{4}\left(\frac{a_i}{K_i}\right)^{\frac34} \varepsilon^t = m'.$$

From this we may conclude that the same formulæ also apply[17] for the quantities a and K (total volumes of labour and capital):

(2.1; 3.1) $\frac{3}{4}\left(\frac{K}{a}\right)^{\frac{1}{4}}\varepsilon^t = l' \qquad \frac{1}{4}\left(\frac{a}{K}\right)^{\frac{3}{4}}\varepsilon^t = m'.$

These equations could be called the demand equations of labour and capital. In case labour and capital are assumed to be complementary, a mutually independent variation of labour and capital volumes it not possible. For a given wage and interest rate, production will take place as long as a profit is left, and it will be terminated if no profit can be squeezed out. However, this is independent of the volume of production. The latter will be expanded—provided it is profitable—to a point where either the capital is fully employed or the demand for labour causes wages to rise to such an extent that no more profit is left.[18] The latter case we call underemployment of capital; we get

(3.2) $al' + km' = u.$

where k is the quantity of capital employed which need not be consistent with the quantity of total capital.

Let us now consider supply. The supply of production factors is —generally speaking—dependent on prices. It may therefore show a certain elasticity. Accordingly, supply can be bigger at one time and smaller at another. If supply were completely inelastic there would be no underemployment of capital or labour. In many of the older theories this underemployment was excluded beforehand. However, since we are interested in unemployment we shall in any case assume a certain elasticity of labour supply.[19] For simplicity's sake we shall

---

[17] For every i it is $\dfrac{K_i}{a_i} = \left(\dfrac{4\,l'}{3\,\varepsilon^t}\right)^4$; therefore also $\dfrac{\Sigma K_i}{\Sigma a_i} = \dfrac{K}{a} = \left(\dfrac{4\,l'}{3\,\varepsilon^t}\right)^4$ or

$\frac{3}{4}\left(\dfrac{K}{a}\right)\varepsilon^t = l'$. This would not apply if DOUGLAS' function were not linear.

[18] The asymmetrical treatment of labour and capital is not necessary but it is a consequence of an asymmetry in the treatment of the supply functions which has been adopted for simplicity's sake and which will be discussed immediately.

[19] This means that we consider the unemployment which will then remain, as voluntary unemployment. Involuntary unemployment will occur only if for any reasons the wage does not adapt itself immediately. This may be the consequence of either a temporary inertia of the market or a permanent

assume an entirely inelastic supply on the capital market. This is by
the way not too far from the results found by DOUGLAS.[20]

With regard to labour supply we shall therefore assume that the
percentage of the population available for employment depends on
the wage rate, that is on the relation between wages and a rate which
is normally considered adequate. If we indicate the flexibility of wages
by λ', the normal wage rate by l^0 and the population by b, the supply
equation may be written as follows:

(4)
$$\frac{l'}{l^0} = \left(\frac{a}{b}\right)^{\lambda'}.$$

The reason for introducing the normal wage rate is to remind us
that wage demands may change in the course of time, in the first place
through improvement of the technical possibilities of production and
in the second, because of a change in social conceptions. It will be
difficult to determine this normal wage statistically; at any rate we
shall not be able to do this directly. We shall be able to give instead,
with the help of our formulæ, an idea of the influence of any possible
changes in these demands on the development of economic variables.

In order to express the possible movement of the normal wage rate
we write
$$\overset{0}{l} = \overset{00}{l} \lambda_0^t$$

where l^{00} is a constant and λ_0 1 the annual rate of increase of the
normal wage.

There is considerable divergence in estimates of the numerical value
of wage flexibility or, inversely, elasticity of labour supply. As DOUGLAS
points out in his book, cited before, there are economists who attribute
to flexibility the value zero and others who think it is infinite and
assert that even negative values are possible, except between 0 and —1.
This is the well-known example of certain tropical races which actually
illustrate such conditions. With an increasing wage rate these people
become less inclined to work because they can make a living in a
shorter time. The same inclination is also found in other races. DOUGLAS
makes extended investigations of geographical comparisons, that is

phenomenon, for example if workers are afraid that an "adaptation" of wages
would lead to inacceptable wages. From the point of view of the working class as a
whole, unemployment is "put up with" and it might for this reason be considered
as voluntary even if for the individual worker it is indeed an involuntary fact.

[20] DOUGLAS, *The theory of wages*, other pages, Chapt. XVIII.

comparisons between different towns in the United States and finds that a negative supply elasticity exists there, too. He states that for certain age brackets and for most women, it is rather high, while for men between the ages of 20 and 60 it is almost zero; which implies that λ' would be very high there.

Another possibility for determining the wage flexibility is a comparison between real wage fluctuations and fluctuations of the employment level. These investigations are based on the entirely plausible assumption that population and normal wages change slowly. Strange to say that here we find a positive correlation, $i.e.$ a positive flexibility: rising employment generally occurs with rising real wages. The correlations in general are not very high—as also with DOUGLAS—and for this reason the values of flexibility are very unreliable. This is shown in Table I where the results for four different countries have been combined. The remarkable thing about these results is that the flexibilities determined according to the diagonal regression are lower where the living standard is higher. The lowest living standard is found in France, next comes Germany, then Great Britain, the highest

TABLE I

WAGE FLEXIBILITY IN GERMANY, GREAT BRITAIN, FRANCE AND THE UNITED STATES, DETERMINED FROM FLUCTUATIONS IN REAL WAGE RATES AND EMPLOYMENT LEVEL*

Country	Flexibility according to			Coefficient of Correlation	Period
	1st	2nd	Diagonal		
	Regression				
Germany	1.25	3.6	2.1	0.59	1887–1913
Great Britain	0.47	3.4	1.3	0.37	1870–1910
France	1.22	20.0	5.0	0.26	1895–1913
United States	0.97	1.2	1.1	0.91	1897–1916

* Sources: For England: Wages: See appendix to this article. Unemployment: Trade union figures from: "Seventeenth abstract of labour statistics of the United Kingdom", *Abstract of Labour statistics, Board of Trade* (Department of Labour), (Cd. 7733) London 1915. – Other countries: J. KUCZYNSKI, "Die Entwicklung der Lage der Arbeiterschaft in Europa und Amerika, 1870–1933", *Statistische Studien zur Entwicklung der Reallöhne und Relativlöhne in England, Deutschland, USA, Frankreich und Belgien,* Basel 1934.

standard being that of the United States. The figures therefore seem to have importance. For the time being, the question of the value of flexibility and whether it is positive or negative remains open.

The last determinant in formula (4) is the size of the population. This we shall consider to be a datum, in other words we neglect the —in my opinion—weak effects of the economic situation on the size of population. We shall assume that it develops according to the exponential law, that is

$$b = b_0 \beta^t,$$

where β is the proportion of population between any given and the previous year and b_0 the size of population for $t = 0$. For the greater part of the nineteenth century the exponential law gives us a good approximation. For the end of the century as well as for the twentieth century a logistic curve would be better. In case of short intervals (10–20 years) the exponential law—which if β is small hardly differs from a straight line—may still be applied as a first approximation. Because of the complexity of the formulæ we shall not operate with the hypothesis of a logistic population development.

In the case of capital supply we shall assume that the interest rate exercises no influence. At this point, however, another much more important fact demands our attention. In principle, the quantity of capital available at a given moment is a product of the accumulation of newly formed capital during all preceding years. Mathematically speaking, this means that it is an integral of the volume of capital formation over time. Thus a logical connection with the past is formed. With regard to new capital formation in any individual period we shall assume it to be proportional to income during such a period, *i.e.* we assume the savings rate to be constant during this time. As a first step this appears justified. For a closer study one might operate with a somewhat more complex relation, although this is not at all ne- cessary. Indicating the savings rate by $\varkappa$, we shall assume that

(5) $$\dot{K} = \frac{dK}{dt} = \varkappa u.$$

5.3. DEMAND AND SUPPLY OF PRODUCTS

The demand equations given in the previous paragraph for labour and capital are at the same time supply equations for finished products.

It must be remembered that we assumed every entrepreneur will expand his production to the point where he receives no additional profit. Evidently, the marketability of the products is of no importance here. This theory is based on the implicit assumption that for every unit produced, there is a corresponding unit of income to buy the product. Production, we must not forget, simultaneously creates income equal to the value of the product. We have here the old view that "les produits s'achètent avec des produits", the "Theorie der Absatzwege" (Say's law). We can also put it in this way: the supply of goods determines the volume of production. It is assumed that K is fully employed, which in turn determines u and a. In general this will be the case when demand equals production capacity or even exceeds it. In times of great enterpreneurial initiative and vast expansion, such as the nineteenth century, this probably applies. In the twenties and thirties of the twentieth century, however, there is more reason to believe that demand lags behind the production capacity. In this case we may not assume that K is completely employed in production. A distinction will have to be made between the quantity of capital available and the quantity of capital employed. The latter shall be written k. The above equations will be supplemented by a demand equation for products. In times of structural depression, therefore, the volume of production is partly determined by demand.

Since classical theory did not deal with these problems, we have here an entirely new field of economics. It has above all been KEYNES who investigated the question of the demand function by, for instance, coining the term "propensity to consume". However, we have to do with demand for both consumer and investment goods. Since we are primarily occupied with economic development between 1870 and 1914 we shall dismiss the details of the demand function. To demonstrate that our theory can also be used for an analysis of the trend movement in the twentieth century, we shall just mention the most important factors controlling the demand for all kinds of goods.

In the first place, income is an important factor in determining the demand for a thing, as we know from both the general theory and from Keynes' arguments as well as from household budgets. Apart from income, the size of the family, *i.e.* population for the economy as a whole, will have a certain influence. The whole income is more likely to be consumed if many persons have to live on it than only a few. This is also what the statistics of household budgets teach us. If we refer to income in this connection it is always in the sense of real income, *i.e.* income corrected for price level fluctuations. For this reason we do not yet have to mention the price level as another factor. Mathematically, the income would simply be stated as u. It is probable, however, that the influence of income on the demand for consumer goods shows a lag, so that u_{t-1} would be decisive for demand in the year t. In addition to the factors mentioned above it is a safe assumption that expenditure is also influenced by habit; such habits will frequently be based on the average prosperity during a somewhat longer and more extended period. This might mean that the average income of the previous ten or fifteen years is also a contributory determinant. The main task of an economic analysis would be to find the exact influence of each individual factor on demand. The first steps in this direction have hardly been taken.[21]

In addition we have the demand for investment goods. Seen over an extended period of time—neglecting fluctuations in demand due to inventory speculation—two components are of significance: the demand for replacement purposes and that for new investments. The first may develop—according to the so-called echo principle—in a wavelike manner, whereby the period is determined by the mean life of the capital goods to be replaced.[22] The latter will in all probability form the most variable component of the total demand, which is decisive for the entire rhythm of the economy. Periods of high investment such as large railway investments alternate with periods of reduced

---

[21] I should like to refer to my attempts to give an explanation of the short-term fluctuations in the total volume of demand in my book: *Les cycles économiques aux Etats-Unis d'Amérique de 1919 à 1932*. (Vérification statistique des théories des cycles économiques, 2. – Série de publication de la Société des Nations, II. Questions économiques et financières, 1939. II. A. 16.) Genève 1939.

[22] Compare J. EINARSEN, *Reinvestment cycles and their manifestation in the Norwegian shipping industry*. (Publication No. 14 from the University Institute of Economics, Oslo), Oslo 1938. – J. MEULDIJK Jr., "Der englische Schiffbau während der Periode 1870–1912 und das Problem des Ersatzbaues", *Weltwirtschaftliches Archiv*, Bd. 52 (1940 II), p. 524 *sq*. – S. DE WOLFF, *Het economisch getij* (Bijdrage tot de verklaring van het conjunctuurverschijnsel, Amsterdam 1929) even tries to explain long waves in trade cycles in this manner.

willingness to make investments. Inventions as well as the opening up of new countries and continents are among the most important determinants. Apart from these, numerous other factors may be of contributory influence. In this field, as in others, research is still in its rudimentary stage.

We shall leave it at that, however, for, as we have seen, the intensity of this demand determines the production volume only when demand decreases. As soon as it exceeds a certain limit, the production increase is stopped by capacity limits, so that the latter is actually decisive. We must make only one qualification: demand for labour in this case, where u is predetermined, must be replaced by another function. This function exhibits a much smaller elasticity than the one derived under section 5, Item 2 above.[23]

5.4. SUMMARY

In the previous paragraphs the formulæ which define the development of production, employment, capital formation, real wages and interest have been stated. Here we should like to briefly repeat and summarize the results.

A. The supply of goods is decisive (periods of expansion)

A 1   *The production process follows the* DOUGLAS *function (capital and labour substitutable)*

A 1 a. Population grows according to the exponential law.

Production equation:

(1.1)
$$u = \varepsilon^t a^{\frac{3}{4}} K^{\frac{1}{4}}$$

Demand equations: Labour:

(2.1)
$$\tfrac{3}{4} \left(\frac{K}{a}\right)^{\frac{1}{4}} \varepsilon^t = l'$$

Capital:

(3.1)
$$\tfrac{1}{4} \left(\frac{a}{K}\right)^{\frac{3}{4}} \varepsilon^t = m'$$

---

[23] See also our publication in the Dutch language on this subject: *Het streven naar efficiency en de werkgelegenheid, loc. cit.*

Supply equations: Labour:

(4)
$$l' = \left(\frac{a}{b}\right)^{\lambda'} l^{00} \lambda_0^t$$

Capital:

(5)
$$\dot{K} = \varkappa u$$

Development of population:

(4')
$$b = b_0 \beta^t$$

A 1 b. Population develops according to a logistic curve. In place of (4') we write now:

(4'')
$$b = \frac{B}{1 + e^{-b_1 t + b_2}}$$

A 2.   *Labour and capital are completely complementary in the production process*

A 2 a. Full employment of capital

Production equations:

(1.2)
$$a = gu$$

(2.2)
$$K = hu$$

Supply equations: Labour:

(4)
$$l' = \left(\frac{a}{b}\right)^{\lambda'} l^{00} \lambda_0^t$$

Capital:

(5)
$$\dot{K} = ku$$

A 2 b. Underemployment of capital

Production equations:

(1.2)
$$a = gu$$

(2.2)
$$k = hu$$

Demand equation: Capital:

(3.2)
$$al' + km' = u$$

Supply equations: Labour:

(4)
$$l' = \left(\frac{a}{b}\right)^{\lambda'} l^{00} \lambda_0^t$$

Capital:

(5.2)
$$m' = \left(\frac{k}{K}\right)^{\mu'}$$

B. The demand for goods is decisive. This case will be considered only for the DOUGLAS function.

Production equation: $u = \varepsilon^t\, a^{\frac{3}{4}}\, k^{\frac{1}{4}}$

Demand equations: comp. section 5.3.

Supply equations: same as under A.

Demand equation for goods: comp. section 5.3.

In the following we shall deal mainly with case A 1 a, the most simple case which represents a usable approximation for the period 1870–1914. The data of the development therefore are: the growth rates of population, efficiency and "normal" wages, the savings rate $\varkappa$ and wage flexibility. To facilitate the following computations we should like to add a few words on the selection of the units. We shall use the statistical data of some countries for certain periods (in general 1870–1914). The most important simplification is to substitute the number 1 for the values of most of the variables in the middle of the period under review; t being assumed for this middle to be equal to zero. The form of the equations, however, does not permit this procedure to be used for every variable. For $t = 0$ we shall therefore make the values for a, u, K and b equal to 1. Hence if follows that $t = 0$, $l' = 3/4$, $m' = 1/4$, whereas $l_{00} = 3/4$. One consequence of our selection is that a and b are not expressed in comparable units; this however is no disadvantage—we are studying only the relative movements. It is clear that $\dot{K}$ cannot be considered as an independent variable.

To end our summary, we should like to point out that the only thing new in our set of formulæ is that K (in DOUGLAS' function) is not assumed to be given, but is the product of previous accumulation. In this way we have obtained a system of development.

6. THE PROBLEM OF INTRODUCING MONETARY VARIABLES INTO THE MODEL

Model A 1 a, which was explained above, can easily be developed into a model including also the most important monetary phenomena. Whereas we do not intend to proceed on the basis of such a model, we should still like to discuss it briefly in order to demonstrate that no serious difficulties arise from the inclusion of monetary variables. If we take the wage rate as l, the interest rate as m, and the price level as p, we get first of all:

$$(6;7) \qquad\qquad l' = \frac{l}{p} \qquad\qquad m' = \frac{m}{p}.$$

The price level may be understood to depend on the quantity of money in circulation M, which in turn may either be assumed to be given (according to WALRAS) or depend on gold reserves (according to CASSEL). If we assume furthermore the speed of circulation to be a technically determined quantity γ—chiefly through terms of payment and the division of labour between the individual enterprises—we get:

$$(8) \qquad\qquad up = \gamma M.$$

This is the simplest way to include monetary aspects in the model. The last equation may be formulated more generally, *e.g.* if we want to consider the demand for money for hoarding. We can also give more consideration to the determinants of banking policy. It would lead too far to particularize, the more so because relations in real terms are not changed as long as we do not alter our equations (1) through (5). In other words: such subtilities influence merely the monetary sphere and not the exchange of goods. Naturally this does not mean that the same is also true for short-term movements or for model B. In these cases the consequences of monetary policy will be much more signifi- cant.

7. THE MATHEMATICAL SHAPE OF THE TREND MOVEMENT

Since the given formulæ determine the movements of the economic system, various conclusions can be drawn from them which shall now be discussed. In order not too much to complicate our formulæ, we have substituted numerical values for λ', *i.e.* the values 0, $\frac{1}{2}$, ∞, and —1. Although we shall have to make four different compu- tations, the formulæ remain simple and there is moreover a method by which they can be checked. The meaning of the four individual values is the following: for $\lambda' = 0$ the wage rates are absolutely rigid, they are, as it were, dictated by the workers' organizations in an economy which is not planned centrally. For $\lambda' = \infty$, on the other hand, they are "absolutely flexible", *i.e.* supply is entirely inelastic and indepen- dent of wage rates, the same number of workers is available at all wages. The values $\frac{1}{2}$ and —1 are, as far as their numerical value is concerned, arbitrary and have been chosen for simplicity's sake.

Qualitatively, $\lambda' = \frac{1}{2}$ gives the situation in case of positive supply elasticity—as we have derived it from the time series—and $\lambda' = -1$ gives the situation in the case of a negative supply elasticity—as DOUGLAS found it in his geographical comparisons. The numerous computations we have made shall not be quoted here in full because they are mathematically simple. Instead, we should like to offer a few examples and merely state the results for the others.

One of the first conclusions to be drawn refers to the mathematical shape of the curve over a period of time. From it we can learn which methods of trend computation are justified by our theory. For this our equations must be solved. Taking $\lambda' = 0$ we get from (1.1) through (5):

$$
(9) \qquad\qquad u = \varepsilon^t \, a^{\frac{3}{4}} \, K^{\frac{1}{4}}
$$

$$
(10) \qquad\qquad \tfrac{3}{4} \left(\frac{K}{a}\right)^{\frac{1}{4}} \varepsilon^t = l' = \tfrac{3}{4} \lambda_0^{\frac{t}{4}}
$$

$$
(11) \qquad\qquad \dot{K} = \varkappa u.
$$

Equation (3.1) may be eliminated because it is useful only for determining m'. From (9) and (11) u can easily be eliminated thus:

$$
(12) \qquad\qquad \dot{K} = \varkappa \, \varepsilon^t \, a^{\frac{3}{4}} K^{\frac{1}{4}}.
$$

In order to eliminate a, too, we have to make use of (10):

$$
(10') \qquad\qquad \frac{K}{a} \, \varepsilon^{4t} = \lambda_0^{4t}
$$

or

$$
(10'') \qquad\qquad a = K \left(\frac{\varepsilon}{\lambda_0}\right)^{4t},
$$

so that we get:

$$
(13) \qquad\qquad a^{\frac{3}{4}} = K^{\frac{3}{4}} \left(\frac{\varepsilon}{\lambda_0}\right)^{3t}
$$

(12) and (13) now lead us to the differential equation for K:

$$
(14) \qquad\qquad \dot{K} = \varkappa \, \frac{\varepsilon^{4t}}{\lambda_0^{3t}} \, K.
$$

The solution is as follows:

$$
(15) \qquad\qquad \frac{\dot{K}}{K} = \frac{d \log K}{dt} = \varkappa \left(\frac{\varepsilon^4}{\lambda_0^3}\right)^t
$$

(16)
$$\log K = \frac{\varkappa}{\log \left(\frac{\varepsilon^4}{\lambda_0^3}\right)} \left(\frac{\varepsilon^4}{\lambda_0^3}\right)^t + C.$$

All the logarithms are natural, and C is an arbitrary constant. The value of C is defined by the condition that for $t = 0$ $K = 1$, i.e. $\log K = 0$, or

(17)
$$0 = \frac{\varkappa}{\log \left(\frac{\varepsilon^4}{\lambda_0^3}\right)} + C.$$

This equation can be expressed a little more elegantly. The figures ε and λ_0 deviate only slightly from 1 and can be written thus:

$$\varepsilon = 1 + \varepsilon'$$

$$\lambda_0 = 1 + \lambda_0'$$

where ε' and λ_0' are small figures. For these we have:

(18) $\qquad\qquad \log \varepsilon = \log (1 + \varepsilon') \simeq \varepsilon'$

(19) $\qquad\qquad \log \lambda_0 = \log (1 + \lambda_0') \simeq \lambda_0'$

A similar expression can later be used for β, viz.:

(20) $\qquad\qquad \log \beta = \log (1 + \beta') \simeq \beta'.$

Since

$$\frac{\varepsilon^4}{\lambda_0^3} = 4 \log \varepsilon - 3 \log \lambda_0, \text{ we get:}$$

(21)
$$C = -\frac{\varkappa}{4\,\varepsilon' - 3\lambda_0'}$$

Thus we have:

(22)
$$\log K = \frac{\varkappa}{4\,\varepsilon' - 3\lambda_0'} \left\{\left(\frac{\varepsilon^4}{\lambda_0^3}\right)^t - 1\right\}.$$

It will be seen that in this simple case already a much more complex time dependency is apparent than in the usual statistical trend determinations. Not only is equation (22) a function which is more complex than the exponential law, it also refers only to $\log K$. In some instances we get the Gompertz-curve. For K the formula is even more complicated. Much the same applies for the other variables.

From (10″) follows:

(23) $$\log a = \log K + 4t(\log \varepsilon - \log \lambda_0).$$

Finally, we get from (9):

$$\log u = t \log \varepsilon + \tfrac{3}{4} \log a + \tfrac{1}{4} \log K$$

(24) $$= t \log \varepsilon + \log K + 3\,t\,(\log \varepsilon - \log \lambda_0)$$

Equations (23 and (24) can be simplified by using ε' and $-\lambda_0'$

(23′) $$\log a = \log K + 4\,t\,(\varepsilon' - \lambda_0')$$

(24′) $$\log u = \log K + 4t\varepsilon' - 3t\,\lambda_0'.$$

Similar computations can be made for those cases where λ' has another value. For $\lambda' = \tfrac{1}{2}$ our equations (1.1) through (5) read as follows:

(25) $$u = \varepsilon^t\, a^{\tfrac{3}{4}}\, K^{\tfrac{1}{4}}$$

(26) $$\left(\frac{K}{a}\right)^{\tfrac{1}{4}} \varepsilon^t = \left(\frac{a}{b}\right)^{\tfrac{1}{2}} \lambda_0^t$$

$$\dot{K} = \varkappa u$$

The differential equation for K can now be somewhat modified. From (26) it follows that:

(28) $$a^{\tfrac{3}{4}} = \frac{K^{\tfrac{1}{4}}}{b^{\tfrac{1}{2}}} \frac{\varepsilon^t}{\lambda_0^t} = K^{\tfrac{1}{4}} \left(\frac{\varepsilon}{\beta^{\tfrac{1}{2}} \lambda_0}\right)^t$$

Thus we get

$$\dot{K} = \varkappa u = \varkappa \varepsilon^t\, K^{\tfrac{1}{4}} \left(\frac{\varepsilon}{\beta^{\tfrac{1}{2}} \lambda_0}\right)^t$$

or:

(29) $$\frac{\dot{K}}{K^{\tfrac{1}{4}}} = K \left(\frac{\varepsilon^2}{\beta^{\tfrac{1}{2}} \lambda_0}\right)^t.$$

The solution of this equation reads:

(30) $$K^{\tfrac{1}{4}} = \frac{\varkappa}{2} \frac{\left(\dfrac{\varepsilon^2}{\beta^{\tfrac{1}{2}} \lambda_0}\right)^t}{\log \left(\dfrac{\varepsilon^2}{\beta^{\tfrac{1}{2}} \lambda_0}\right)} + C.$$

The arbitrary constant C must again meet the condition that for $t = 0$ $K = 1$; that is:

(31)
$$1 = \frac{\varkappa}{2 \log \frac{\varepsilon^2}{\beta^{\frac{1}{2}} \lambda_0}} + C.$$

Here again it is advisable to make use of the symbols ε' and λ_0', as well as of β', so that we get:

(32)
$$K^{\frac{1}{2}} = 1 + \frac{\varkappa}{2} \frac{\left(\frac{\varepsilon^2}{\beta^{\frac{1}{2}} \lambda_0}\right)^t - 1}{2\,\varepsilon' - \frac{1}{2}\,\beta' - \lambda_0'}.$$

The formula for K which would result if we were to raise it to the second power would again be very complicated: it results in a sum of various exponential terms.

Further computations will not be given here, only a few results. For $\lambda' = -1$ we get:

(33)
$$K = 1 + \frac{\varkappa}{\lambda_0' + \beta'} \{(\lambda_0 \beta)^t - 1\},$$

and for $\lambda' = \infty$:

(34)
$$K^{\frac{3}{2}} = 1 + \frac{k}{\beta' + \frac{4}{3}\varepsilon'} \{(\beta^{\frac{3}{2}} \varepsilon)^t - 1\}.$$

All these formulæ have one disadvantage in common: we cannot readily determine the influence of the individual data on the development of the quantities K, a and u. In order to get a reliable impression of the relations, it is necessary to make use of other methods. The details of the mathematical form of the trend development are lost this way, just as if we replaced a curve by a straight line. Such details, therefore, can be found only with the help of the exact formulæ (22), (33) and (34).

8. THE GROWTH RATE OF CAPITAL, EMPLOYMENT AND PRODUCTION AND ITS EXPLANATION

One of the first methods of approximation consists in the computation of the growth rates of our three main variables K, a and u for the middle of the period under review, *i.e.* for $t = 0$. We should like to quote a few examples to illustrate the computation and for the rest give results only. For $\lambda' = 0$, for instance, the starting point for K is equation (22). Since the growth rate is equal to $\dot{K}/K = d \log K/dt$, all we have to do is differentiate (22) with respect to time.

$$(35) \qquad \frac{d \log K}{dt} = \frac{\varkappa}{4\,\varepsilon' - 3\,\lambda_0'} \left(\frac{\varepsilon^4}{\lambda_0^3}\right)^t \log \frac{\varepsilon^4}{\lambda_0^3} = \varkappa \left(\frac{\varepsilon^4}{\lambda_0^3}\right)^t.$$

For $t = 0$ we get from the above: $d \log K/dt = \varkappa$. A simpler way to do this would have been just to divide equation (11) by K:

$$\frac{\dot{K}}{K} = \frac{\varkappa u}{K}.$$

For $t = 0$, $u = K = 1$, therefore $\dot{K}/K = \varkappa$. This method cannot be applied, however, to the other variables, and moreover it does not give us a chance to work out second approximations (*i.e.* find the results for $t \neq 0$).

For $\lambda' = \frac{1}{2}$ we use formula (32) and remember that

$$\frac{\dot{K}}{K} = \frac{d \log K}{dt} = \frac{d \frac{1}{2} \log K}{\frac{1}{2}\, dt} = \frac{d \log K^{\frac{1}{2}}}{\frac{1}{2}\, dt} = \frac{1}{\frac{1}{2} K^{\frac{1}{2}}} \frac{dK^{\frac{1}{2}}}{dt}$$

We finally get the following results:

TABLE II

GROWTH RATES FOR CAPITAL QUANTITY, EMPLOYMENT, AND PRODUCTION FOR THE MIDDLE OF THE PERIOD AND FOR DIFFERENT VALUES OF λ'.

$\lambda' =$	0	$\dfrac{1}{2}$	∞	-1
$\dot{K} =$	$\varkappa$	$\varkappa$	$\varkappa$	$\varkappa$
$\dot{u} =$	$\varkappa + 4\varepsilon' - 3\lambda_0'$	$\dfrac{\varkappa}{2} + \dfrac{\beta'}{2} + 2\varepsilon' - \lambda_0'$	$\dfrac{1}{4}\varkappa + \dfrac{3}{4}\beta' + \varepsilon'$	$\beta' + \lambda_0'$
$\dot{a} =$	$\varkappa + 4\varepsilon' - 4\lambda_0'$	$\dfrac{\varkappa}{3} + \dfrac{2}{3}\beta' + \dfrac{4}{3}\varepsilon' - \dfrac{4}{3}\lambda_0'$	β'	$-\dfrac{\varkappa}{3} + \dfrac{4}{3}\beta' - \dfrac{4}{3}\varepsilon' + \dfrac{4}{3}\lambda_0'$

The table shows primarily the influence of the data on the growth of u and a. It also appears, however, that this influence is strongly dependent on λ'. There are even changes from positive to negative signs and *vice versa:* the influence of the normal wage growth rate λ_0' on the growth rate of both production and employment is negative for positive values of λ' and positive for negative values of λ'. This means that a rapid increase in wage demands with negative supply elasticity leads to an even more rapid increase of production compared to a slow increase in wage demands. At first sight this may appear strange. The explanation lies in the fact, that if wage demands rise rapidly, a given wage is more readily felt to be inadequate than if they rise slowly. In case of a negative elasticity of labour supply, the compensation is sought in a bigger labour supply. This leads to higher production. At the same time it leads to a lower (or more slowly rising) real wage level.

A second change of signs is recognized in the influence of ε' on employment: this influence is positive for positive values of λ', negative for negative values of λ'. The explanation is obviously found in the fact that an increase in the efficiency of production, under otherwise identical circumstances, causes a rise in wages; if the supply elasticity of labour is negative, this leads to a reduction in supply and employment. The table shows that production is not affected thereby: the increased production per workman manifestly compensates exactly the reduced number of workers.

A third change of signs shows the influence of $\varkappa$ on employment. It appears that a more rapid capital formation, and consequently the increase in labour productivity, has similar effects as in the former case. Production is not affected here either. All this shows that an exact knowledge of the supply elasticity of labour is very important and interesting.

Quite apart from the change of signs in the cases discussed above, the value of λ' shows a considerable influence on the results of Table II. For example for $\lambda' = 0$—i.e. in the case of rigid wages—the increase in population has no effect on the growth rate of production or employment. Rising values of λ' cause a corresponding rise of the influence of population growth; for $\lambda' = \infty$—i.e. rigid labour supply—employment naturally rises hand in hand with population. Not so production: it only rises at 3/4 of the population growth. The per capita production therefore drops, i.e. the living standard diminishes. For $\lambda' = -1$, employment rises even more briskly than population, precisely by 1/3. The influence of efficiency on production and employment, by contrast, becomes stronger as we move toward the left in our table. For $\lambda' = 0$ (rigid wages) the growth rate of production and employment is even four times the speed of efficiency growth. (It should be remembered that the meaning of the word efficiency is not absolutely identical here with increase in labour productivity. It comprises a simultaneous and equally strong increase in capital productivity (see section 5)). For $\lambda' = \infty$, *i.e.* for rigid labour supply, efficiency as we take it has no effect on employment, and for $\lambda' = -1$ even a negative one.

Finally, we should like to ascertain in which respect our table leads to unambiguous conclusions. There are several, of which we will single out a few. As far as the growth rate of production is concerned, the signs of $\varkappa$, β' and ε' are all alike, that is to say positive. This means that an increased rate of capital formation, population growth and efficiency result in a rising rate of production. To arrive at this conclusion, it is true, it would not have been necessary to establish all these formulæ. However, there is more to be inferred from this. The coefficients of $\varkappa$ and β never exceed 1; and they reach these values only in extreme cases. This means that an increase of the growth rate of capital formation and population does not lead to a proportional increase of the growth rate of production. An increase in the rate of population growth, therefore, does not enable us to increase per capita production, but in general only to lower it. Capital formation must proceed at a quicker pace than population growth if the living standard is to be raised. As far as capital formation goes, the same conclusion can be drawn for employment.

We should like to add a few remarks on the question: what are the consequences of technical development for the level of production and employment? As we have already seen, the term "technical development" is interpreted in different ways. It is often used synonimously with the term "increase in labour productivity"; however, there it is more inclusive. The following is of importance for the present problem. The question of the influence of a certain phenomenon on the development of certain economic variables is truly significant only if such a phenomenon is a datum in the economic sense of the word. However, we have already seen that it depends on the production function whether labour productivity is a datum or not. We might add that it is moreover dependent upon the supply functions of the production factors. Thus, the number of workers forms a datum if supply is assumed to be absolutely inelastic, and does not if supply is assumed to be elastic. In the latter case only the number of population—as it were an even more "distant" phenomenon—forms a datum *etc.*

In our model A 1, in which the DOUGLAS production function is used, labour productivity forms no datum. The question of its influence on the development of production and employment would therefore have no definite meaning. Only in the case of a rigid wage rate, that is for $\lambda' = 0$, can the question have meaning. It must be understood that the wage is always equal to the marginal productivity of labour, the latter being—if we are using the DOUGLAS function—always proportional to the mean labour productivity in the statistical sense. Therefore, variations in labour productivity can only occur provided that equal variations in the wage rate take place. The latter is, as must be borne in mind, a datum for $\lambda' = 0$ and thus can be independently varied. It is in this case equal to the normal wage (*i.e.* the wage demand); as may be seen from Table II, the influence of the wage rate on the development of production as well as of employment is negative. The influence of an increase of labour productivity on the development of production and employment is therefore also negative. In the present case this is explained by the fact that such an increase in productivity can only be brought about by an increase in the capital intensity of production and that in addition the capital quantity only be sufficient to produce a slow rise in production. It may be shown, however, that a negative effect on employment may also occur in the case of an underemployment of capital.

At first sight it may be hard to believe that raising the labour productivity has an depressing effect on the trend movement of employment. It is frequently argued that the development in the nineteenth and the twentieth century denied this. It must not be forgotten, however, that the development was not characterized by a rising labour productivity alone. Both capital goods and arable acreage rose materially. Another argument is that technical development is not equivalent to an increasing labour productivity, as we have stressed several times. We believe, therefore, that our conclusion is justified and should like, at the end, to formulate the result a little differently: for employment, an increase in capital productivity and capital quantity has a favourable effect, is not in all cases true for an increase in labour productivity.[24]

9. STATISTICAL INVESTIGATIONS FOR GERMANY, GREAT BRITAIN, FRANCE AND THE UNITED STATES BETWEEN THE YEARS 1870–1914

After all these theoretical considerations we should like to come to some statistical investigations in order to convey a general idea of the magnitude of the variables studied above. For this purpose we have compiled statistics for Germany, Great Britain, France and United States – for the period 1870 to 1914.

For research in trade cycles this period might be called classic in a double sense. In the first place, it has been the subject of several well-known works, and in the second, economic development during this period shows a certain smoothness. At the same time one gets the impression that many of the difficulties encountered during the years 1919–1939 can only be understood against the background of trends during the period from 1870–1914.

We have now compiled the following data for each of these countries during the said period: the growth rates of total population (β'), working population (a), real wage $(\dot{l}'/l')$, total production volume $(\dot{u})$, and volume of capital $(\dot{K})$ in the sense that we understand it, *i.e.* including land. There is probably no need to emphasize that with regard to the last two quantities this procedure is rather hazardous. Some of the material that had to be used was very incomplete and its reliability could not be checked in all cases. We therefore recommend that the reader regard our attempt as preliminary. Perhaps the statistical agencies in the individual countries—but only perhaps—can furnish better estimations. The computation of the first three quantities will need no explanation; the method will be clear and the sources are listed in the appendix. When determining the total production volume, an effort has been made to give a weighted index for the production of agriculture, industry, transportation and services. In

---

[24] See also our publications in the Dutch language on this subject: "Technische ontwikkeling en werkgelegenheid", *Uit leven en wetenschap*, Amsterdam 1940. – *Het streven naar efficiency en de werkgelegenheid*, other pages.

principle, the weights have been based on the size of the working population or its contribution to national income. The estimation of the capital quantity is based—unless other estimations were available—on the same conception, *i.e.* we have made use of weighted indices of the quantitative development of the individual components of the capital goods stock. These components are: the number of live stock, transportation (length of the railway network, number of engines, passenger and freight cars, tonnage of ships), the industrial apparatus (horsepowers), available housing and acreage. The weights are proportional to the value of the components in the base year.

The annual growth rate has been computed from the available figures in the following way: if data were available only from enterprises' censuses, such data were used, and if annual data were available, from figures with, for example, ten year intervals. Since the trade cycle movement during this period is rather moderate, it causes only a very small element of error in such computations. The results have been combined in Table III. In this table we recognize first a few familiar facts, especially with regard to population growth. In the second place we find that in all four countries the working population grew more rapidly than population as a whole. In Great Britain, where the process of industrialization was nearly at an end, the difference between the two growth rates amounts to very little. In Germany the gap is not great either, probably because the process had only been under way for a short time. The greatest difference is found in France and the United States where the process had reached its climax.

TABLE III

ANNUAL GROWTH RATES OF SOME IMPORTANT ECONOMIC VARIABLES IN GERMANY, GREAT BRITAIN, FRANCE AND THE UNITED STATES 1870–1914 (%)

Symbol	Variable	Germany	Great Britain	France	US
β'	Total population	1.1	0.9	0.1	2.1
a	Working population	1.6	1.1	0.8	3.0
l'/l'	Real wages	0.9	0.8	1.2	0.8
u	Production	3.4	1.6	1.9	4.1
$\dot{K} = \varkappa$	Capital quantity *	2.6	1.8	0.8	2.9

* (including land)

It is remarkable that the figures for the real wage increase differ only slightly; the difference is less substantial than with the figures for per capita production of working population as demonstrated by this comparison:

TABLE IV

GROWTH RATES OF REAL WAGE AND PRODUCTIVITY IN GERMANY, GREAT BRITAIN, FRANCE AND THE UNITED STATES

Growth rate (%)	Germany	Great Britain	France	US
Real wage	0.9	0.8	1.2	0.8
Per capita production of working population	1.8	0.5	1.1	1.1

The reason for the real wage increases being more or less uniform in the four countries is perhaps that during this period there was still a certain freedom of movement on the part of the workers, manifest chiefly in the opportunity to emigrate to America. This might also be the explanation for the fact that the increases in Great Britain and the United States—the countries with the highest real wages—is the lowest, whereas in France where real wages were lower, it is the highest.

When making an analysis of the growth rates of the amount of capital we must not forget that these refer to the capital inside a country. In the European countries they are therefore exclusive of capital exports, in America inclusive of capital imports. The growth rates say little about the savings quota because they bear no reference to income but only to the existing quantities of capital. What we can show with these statistics is the speed of growth of efficiency. Computed according to our formula (1.1) this quantity turns out to be:

$$\varepsilon' = \dot{u} - \tfrac{3}{4}\dot{a} - \tfrac{1}{4}\dot{K}.$$

This computation has been tabularized in Table v.

The sequence of these magnitudes is the same as with the increase in the rate of per capita production and is probably correlated with the corresponding phase of the industrialization process.

Table V

Computation of the Rate of Growth of Efficiency ε' in Germany, Great Britain, France and the United States During the Period 1870–1914

No.	Symbol	Germany	Great Britain	France	US
1	$\frac{3}{4}\,\dot{a}$	1.2	0.8	0.6	2.3
2	$\frac{1}{4}\,\dot{K}$	0.7	0.5	0.2	0.7
3	Sum (1) + (2)	1.9	1.3	0.8	3.0
4	$\dot{u}$	3.4	1.6	1.9	4.1
5	$\varepsilon' = (4) - (3)$	1.5	0.3	1.1	1.1

In conclusion we should like to take another look at Table II. As we have already seen, the production increase $\dot{u}$ can be explained by capital formation for at most an amount $\varkappa$ and by population increase for at most β'. Since the coefficients together are 1, the sum of these two factors together will never explain a value of $\dot{u}$ exceeding the larger of the two quantities $\varkappa$ and β'. Since $\varkappa$ is always the larger of the two figures, Table III shows also that a maximum of 2.6% out of 3.4% can be thus explained in the case of Germany, at the most 1.1% out of 1.9% in the case of France, and in the case of the United States a maximum of 2.9% out of 4.1%. Only in the case of Great Britain is it possible to explain the total production increase by capital formation and population increase.

Were we to adopt Douglas' view that λ' is negative, the influence of capital and population increases would not surpass $\frac{1}{4}\varkappa + \frac{3}{4}\beta'$,

Table VI

Explanation of Production Increase in Germany, Great Britain, France and the United States if Wage Flexibility Is Assumed to be Negative

	Germany	Great Britain	France	US
Production increase explained from:	3.4	1.6	1.9	4.1
Capital & population increase	1.5	1.2	0.3	2.3
Efficiency increase	1.5	0.3	1.1	1.1

i.e. 1.5%, 1.2%, 0.3% and 2.3% for the respective countries. Hence it follows that the effect of the efficiency increase ε' on production increase u would be limited to not more than $1 \times \varepsilon'$, *i.e.* 1.5% for Germany, not more than 0.3% for Great Britain, 1.1% for France and 1.1% for the United States. The results have been combined in Table VI.

Thus we have made an attempt, at least for these cases, to estimate the relative importance of the components assumed in our theory. There is surely no need to stress that our attempt can only claim to be accurate provided that 1) our theory is accepted, 2) our statistical information is assumed to be correct and 3) DOUGLAS' view concerning the sign of λ' is agreed to.

Up to this point we have always interpreted the statistical results in the sense of our model A1a, in other words we have assumed that the DOUGLAS function is valid, that population growth follows an exponential law, that capital supply is entirely inelastic. It is not our intention to go into the details of another interpretation, because we are of the opinion that for the period under review our interpretation is a usable first approximation. However, we will mention other possibilities of interpretation such as the one incorporated in our model A 2 a. In this model a different production function was assumed in which labour and capital were thought of as being entirely complementary, and the (statistical) labour productivity and capital productivity u/a and u/K, or, if so preferred, labour productivity and capital intensity u/a and K/a, figure as independent data. Their annual growth rates may be easily computed from Table III:

TABLE VII

ANNUAL GROWTH RATES OF LABOUR PRODUCTIVITY, CAPITAL PRODUCTIVITY AND CAPITAL INTENSITY IN GERMANY, GREAT BRITAIN, FRANCE AND THE UNITED STATES 1870–1914 (%)

Quantity	Germany	Great Britain	France	US
Labour productivity	1.8	0.5	1.1	1.1
Capital productivity *	0.8	— 0.2	1.1	1.2
Capital intensity *	1.0	0.7	0.0	— 0.1

* including land

An interpretation of our figures within the definition of our models A 2 b and B is pointless for the period under review because these models refer to periods of structural underemployment of capital.

10. APPENDIX

Sources and computational bases for the statistical investigation: In this appendix some detailed information concerning the sources and computational bases for the statistical analysis are given. A complete survey would be much too voluminous for practical purposes.

Total population and working population:

These figures are taken from the censuses of occupational surveys of the various countries.

Real wages:

Germany and France: C. VON TYSZKA, "Löhne und Lebenskosten in Westeuropa im 19. Jahrhundert (Frankreich, England, Spanien, Belgien). With annex: "Lebenskosten deutscher und westeuropäischer Arbeiter früher und jetzt, *Schriften des Vereins für Sozialpolitik,* Bd. 145, T.3) München u. Leipzig 1914. (Für Deutschland: "Löhne in Preussen", *Idem* p. 289).

Great Britain: The wage rate is that of Bowley and Wood, taken from: W. L. LAYTON, *An introduction to the study of prices. With special reference to the history of the nineteenth century,* London 1920, p. 184. The index of living costs is that of C. CLARK, *National income and outlay,* London 1937, p. 231. By way of comparison the figures of A. H. HANSEN, "Factors affecting the trend of real wages", *The American Economic Review,* Vol. 15 (1925), p. 27 *sq.* have been used; they showed a growth rate of 0.81 % per annum as against 0.83 % in our computations.

United States: Wage rate from: W. I. KING, "The wealth and income of the people of the United States", *The Citizen's Library of Economics, Politics and Sociology, N.S.,* New York 1923, p. 168. Living costs: own computations from data of C. SNYDER and R. S. TUCKER. By way of comparison figures from HANSEN (*loc. cit.*) were again used showing a growth rate of 0.85 % as against our 0.69 %.

Production:

Germany: The growth rate is an estimated average of the rates for the index of goods (industry and agriculture) according to R. WAGEN-FÜHR, "Die Industriewirtschaft, Entwicklungstendenzen der deutschen und internationalen Industrieproduktion 1860 bis 1932", *Vierteljahres-hefte zur Konjunkturforschung*, Sonderh. 31, Berlin 1933) and for an index of transportation services. The weights are 18.6 and 3.8 according to the contributions to the national income in the year 1895 according to Helfferich. The transportation index was combined from the figures for railway and mail traffic.

Great Britain: Own computation using: W. HOFFMANN, "Ein Index der industriellen Produktion für Grossbritannien seit dem 18. Jahr-hundert", *Weltwirtschaftliches Archiv*, Bd. 40 (1934, II), p. 383 *sq.*, L. DRESCHER, "Die Entwicklung der Agrarproduktion Grossbritan-niens und Irlands seit Beginn des 19. Jahrhunderts", *Bemerkungen zum Index der Agrarproduktion, idem* Bd. 41 (1935 I), p. 270 *sq.* and from official data on transportation (railways, tramways and mail) and services (housing and domestic services). The weights are based on the data of FLUX for the national income in the year 1907.

France: The growth rate is a weighted average of the rates of in-dustrial production, agricultural production and transportation. Index of industrial production according to WAGENFÜHR (*loc. cit.*); agri-cultural production computed from data in: "L'évolution de l'économie française, 1910–1937" *Tableaux, statistiques, publ. par l'Institut scien-tifique de recherches économiques et sociales* sous la direction de Ch. Rist, Paris 1937) for all data on agricultural products and estimations of the meat production; transportation index from official data on railway traffic, inland navigation and mail traffic. Weights accord-ing to the number of employees in the year 1911 (industry 7, agricul-ture 8.5 and transportation including mail 1.2 million).

United States: The production figures were obtained from data by KING (*loc. cit.*) by dividing them by the index of living costs (see above under real wages) or an index of investment goods prices (own computation from data in: *Wholesale prices for 213 years, 1720 to 1932*, P.I.: G. F. WARREN AND F. A. PEARSON, *Wholesale prices in the United States for 135 years, 1917 to 1932*, Cornell University, Agricultural Experiment Station, Memoir 142, Ithaca, New York, 1932, p. 98, 100, and KING, (*loc. cit.*).

Capital quantity:

Germany: Quantities used: Length of railways, number of engines, passenger and freight cars, number of horses, cattle, pigs, sheep and goats, freight capacity of inland craft, net tonnage of sea craft, number of dwellings, horsepowers of machines in industrial enterprises, arable acreage. Weights: Railways 2, ships 1, live stock 1, dwellings 6, industrial apparatus 9, acreage 10. These figures correspond, in billion Marks, to the national wealth in the year 1909 according to: A. STEIN-MANN-BUCHER, *350 Milliarden deutsches Volksvermögen (Das Volksvermögen Deutschlands, Frankreichs, Grossbritanniens und der Vereinigten Staaten von Amerika, Neue Massstäbe und Wege für deutsche Politik und Finanzwirtschaft,* Berlin 1909) and according to estimates from other sources.

Great Britain: According to: P. H. DOUGLAS, "An estimate of the growth of capital in the United Kingdom 1865–1909", *Journal of Economic and Business History",* Cambridge, Mass., Vol. 2 (1929/30), p. 675. To the "active capital" according to DOUGLAS, other quantities pertaining to land and residential buildings have been added.

France: Quantities used: Same as for Germany except those for inland navigation. Weights: Railways 2, cattle 1, buildings 4, ships 0.3, industrial apparatus 4, land 5. These figures correspond in billion ffrs.) to the national wealth in the year 1912 according to E. THÉRY. Compare *Volksvermögen* (W. WINKLER), Handwörterbuch der Staatswissenschaften, 4, gänzlich umgearb. Aufl., Jena, Bd. 8 (1928), p. 780.

United States: All figures according to KING (loc. cit.); monetary data have been corrected with the help of computed price indices (*cf.* under production).

THE INFLUENCE OF PRODUCTIVITY ON ECONOMIC WELFARE

1. It is a well-known old thesis that an *increase in labour productivity leads to an increase in economic "welfare"*. Assuming for a while that the meaning of these two concepts is clear, we may say that the statement is correct for a Robinson Crusoe economy as we know it from our books. If Crusoe can get more products for the same effort, then probably he will shorten somewhat his working-day and get more products, and by doing so feel happier. The statement seems guaranteed for an economy: (I) without foreign trade, (II) without working-hours regulations, (III) without problems of capital scarcity and (IV) without monetary complications.

Many times already, however, doubt has arisen concerning the validity of that thesis. There are the old nineteenth-century discussions on technological unemployment, and we all know their modern versions from the thirties. During the recent full-employment years the old optimism as to the consequences of increased productivity has been revived. Only quite recently new reasons for some qualifications have come up, among other things in connection with problems of capital scarcity and balance-of-payments equilibrium. I propose to reformulate some of these qualifications to the old thesis. This may prove to be of some use to practical policy in the field of productivity-furthering measures, now very much in the centre of public interest. In order to avoid misunderstanding I want to stress from the outset, however, that in its essence I consider the thesis as sound; we should be careful, however, not to apply it mechanically.

2. As is usual in economic science, much depends on a careful *statement of the problem* we want to consider. Discussing the influence of an increase in labour productivity on welfare first of all implies that we consider labour productivity as one of the *data* to the economy considered. This, I think, can be easily admitted. The next thing we have to do is to give a clear definition of what we understand by *"welfare"*.

This is already less simple. I do not propose to go into all the well-known questions of comparability of individual utilities[1]; I want to take a "practical" point of view as my starting point. We may say, then, that perhaps the best single figure representing a nation's welfare is the value of its *real expenditure* on consumer and investment goods (to be written as x in what follows). But welfare cannot be considered essentially as a one-dimensional concept; and at least some rough indications about the distribution of x over certain groups of the population are needed in order to complement the figure x. I propose that two further figures are very useful: first, total real labour income L' as an indication of the distribution between the two big "classes" of society and, second, employment a as an indication of the distribution between employed and unemployed.

The way in which these figures should be used in order to judge a change in the economy is different from the way in which we look at x. Here it is not so that L' and a should be a maximum, but they may have optimum values. It is well known that any judgment in these figures is even more a matter of taste than a judgment on x. But serious declines in L' or a generally should be a matter of concern.

It seems useful already to point to one feature of our main measure of welfare: real expenditure of a nation. This measure x is not identical with the concept of the nation's product. For the product to become the nation's expenditure it is necessary to be exchanged, partially at least, at the world market. And this exchange, in dependence of the terms of trade prevailing, may change its value in a different way with one level of productivity than with another. An isolated increase in productivity will, generally speaking, worsen the country's terms of trade and hence the relation between real expenditure and product.

3. The third element in a careful statement of our problem consists in the set of hypotheses we introduce with regard to the *structure of the economy* considered. This concept we want to give a rather wide meaning. Not only have we to include in our concept of structure the particulars about the type of products and of productive agents charac-

---

[1] For a very clear summary of these problems, *cf.* NANCY RUGGLES, "Recent Developments in the Theory of Marginal Cost Pricing", *Review of Economic Studies*, 1949–50, Vol. xvii (2), No. 43, pp. 107–26.

teristic of the country and the behaviour of its citizens as portrayed by the demand and supply functions, *etc.* but we have also to include hypotheses as to the *governmental policy* pursued, and, perhaps, as to what I want to call *group behaviour*. In modern economies the consequences of certain changes in data, such as an increase in productivity, not only evoke individual reactions implied in the set of demand and supply relations, but also collective reactions as, *e.g.*, government measures to protect the balance of payments, trade-union demands as to wages, demands by organized farmers as to farm prices, *etc.*, and it is sometimes useful to distinguish between individual and collective policies.

Finally, when stating our problem we shall also have to pay attention to whether we think of short-run or of long-run reactions.

4. In terms which are customary nowadays this comes to saying that the consequences of an increase in labour productivity depend on the model we use. It is the purpose of this paper to present a number of models each of which may throw some light on our main problem.

TABLE I

SUMMARY OF FEATURES OF MODELS USED[1]

Model No.	Short (s)- or long (l)-run	Foreign trade	Capital as a limiting factor	Number of products	Balance of payments equilibrium	Government or Group policies.			
						Instruments			Targets
						Wages	Taxes	Profit margins	Target of policy indicated by +
I	l	—	+	1	.	+	—	—	.
II	l	+	—	1	+	—	—	—	.
III	s	+	—	1	—	—	—	—	.
IV	s	+	—	1	+	+	—	—	"Social equilibrium"
V	s	+	—	1	+	—	+	—	Equilibrium in balance of payments
VI	s	+	—	1	—	—	+	—	Maintenance of employment
VII	s	+	—	1	—	—	—	+	ployment
VIII	s	+	—	2	—	+	—	—	"Social equilibrium"

[1] + means present; — means absent; . means does not apply.

Some of these models (I, II and VIII) will be described in full; for the others the reader will be referred to other publications of the author. Before giving more details and a treatment of our problem, we may summarize in Table I some of the features of the models to be presented.

5. *Long-term, isolated-state, capital-shortage model* (I). The first model to be discussed represents an attempt to portray the pure form of technological unemployment; in order to concentrate on this phenomenon the complications of short-term-spending reactions and of international-trade connections have been eliminated. Adopting the style of the old models used in production theory (J. B. CLARK, DOUGLAS), a barter economy is assumed to exist, where one product for general use is produced by the combination of capital and labour. Capitalist and employer are the same person. The economy is a "multiple" of an optimum-size enterprise, working with a capital k of infinite fluidity, technically adapted to the optimum method of production. The range of possible methods between which the employer may choose is indicated by a function $h(i)$, where i is the "capital intensity" of a process, *i.e.*, the amount of capital needed in order to employ one man according to that method and h is the productivity of that man. The curve $h = h(i)$ represents the "curve of the technical possibilities". The employer has to pay a real wage l to each worker employed; this wage he considers as given (free competition between employers at the labour market). Indicating total production of the enterprise by u, the employer will choose i such as to make his profit a maximum, *i.e.*, $u - al$; hence

$$\frac{du}{di} - l\frac{da}{di} = 0$$

where $u = ah(i)$ and

$$a = \frac{k}{i}, \text{ or}$$

$$\frac{d}{di}\left\{\frac{k}{i}h(i)\right\} - l\frac{d}{di}\frac{k}{i} = 0.$$

It follows that

(5.1)
$$h' = \frac{h - l}{i}$$

meaning that the equilibrium point E at the curve of technical possibilities (*cf.* Fig. 1) has a tangent passing through the point P(0, *l*). The
production of one man is indicated by EQ, of which RQ is his wage.
Total production is as long as *k* is constant, represented by tg $\angle$EOQ.

The value of *i*, found from (5.1), determines how many workers
$a = k/i$ will be absorbed. In its turn, *i* depends on the curve $h(i)$, as
well as on the value of *l*. We assume that in an initial position there is
full employment.

6. Suppose now that, with total capital *k* per enterprise given, new
technical possibilities are introduced, *i.e.*, a new curve $h_1(i)$ develops.
What will happen depends on the shape of that curve. As long as
wages are constant, it may very well happen that not all workers can
be absorbed. Adaptation of *l* may be the consequence. But it may be
that only at a wage rate zero or a negative wage rate will all labour be
absorbed. If only the curve of technical possibilities is sufficiently
steep in its relevant parts, very strange things may happen (*cf.* Fig. 1,
curve $h_1(i)$). The rather revolutionary changes in labour productivity
represented by the change from curve *h* to curve h_1 are characterized

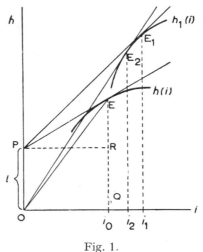

Fig. 1.

by two features. First, there is an increase in productivity for all
capital intensities considered; and secondly, the increase is particularly
large for ranges of capital intensity higher than those used so far. This

means that if considerable investments are made, unprecedented increases in productivity are possible. The picture has been suggested by the development in the United States[2] of new automats for which these features apply. Our picture shows that if such a development was general, a shift of E towards the right, *i.e.*, unemployment, would be the consequence. The causes for it could be formulated as capital scarcity. The new methods (using automats) are, in our picture, of such a productivity that private employers will irresistibly be driven towards their application, whereas at the same time they are so capital-intensive that only part of the workers can be employed, even if wage rates are very low (point E_2).

What, then, happens to "welfare"? The first yardstick we proposed, total real expenditure, now coinciding with total production, may increase, even considerably, as in Fig. 1. But employment and total real labour income would fall considerably. The result for welfare would be dubious. It is even conceivable (*cf.* Fig. 2) that total production would fall and employment too. Here the result would be positively unfavourable for welfare.

7. *Long-term open-economy model* (II). As the next model we consider a nation with foreign trade, producing, with the aid of labour and organization as productive agents, one product out of imported raw materials. The product is sold both at home and abroad. Monetary equilibrium, and hence equilibrium in the balance of payments, is maintained throughout. As the data of the economy we consider, apart from the usual structural data, the degree of labour productivity h. Provisionally the wage rate l and the autonomous profit margin π_0 (to be defined later) per unit of product are supposed to be independent of h. As the dependent variables of the system we consider: Y, national income in monetary units; X, national expenditure in monetary units; v, volume of production; x, real national expenditure; p, price level of product; L', real labour income; a, volume of employment.

We compare two situations, an initial one, in which $Y = X = y = x = p = a = h = l = 1$,[3] and one in which h shows a variation dh. We

---

[2] F. L. POLAK, *De wentelgang der Wetenschap en de Maatschappij van morgen*, Leiden, 1949 (Dutch).

[3] *Cf.* the model used and described in some detail in J. TINBERGEN, *Econometrics*, The Blakiston Co., Philadelphia, 1951, § 44 *sq.*

propose to determine the corresponding variations in the dependent variables, in particular in x, a and L', considered as measures of welfare.

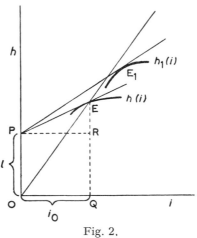

Fig. 2.

Our structural relations are:

Income definition:

(7.1) $$Y = (1 + \mu)yp - \mu y p^{\varepsilon}.$$

Here μ represents the nation's import quota, which we consider constant (a loss of generality which may be shown not to be relevant for our purpose), and ε represents the price elasticity of imports with respect to the price level of the product.

Home demand equation:

(7.2) $$X = Y.$$

Foreign demand equation:

(7.3) $$\mu y p^{\varepsilon} = \mu p^{1-\eta}.$$

Here the left-hand side represents the value of imports, which, as a consequence of balance-of-payments equilibrium, must be equal to the value of exports. The right-hand side represents the value of exports, which is equal to the price level p multiplied by the demand function. The demand function $\mu p^{-\eta}$ shows an elasticity of η with respect to prices; the constant factor μ is found by the condition of balance-of-payments equilibrium in the initial situation.

Supply equation:

(7.4) $$p = \pi_0 + \pi_1 \frac{l}{h} + \pi_2(y - 1) + \pi_3.$$

This equation should be considered as an approximation for small variations in the variables. It expresses the price level as a sum of the following components:

(I) the autonomous part of the profit margin π_0;

(II) labour costs, where π_1 represents the marginal wage quota;

(III) the automatic part of the profit margin, assumed to vary linearly with the volume of production, where π_2 represents the price flexibility in the initial situation; and

(iv) the import quota π_3, assumed constant in our problem.

Definition of home expenditure:

(7.6) $$X = xp.$$

Definition of employment:

(7.6) $$a = \frac{y}{h}.$$

Definition of real labour income:

(7.7) $$L' = \Lambda \frac{yl}{hp},$$

where Λ represents the ratio of labour income to national income in the initial situation.

8. From these equations we deduce:

$$dY = (1 + \mu)(dy + dp) - \mu dy - \mu \varepsilon dp$$
$$= dy + (1 + \mu - \mu \varepsilon)dp$$
(7.8) $$dX = dx + dp = dY \therefore dx = dy + \mu(1 - \varepsilon)dp.$$

$$\mu dy + \mu(\varepsilon + \eta - 1)dp = 0$$
(7.9) $$\therefore dy + (\varepsilon + \eta - 1)dp = 0$$
(7.10) $$dp = \pi_1(dl - dh) + \pi_2 dy + d\pi_0$$
(7.11) $$dL' = \Lambda(dy + dl - dh - dp)$$
(7.12) $$da = dy - dh.$$

Equations (7.8) to (7.12) enable us to calculate dx, da, dL', dy and

dp as functions of the independent variations dh, dl and $d\pi_0$. For our purpose only the expressions for dx, da and dL' in terms of dh are relevant; hence we put $dl = d\pi_0 = 0$ and find:

$$(7.13) \qquad dx = \pi_1 \frac{\eta - (1 + \mu)(1 - \varepsilon)}{\pi_2(\varepsilon + \eta - 1) + 1} \, dh$$

$$(7.14) \qquad da = \frac{(\pi_1 - \pi_2)(\varepsilon + \eta - 1) - 1}{\pi_2(\varepsilon + \eta - 1) + 1} \, dh$$

$$(7.15) \qquad dL' = \frac{(\pi_1 - \pi_2)(\varepsilon + \eta - 1) + \pi_1 - 1}{\pi_2(\varepsilon + \eta - 1) + 1} \, dh.$$

It follows that the changes in each of our welfare indicators depend on the productivity change in a rather complicated way: the price elasticities of foreign trade, the price flexibility and the marginal labour quota entering into each relation, and the import quota in the first only. The signs of the coefficients will be different according to the numerical values of the data just enumerated. The reader may try several sets of values. Since the purpose of this model is to show some of the implications for countries with a considerable portion of foreign trade, we will substitute figures found to be a fair approximation to the situation in a small country like the Netherlands. It was found that $\pi_1 = 0.3$; $\pi_2 = 0.1$; $\eta = 2$; $\varepsilon = 0.3$ and $\mu = 0.4$, leading to the formulae: $dx = 0.3 \, dh$; $da = -0.7 \, dh$; $dL' = -0.4 \, dh$.

Total real expenditure therefore increases, but employment, as well as real wage income, decrease with increasing productivity. The influence on "welfare" therefore depends on how heavily the decrease in employment and labour income count for us. Moreover, it is interesting to note that even $dx < 0$ for $0.7\eta + \varepsilon < 1$, i.e., for values of the elasticities considerably less stringent than the well-known "critical values" in the unstable balance-of-payments case.[4]

9. *Short-run open-economy models* (III–VIII). The models to be discussed in what follows are all short-run models in the sense that expenditures are supposed to react on income changes in the Keynesian way.

[4] Cf. e.g., G. STUVEL, *The Exchange Stability Problem*, Leiden, 1950, where all previous authors are also cited.

This means that equation (7.2) of the previous model is replaced by a more general one:

(9.1) $$x = L' + (1 - \sigma)Z' + c',$$

where Z' is real entrepreneurial income, σ their "marginal propensity not to spend" and c' a constant; c' depends on the initial situation. This model has been used for other purposes and described elsewhere.[5] Apart from slight differences that are irrelevant for the present purpose, the other relations in it are based on the same assumptions as in Model II.

In some of the versions there are, however, added one or two further variables representing instruments of economic policy that may possibly interfere with our problem and contribute to the consequences of an increase in labour productivity. In Model III no such additional instruments are considered, but since balance-of-payments equilibrium is no longer presupposed, the deficit D on current account of this balance is an additional symbol used.

Dealing with the equations in the same way as in the previous model (II) and taking $\sigma = 0.3$, we find:

(9.2) $$dx = -0.1(dh - dl)$$

(9.3) $$da = -0.9\,dh - 0.1\,dl$$

(9.4) $$dL' = -0.6(dh - dl)$$

(9.5) $$dD = -0.1(dh - dl).$$

The choice of σ is based upon the assumption that additional income is heavily taxed and government expenditure only partially reacts on an increase in tax receipts. Taking $\sigma = 0.2$ or 0.4 does not essentially change our results.

Comparing these results with those obtained for Model II and assuming, as a start, that wage rates do not change ($dl = 0$), we see that again the influence of h on a and L' is negative. The balance-of-payments deficit appears to react in the "classical" way: decreasing with an increase in productivity.

In addition, we now find that even the influence on x is slightly negative. This is evidently due to the tendency, now assumed, to hoard part of an additional income Z'. Given the fact that workers' income

---

[5] *Cf.* note 3 on p. 64.

declines and non-workers hoard part of the increase, the possibility arises of a decrease in total expenditure; and with the numerical values of our coefficients this appears actually to happen.

In this case the negative effect on total real expenditure, explained by the tendency to hoard, is the more remarkable, as the influence of h on the volume of production y is easily found to be positive; since $dy = da + dh$, we have

$$(9.6) \qquad dy = 0.1(dh - dl).$$

Here we have a clear example of the adverse influence of the terms of trade: the increase in h causes prices to go down, and this fall explains the divergency between dy and dx.

Our conclusion must be that an increase in labour productivity in this model turns out to be detrimental to welfare, although the effect on the balance of payments appears to be slightly favourable.

10. *Wages fully responding to productivity increases* (Model IV). The first alternative on Model III we shall deal with assumes that wages are not kept constant, but move along with the change in productivity; hence $dl = dh$. This behaviour of wages may be interpreted as the realization of "social equilibrium", if by that phrase we mean the maintenance of the distribution of national income between labour and non-labour income. In fact, it may be easily seen that only by this wage policy will distribution remain unaltered. This assumption leads us to the remarkable result that:

$$(10.1) \qquad dx = dy = dL' = dD = 0,$$

and

$$(10.2) \qquad da = - dh.$$

This result may also be obtained in a verbal and more general way.[6] The only assumptions to be made are:

(a) The price level depends on wage rates and productivity only as far as the ratio between these two variables changes; in addition, it depends on the volume of production.

(b) The volume and the value of exports depend on wage rates and productivity only through their dependence of prices.

---

[6] *Cf.* J. TINBERGEN, "The Significance of Wage Policy for Employment", *International Economic Papers* (I), 1951.

(c) With constant foreign prices, the volume and value of imports depend only on the volume of production and the price level of national products.

(d) National income is a function of national expenditure, exports and imports.

(e) National expenditure is a function of national income, labour income and the price level.

(f) Labour income is the product of the volume of production and labour costs per unit of product (which equal the ratio between the wage rate and productivity).

From these assumptions, which together with some definitions represent a sufficient number of relations to determine, among other things, the volume of production y, total real expenditure x, real labour income L' and the balance-of-payments deficit D as functions of productivity and the wage rate, it will be found that y, x, L' and D depend only on the ratio of l and h and, besides that, in no other way on l and h. Any changes in l and h that do not affect their ratio will not change, therefore, y, x, L' and D, as indicated by (10.1). Since, in addition, $a = y/h$, $da = -dh$ as long as $dl = dh$.

The result for our topic is that with this wage policy an increase in productivity will not affect x, L' or D and adversely affect employment. The result might be interpreted by stating that national welfare of an open economy cannot increase if exports do not increase and that the assumed wage policy prevents this possible effect of an increase in productivity from materializing.

11. *Tax policy in order to maintain balance-of-payments equilibrium* (Model v). Introducing now, as an additional instrument of economic policy, a possible increase in indirect taxes and assuming this instrument to be used in order to maintain balance-of-payments equilibrium, we obtain relations[7] in which the change in the rate τ of indirect taxes appears as an additional variable:

(11.1) $dx = -0.1(dh - dl) - 2.0 d\tau$

(11.2) $da = -0.9 dh - 0.1 dl - 1.3 d\tau$

(11.3) $dL' = -0.6(dh - dl) - 2.1 d\tau$

(11.4) $dD = -0.1(dh - dl) - 0.7 d\tau.$

[7] *Loc. cit.*

The first two terms at the right-hand side are the same as in equations (9.2) to (9.5).

Assuming that again wage rates will not be changed, but that tax rates will be altered in such a way as to maintain balance-of-payments equilibrium, we have to find $d\tau$ from the relation

$$0 = dD = -0.1\,dh - 0.7\,d\tau,$$

or

(11.5) $d\tau = -0.15\,dh$

leading to:

(11.6) $dx = 0.2\,dh$

(11.7) $da = -0.7\,dh$

(11.8) $dL' = -0.3\,dh.$

This change in policy appears to bring about a positive influence of labour productivity on real expenditure, leaving us still, however, with a negative influence on employment and real workers' income.

12. *Tax policy in order to maintain employment* (Model VI). Let us now suppose that tax policy is not used in order to maintain balance-of-payments equilibrium but in order to maintain employment. This comes to choosing, in formulae (11.1) to (11.4), τ so as to make $da = 0$ (taking still $dl = 0$). The results are:

(12.1) $d\tau = -0.7\,dh$

and

(12.2) $dx = 1.3\,dh$

(12.3) $dL' = 0.7\,dh$

(12.4) $dD = 0.4\,dh.$

"Welfare" in our sense will now be favourably influenced to a slight degree but at the expense of a considerable increase in the balance-of-payments deficit. Similar results would have been obtained if we had taken $dl = dh$.

13. *Price policy in order to maintain employment* (Model VII). Similar calculations were made with still another additional instrument, *viz.*, by introducing price policy (profit-margin regulations) as a means of

maintaining employment. With this instrument as an additional variable π_0, the formulae (9.2) to (9.5) become:

$$(13.1) \qquad dx = -0.1(dh - dl) - 0.9 d\pi_0$$

$$(13.2) \qquad da = -0.9 dh - 0.1 dl - 1.1 d\pi_0$$

$$(13.3) \qquad dL' = -0.6(dh - dl) - 2.0 d\pi_0$$

$$(13.4) \qquad dD = -0.1(dh - dl) - 0.0 d\pi_0.$$

Choosing $d\pi_0$ so as to make da vanish we get:

$$(13.5) \qquad d\pi_0 = -0.8 dh,$$

leading to:

$$(13.6) \qquad dx = +0.6 dh$$

$$(13.7) \qquad dL' = +dh$$

$$(13.8) \qquad dD = -0.1 dh.$$

This version appears to be favourable to welfare in the various aspects used so far and to the balance of payments. But here, as could be expected, it is non-workers that have to bear the burden, and again the effect is questionable.

14. *Two-industry version of short-term model* (Model VIII). The models so far analysed have shown us that the influence of productivity on economic welfare and the balance of payments is by no means as unambiguous as is often believed. It very much depends on a number of circumstances whether an increase in productivity has or has not a favourable effect—however the term favourable be interpreted. This conclusion is of some importance, as has been pointed out already in section 1, for present-day economic policy in a number of countries, since there is a strong tendency to advocate increases in productivity in a general way. It would appear that at least certain qualifications might be useful and that, perhaps, a policy of furthering productivity deserves to be directed towards specific industries in order to have a maximum of success. Some of the adverse reactions so far detected probably work out in a more pronounced way in one and in a less pronounced way in another type of industry; this applies, *e.g.*, to the capital-shortage argument, whereas, on the other hand, the significance

for foreign trade also varies considerably between one industry and the other.

For these reasons the macro-economic approach of the preceding sections cannot be the only basis of devices for practical policy. Divergencies between industries are ruled out beforehand in these models. They may have made us cautious *vis-à-vis* too simple ideas about the desirability of a general increase in productivity in one country, but they cannot show us the way towards alternative policies. Micro-economic models will be necessary; but we know by now that their handling is no simple affair. There seems to be some wisdom in a modest start, and this is why I propose only to contrast the previous models to the simplest conceivable alternative in this connection: a two-industry model, leaving it to others more courageous than I to expand the number of industries.

In order to find out in exactly what way the two-industry version leads to results different from a one-industry version we will discuss one and the same problem in both ways; in order to reduce the problem to its simplest kernel we will even simplify the one-industry model still further. The problem to solve will be the following: suppose we want (I) to maintain employment, (II) to maintain social equilibrium as defined in section 10 and (III) to restore equilibrium in the balance of payments, how have we to vary labour productivity?

The reader will observe that by posing this problem I have shifted from a problem of explanation to a problem of policy, or, as we now say, to a "decision model" (FRISCH). This will probably accentuate some of our findings so far in a useful way.

We will use Model II of section 7 with the exception of the hypothesis of monetary equilibrium, meaning that we assume a more general spending reaction. Moreover, we will simplify our supply equation by taking $\pi_2 = 0$ (which does not influence our results very much). Since the balance-of-payments deficit D = value of imports — value of exports, we find from (7.3) and (7.9):

(14.1) $$dD = \mu dy + \mu(\varepsilon + \eta - 1)dp$$

and from (7.4) and (7.10):

(14.2) $$dp = \pi_1(dl - dh),$$

ruling out the possibility of changes in π_0.

For our problem it is useful to replace dy by $da \mid dh$ (*cf.* 7.12) in equation (14.1). The condition of social equilibrium may be written as

$$\frac{dp}{p - \pi_3} = \frac{dl - dh}{l/h} \quad \text{or}$$

(14.3)
$$dp = \lambda(dl - dh),$$

there λ is the initial value of

$$\frac{p - \pi_3}{l/h} = 0.7.$$

Equations (14.1) to (14.3) are then three equations enabling us to find the three political instruments dl, dh and dp when the three targets da, λ and dD are given. The solution is easy: we find $dp = 0$, $dl = dh$ and $\mu dh = dD$. The latter result tells us that in order to reduce D we have to reduce h, and therefore represents some of the paradoxical conclusions reached so far.

15. This set-up we will now refine by considering two industries instead of one. By so doing we shall meet some of the more general difficulties of "micronising" macro-models; but we shall not go into this side more systematically.

We have now to deal with two branches, each of them characterized by their own a, y, x, e, h, p, μ and π, which we shall distinguish by super-scripts 1 and 2. Of these, the hs and the ps will remain index-numbers with an initial value of 1, but the as, ys, xs and es are sup-posed to add up to the corresponding macro concepts. We shall assume wage rates and export elasticities to be the same in the two industries and therefore maintain our symbols l and ε. As targets we consider:

(I) to maintain employment a^1 and a^2 in the two industries, *i.e.*, $da^1 = da^2 = 0$;

(II) to maintain social equilibrium, *i.e.* $dp = \lambda(dl - dh)$, where h and p now represent weighted averages of h^1, h^2 and p^1, p^2, to be defined later; and

(III) to restore equilibrium in the balance of payments, *i.e.*, to give a certain negative value to dD.

Our unknowns are p^1, p^2, l, h^1 and h^2.

Our equations will be the analogues to (14.1) to (14.3); but we want more equations, since we have more unknowns. On the other hand, the existence of more than one industry also implies the existence of more relations.

The following equations are easily found:

$$(15.1) \qquad dD = \mu^1 dy^1 + \mu^2 dy^2 - de^1 - e^1 dp^1 - de^2 - e^2 dp^2$$

$$(15.2) \qquad dp = \frac{\overset{1}{v} dp^1 + \overset{2}{v} dp^2}{\overset{1}{v} + \overset{2}{v}} = \frac{\overset{1}{v} \pi_1^1 (dl - dh^1) + \overset{2}{v} \pi_1^2 (dl - dh)}{\overset{1}{v} + \overset{2}{v}}$$

$$(15.3) \qquad dp^1 = \pi_1^1 (dl - dh^1)$$

$$(15.4) \qquad dp^2 = \pi_1^2 (dl - dh^2)$$

$$(15.5) \qquad de^1 = - e^1 \varepsilon dp^1$$

$$(15.6) \qquad de^2 = - e^2 \varepsilon dp^2$$

$$(15.7) \qquad \frac{dy^1}{y^1} = \frac{da^1}{a^1} + \frac{dh^1}{h^1}$$

$$(15.8) \qquad \frac{dy^2}{y^2} = \frac{da^2}{a^2} + \frac{dh^2}{h^2}.$$

In these equations v^1 and v^2, used as weights for p^1 and p^2, are the volumes of gross production, as distinguished from the volumes of net production y^1, and y^2; for an industry with a higher import quota v^2 is relatively larger than y^2; but we assume that v^1 varies proportionally to y^1 and v^2 to y^2. Further $h^1 = h^2 = 1$ and $da^1 = da^2 = 0$.

The above eight equations are not sufficient in number to yield us all the nine unknowns dy^1, dy^2, de^1, de^2, dp^1, dp^2, dh^1, dh^2 and dl. It is necessary now to give some attention to the variables dx^1 and dx^2; and their role is understood most easily if we also consider dv^1 and dv^2. Hence, four new unknowns and five more equations are introduced. Four of them give no trouble:

$$(15.9) \qquad dv^1 = dx^1 + de^1$$

$$(15.10) \qquad dy^2 = dx^2 + de^2$$

$$(15.11) \qquad \frac{dv^1}{v^1} = \frac{dy^1}{y^1}$$

$$\text{(15.12)} \qquad \frac{dv^2}{v^2} = \frac{dy^2}{y^2}.$$

The fifth has to tell something about the relation between dx^1 and dx^2. This was not necessary in our one-industry model, since total real expenditure dx depends on dy through the spending relation which is no longer free once we make a certain assumption on the balance of payments: the deficit on that balance is identical with the monetary deficit in internal spending. In the two-industry model, however, the distribution of dx over dx^1 and dx^2 also comes in, and that is not implied in any of the other relations. This distribution will, generally speaking, depend on the relative prices of goods 1 and 2. Only as a limiting case may we assume, which we will do for simplicity, that it is independent of prices. Next, the distribution will depend on the size of x^1 and x^2; there will be a tendency for dx^1 and dx^2 to be proportional to x^1 and x^2. But a third tendency is present, determined by income elasticities of x^1 and x^2; the higher the elasticity of x^1, the higher dx^1. Putting

$$\text{(15.13)} \qquad \frac{dx^1}{x^1} = \varrho \, \frac{dx^2}{x^2}$$

ϱ represents the ratios of the income elasticities for x^1 and x^2.

16. We are now able to solve our equations. Leaving the algebra to to the reader and using the relations $(1 + \mu^1)y^1 = v^1 = x^1 + e^1$ and $(1 + \mu^2)y^2 = v^2 = x^2 + e^2$, we may first reduce our system to three equations in dl, dh^1 and dh^2:

$$
\text{(16.1)} \qquad
\begin{aligned}
\overset{2}{x}\{(\overset{1}{x} + \overset{1}{e})d\overset{1}{h} + \overset{1}{e}\,\varepsilon\overset{1}{\pi_1}(dl - d\overset{1}{h})\} = {}& \varrho\overset{1}{x}\{(\overset{2}{x} + \overset{2}{e})d\overset{2}{h} + \\
& \overset{2}{e}\,\varepsilon\overset{2}{\pi_1}(dl - d\overset{2}{h})\}
\end{aligned}
$$

$$\text{(16.2)} \qquad (\overset{1}{x} + \overset{1}{e})\overset{1}{\pi_1}(dl - d\overset{1}{h}) + (\overset{2}{x} + \overset{2}{e})\overset{2}{\pi_1}(dl - d\overset{2}{h}) = 0$$

$$
\text{(16.3)} \qquad
\begin{aligned}
& \frac{1}{1 + \overset{1}{\mu}}(\overset{1}{x} + \overset{1}{e})d\overset{1}{h} + \frac{\overset{2}{\mu}}{1 + \overset{2}{\mu}}(\overset{2}{x} + \overset{2}{e})d\overset{2}{h} + (\varepsilon - 1) \\
& \{\overset{1}{e}\overset{1}{\pi_1}(dl - d\overset{1}{h}) + \overset{2}{e}\overset{2}{\pi_1}(dl - d\overset{2}{h})\} = dD.
\end{aligned}
$$

Equation (16.2) enables us to express dl in terms of dh^1 and dh^2:

$$\text{(16.4)} \qquad (b^1 + b^2)dl = b^1 dh^1 + b^2 dh^2$$

where

(16.5) $$b^1 = \pi_1^1(x^1 + e^1) \text{ and } b^2 = \pi_1^2(x^2 + e^2),$$

representing total wages in the initial situation in branches 1 and 2, respectively. Substituting (16.4) into (16.1), we find dh^1/dh^2:

(16.6) $$\frac{dh^1}{dh^2} = \frac{\varrho(x^2 + e^2)x^1 - E\{x^2e^1(x^2 + e^2) + \varrho x^1e^2(x^1 + e^1)\}}{(x^1 + e^1)x^2 - E\{x^2e^1(x^2 + e^2) + \varrho x^1e^2(x^1 + e^1)\}},$$

where

$$E = \frac{\varepsilon \pi_1^1 \pi_1^2}{b^1 + b^2}.$$

Finally, we may find, e.g., dh^1 from a substitution of (16.6) into (16.3).

It would lead us too far to discuss all the implications of the solutions. We want to stress, however, the following points:

A. The example clearly shows how rapidly matters become more complicated with an increase in the number of branches.

B. It may be shown that not only different values for dh^1 and dh^2 will be found, but that even different signs of dh^1 and dh^2 are possible. According to formula (16.6), this depends on the values of x^1, x^2, e^1, e^2, ϱ and E, i.e., on the sales composition of each of the industries, on the ratio of their income elasticities ϱ, on the price elasticity ε (taken equal for both industries) and the product of their labour quota π_1^1 and π_1^2. Taking, to begin with, $\varrho = 1$, $\varepsilon = 2$, $b^1 + b^2 = 0.5$ and $\pi_1^1\pi_1^2 = 0.09$, we find for dh^1/dh^2:

TABLE II

Two-Industry Model.   Values for dh^1/dh^2 with

$\varrho = 1$, $\varepsilon = 2$, $b^1 + b^2 = 0.5$ and $\pi_1^1\pi_1^2 = 0.09$

x^1 \ e^1	0	0.1	0.2	0.3	0.4
0	indet.	— 0.9	— 0.8	— 0.7	— 0.6
0.1	1.5	0.6	0.2	— 0.0	— 0.1
0.2	1.5	0.9	0.5	0.3	0.2
0.3	1.6	1.1	0.7	0.5	0.3
0.4	1.7	1.2	0.9	0.6	0.4
0.5	1.9	1.4	1.0	0.7	0.5

Evidently the negative sign for dh^1/dh^2 occurs here only if x^1 is very small, *i.e.*, if industry 1 is mainly an export industry. It is clear that in that case indeed an increase in productivity will yield a positive contribution to the balance of payments. From the structure of the formula for dh^1/dh^2 it is also clear that with higher values for E, *i.e.*, for higher export elasticities as well as for higher labour quota, negative values for dh^1/dh^2 will occur more frequently. The same is true for lower values of ϱ, *i.e.*, if industry 1 shows a relatively lower income elasticity of home demand than industry 2.

C. On the other hand, it is remarkable that μ^1 and μ^2, the import quota, do not directly influence the value of dh^1/dh^2; they do not occur in formula (16.6). This statement should, however, be supplemented by the consideration that μ^1 and μ^2 are not completely free, once that the x and the e are given. Since, in our system of units $y = 1$ or $y^1 + y^2 = 0$, we have:

$$(16.7) \qquad \frac{x^1 + e^1}{1 + \mu^1} + \frac{x^2 + e^2}{1 + \mu^2} = 1,$$

meaning that μ^1 and μ^2 are situated on an equilateral hyperbola. As a consequence of boundary conditions for the x and e (all of them should be positive), not all values of μ^1 and μ^2 are permitted.

D. The condition for dh^1 to be equal to dh^2 is also easily found; it is

$$(16.8) \qquad \varrho(x^2 + e^2)x^1 = (x^1 + e^1)x^2.$$

In this case there is no need for a micro-model.

17. *Summary.* Let us try to summarize our findings. The old thesis that an increase in productivity leads to an increase in welfare should not be misunderstood. Not under all circumstances does it lead to consequences that are in all respects attractive. In a number of cases the consequences are definitely mixed; some of them favourable, others unfavourable. It does not always entail an increase in total real expenditure; nor does it always yield an increase in real workers' income. Often it reduces the volume of employment. If it acts favourably on all these aspects of welfare it may deteriorate the balance of payments or real non-workers' income.

Of course, some of these statements have an element of self-evidence.

If we find, in Model III, that x, a and L' all diminish but the balance of payments improves, one may object that this balance-of-payments surplus should somehow be added to the results. This is, to some extent, correct. But on the other hand, the tendency to hoarding which is the reason for the balance-of-payments surplus does cause total real expenditure, and hence presumably consumption, to go down, be it only temporarily.

Another objection may be that a decline in employment is in fact an element of welfare, since it represents leisure, and that an increase in leisure is one of the natural ways of enjoying the advantages of increased productivity. This is also in some sense true; here the difficulty is that in present-day society the decline in employment is often borne by a small group of unemployed and if so is certainly an evil. A final remark may be that we studied only isolated increases in productivity in one country and that some of the adverse effects may vanish if all countries show an increase in productivity at the same time. This again does not help countries now summoned to raise productivity more than others.

In fact it may be said that an increase in productivity in one country (without an increase in the other countries)—just as an increase in productivity in one firm—to a large extent comes to the advantage of the buyers, *i.e.* the other countries.

As I said already, the interpretation of this study should nevertheless not be that increases in productivity are of no use. They decidedly are, but they should at the same time be well-selected and well-directed increases in productivity.

ON THE THEORY OF INCOME DISTRIBUTION[*]

CONTENTS

1. THE STATISTICAL FACTS OF INCOME DISTRIBUTION

The frequency distribution of incomes has aroused the interest of statisticians for a long time. Pareto's Law is one of the forms in which the regularities of income distribution have been expressed. Both VAN DER WIJK[1] and GIBRAT[2] have proposed another formula, known as the logarithmic normal distribution. Their formula says that the logarithms of incomes are normally distributed, *i.e.* according to Gaussian law. The results of the two approaches are not very different and it would be difficult, from a statistical point of view, to decide which of the two formulae deserves preference. Most of the statistical research on comparisons between countries and periods has been done

---

[*] Published in Weltwirtschaftliches Archiv 77 (1956), pp. 155-175 Some errors have been corrected.

[1] J. VAN DER WIJK, *Inkomens- en vermogensverdeling*, Nederlandsch Economisch Instituut Nr. 26, Haarlem, 1939.

[2] R. GIBRAT, *Les inégalités économiques, Applications: Aux inégalités des richesses, A la concentration des entreprises, Aux populations des villes, Aux statistiques des familles, etc. d'une Loi nouvelle, La loi de l'effet proportionnel*, Paris, 1931.

with the aid of Pareto's Law. The experience so far gained may be very briefly summarized as follows. Except for cyclical fluctuations, Pareto's constant a for incomes before taxes has moved upward in most countries, indicating a gradually decreasing inequality in incomes. From a figure of around 1.3 in the early phase of industrial revolution (and this figure applies also to under-developed countries in our times) the level has risen to about 2 in the socially advanced countries. In several western countries incomes after taxes show an a some 0.2 higher, pointing to a further decrease in inequality.[3]

2. THE NEED FOR A THEORETICAL INTERPRETATION

The fairly satisfactory state of affairs with respect to the statistical description of income distribution contrasts with an unsatisfactory state in the area of economic interpretation. No generally accepted interpretation of the statistical regularities seems to exist, and most economic text books do not even deal with such an interpretation.[4] This is the more remarkable since the inequality in income distribution is at the bottom of some of the most important problems of economic policy.

To be sure some attempts, and even a few very interesting ones, have been made to throw light on the forces behind the distribution of income. The distribution of wealth, as well as that of certain physical and psychological properties of man, has rightly been mentioned as basic for the understanding of income distribution.

Some interesting partial investigations into the distribution of incomes within homogeneous groups have tried to shed some light on the details of the mechanism.

Recently, TUCK[5] has made a very interesting attempt to explain not only the distribution of incomes, but also the frequency distribution of enterprises with regard to size, with the aid of a rather complex property of man, the ability to guide other people.

What seems to be lacking in all these attempts is, in the author's

[3] *Cf.* JAN TINBERGEN, *Redelijke inkomstenverdeling*, Haarlem, 1953, p. 15 *sq.*
[4] The interpretation given by CHAMPERNOWNE also does not seem to aim at an economic analysis of the process. *Cf.* D.G. CHAMPERNOWNE, "A Model of Income Distribution", *The Economic Journal*, Vol. LXIII, London, 1953, p. 318 *sq.*
[5] R. H. TUCK, *An Essay on the Economic Theory of Rank*, Oxford, 1954.

opinion, a precise description of the mechanism of income formation in terms of the usual instruments of economic analysis. The present article, while elaborating some ideas put forward earlier, tries to make a contribution in this field. This attempt is very provisional, since an essential ingredient for building an acceptable theory is still lacking: *i.e.* sufficient statistical and factual information.[6] Therefore, any theory now presented cannot have been tested; it can only serve as a basis for collecting the necessary data.

A theory of income distribution is needed not only for purely scientific reasons; it is also needed if a policy is to be devised to influence income distribution in the future.

3. DEMAND FOR AND SUPPLY OF PRODUCTIVE CONTRIBUTIONS

The usual instruments of economic analysis just referred to consist of the concepts of demand and supply applied to the system of markets which determine income distribution. Since incomes derive from production, we have to consider the markets for productive contributions. By this term, not only the labour market, but the markets of the other factors of production as well are indicated, although labour, in the widest sense of this word, will play a predominant role. For this reason we will sometimes speak of the demand for and supply of labour in our examples; it should be kept in mind, however, that the demand for and supply of capital and land are implied as well.

It is essential for our problem that this market for productive contributions consists of a very large number of compartments. Demand, supply and price have to be distinguished for each of these compartments but, at the same time, there will be a considerable degree of interdependence. We might deal with this situation by introducing an index for each compartment, say j, and separate symbols for the supply, the demand and the price in each of them, bearing in mind that supply in compartment $j = 767$ depends not only on the corresponding price but also on a number of other prices. The system of equations describing the equilibrium conditions for all of these compartments would be very large and difficult to handle. We will use another instrument which will considerably simplify this description.

---

[6] *Cf.* section 10.

We will not use a discontinuous index but a set of continuously changing variables characterizing the many compartments; and we will assume that the price system can be described by one single function of
these variables. Instead of saying that supply in a given compartment
depends on all the prices in the various compartments we will say that
that supply depends on the function just mentioned, *i.e.* on the parameters of that function. This mathematical set-up appears to be much
more efficient for the treatment of our problem. In order to clarify the
method, we will first specify what variables we are going to use for the
description of the market for productive contributions.

4. CHARACTERIZING PRODUCTIVE CONTRIBUTIONS BY THE "DEGREES" OF THEIR ATTRIBUTES OR QUALITIES

The variables to be used will be called the "degrees" to which certain
attributes or qualities are needed for the contribution to be made.
These attributes or qualities may be intelligence, ability to work under
unfavourable physical conditions, ability to deal with other people,
and so on. These attributes are partly those known from job evaluation. In addition, there will be others needed for jobs not yet evaluated
—especially the most qualified—and there may be such attributes
as do not necessarily refer to the personal abilities of a man, but to his
wealth, relations *etc.* In contradistinction to the usual approach in
job evaluation we will not only use these concepts for the description
of "jobs", which are indicative of the demand side of our markets, but
also for the description of individuals which represent the supply side.

As already observed, the variables which we are going to use to
characterize the various market compartments are the *degrees to which*
certain attributes are required or present in that compartment. We will
indicate by s_i the degree to which an attribute i is required, and by t_i
the degree to which it is present in those compartments supplying a
contribution. If we used, say, 25 attributes for the characterization of
our market, each compartment would be described by 25 figures
$s_1, s_2 \ldots s_{25}$ on the demand side. Because of the use of continuous
variables we are free ourselves to choose the size of the compartment;
this size will be indicated, on the demand side, by the intervals ds_1, ds_2
$\ldots ds_{25}$ admitted. In a space with 25 dimensions this represents a
little hypercube if all ds_i chosen are of equal size. Small values of ds_i

will describe a sharply defined "occupation", larger values a whole group of neighbouring occupations; neighbouring, that is, in the sense of requiring almost the same abilities.

In order to simplify our illustrations we will base them on a much more restricted number of attributes, namely 2. This may be justified by the fairly high correlation which appears to exist between several of the "degrees" needed for a number of jobs; such "degrees" may then be represented by one single s_1 and a few others by s_2. The existence of such correlation is illustrated by the fact that for a long time it was assumed that intelligence alone is the relevant criterion, or by Mr. Tuck's approach of using the ability to guide (or command) other people as his sole variable.

The demand in our market system may be said to be exerted by the "organizers of production", who are supposed collectively to specify a frequency distribution $m(s_1, s_2 \ldots)$ of the number of contributions they want in each region of the variables s_i.

On the supply side it is assumed that a similar frequency distribution describes the availability of attributes on the part of the individuals forming the economy; this distribution will be indicated by $n(t_1, t_2 \ldots)$. In principle this frequency distribution can be observed by psycho-technical tests; in a rudimentary form these are available as army tests or as sets of school reports for young people.[7]

5. THE INCOME SCALE AND ITS INFLUENCE ON THE CHOICE OF A "JOB"

If the two frequency distributions just introduced were identical, *i.e.* the number of contributions of each type wanted were equal to the number of contributors available, it would be possible to organize pro-

---

[7] For such tests to be conducted correctly, the circumstances under which the "degrees" are measured have to be specified. When put under pressure, as *e.g.* in competitions, most people will be able to deliver higher performances than without such pressure. For the economic application of such measurements one of the important "circumstances" is the income that may be derived from a certain performance. Strictly speaking we should specify our definition $n(t_i)$ by saying that it represents the supply distribution over the various jobs when all remunerations are equal. Alternatively we may specify any given system of remunerations or "income scale". *Cf.* also U.S. Employment Services, *Guide to the Use of General Aptitude Test Battery B*–1002, Washington.

duction so that each "job" would be done by a man just fit for it.
Apart from the availability of the necessary information, there would
be no problem of choosing a job. In reality the two frequency distributions do not coincide and this introduces an element of tension between
attributes required and attributes available. In order to get every
"vacancy" filled the organizers will have to offer remunerations attract-
ing people to the jobs for which supply is insufficient and repelling
them from jobs with oversupply. This system of tensions seems to
represent the essence of our problem since the function of income distribution is to induce people to choose the proper contribution to
production.

We will assume, as already announced, that the incomes paid in the
various compartments may be represented by a system, to be called
the *"income scale"*. This scale will be represented mathematically by
assuming that income l in each compartment $s_1, s_2 \ldots$ can be determined from the values $s_1, s_2 \ldots$ by a certain function $\Lambda(s_1, s_2 \ldots)$.
This scale, then, is the unknown of our problem; and we will have to
fix it in such a way as to equilibrate demand and supply in each compartment. It is this scale, at the same time, which influences both the
supply and the demand side of the market so as to bring them together.
Fort he time being we will assume that the demand side is not influenced,
i.e. that demand is inelastic; later on, however, this assumption will be
removed.[8] We will first consider the way in which supply adapts itself
by studying in more detail the choice the individual makes as to his
contribution. Also here we will use a traditional instrument of economic analysis, namely the utility or indifference function. It will be
assumed that each individual tries to maximize his utility function ω,
supposed to depend on (I) the income l received for the "job" he
chooses, (II) the degrees of the attributes of the job s_i representing its
difficulty and (III) the degrees of the attributes t_i characterizing the
individual, *i.e.* his "abilities". More specifically we assume that the
two latter groups of variables—the s_i and the t_i—affect the individual's well-being only to the extent that there are "tensions" between
them. Still more specifically we assume ω to be of the form

(5.1) $$\omega = \omega_3 \log l - \tfrac{1}{2}\omega_1(s_1 - t_1)^2 - \tfrac{1}{2}\omega_2(s_2 - t_2)^2.$$

---

[8] *Cf.* section 8.

One way of interpreting this formula is that utility is measurable, that equal percentage increases in income cause equal additions to utility and that equal increases in "tensions" between s_i and t_i— whether positive or negative—cause parabolic increases in disutility with a disutility $\frac{1}{2}\omega_i$ for the first unit of tension. It is by no means necessary, however, to adhere to the interpretation of measurability. Formula (5.1) may simply be said to define the shape of indifference curves. As long as only small "tensions" $s_i - t_i$ appear, the form of (5.1) may be considered to be an approximation which is sufficiently general; the really restrictive hypothesis is that the compensation wanted by different individuals for a unit tension is a given percentage increase in income. Evidently, the final decision about such assumptions can be made only on the basis of empirical evidence.[9]

When confronted now with an income scale

(5.2) $$\log l = \lambda\,(s_1,\, s_2 \ldots),$$

the individual will choose his "job" $s_1,\, s_2\, \ldots$ so as to maximize ω, leading to:

(5.3) $$\frac{\partial \omega}{\partial s_1} \equiv \omega_3\,\frac{\partial \lambda}{\partial s_1} - \omega_1\,(s_1 - t_1) = 0$$

(5.4) $$\frac{\partial \omega}{\partial s_2} \equiv \omega_3\,\frac{\partial \lambda}{\partial s_2} - \omega_2\,(s_2 - t_2) = 0 \; etc.$$

In the special case where λ is of the shape:

(5.5) $$\lambda \equiv \lambda_{00} + \lambda_{10}s_1 + \lambda_{01}s_2 + \tfrac{1}{2}\lambda_{20}s_1^2 + \lambda_{11}s_1s_2 + \tfrac{1}{2}\lambda_{02}s_2^2,$$

these equations take the form:

(5.6) $$t_1 = (1 - \omega_3'\lambda_{20})\,s_1 - \omega_3'\lambda_{11}s_2 - \omega_3'\lambda_{10}$$

(5.7) $$t_2 = -\omega_3''\lambda_{11}s_1 + (1 - \omega_3''\lambda_{02})\,s_2 - \omega_3''\lambda_{01}$$

where

(5.8) $$\omega_3' = \frac{\omega_3}{\omega_1}; \quad \omega_3'' = \frac{\omega_3}{\omega_2}.$$

---

[9] There is no lack of generality in our assumption that one and the same function ω can be used to describe the behaviour of different individuals, since the parameters t_i may always be used in a number sufficient to bring out all relevant differences between individuals.

In our illustration[10] we will use this particular assumption about λ in order to solve the problem.

6. ILLUSTRATION OF THE PROCESS OF INCOME FORMATION

The process of income formation now may be further illustrated by an attempt to solve the problem posed, *i.e.* to determine the unknown function λ, in the case of only two attributes where (a) the demand frequency distribution is inelastic and (b) both the demand and the supply distribution are normal distributions in their variables. In formulae this implies that

$$m(s_1, s_2) = \frac{m_0}{2\pi\sigma_1\sigma_2\sqrt{1-r_s^2}} \exp \frac{1}{1-r_s^2} \left[-\frac{1}{2\sigma_1^2}(s_1-\bar{s}_1)^2 \right.$$

(6.1)
$$\left. + \frac{r_s}{\sigma_1\sigma_2}(s_1-\bar{s}_1)(s_2-\bar{s}_2) - \frac{1}{2\sigma_2^2}(s_2-\bar{s}_2)^2 \right]$$

$$n(t_1, t_2) = \frac{n_0}{2\pi\tau_1\tau_2\sqrt{1-r_t^2}} \exp \frac{1}{1-r_t^2} \left[-\frac{1}{2\tau_1^2}(t_1-\bar{t}_1)^2 \right.$$

(6.2)
$$\left. + \frac{r_t}{\tau_1\tau_2}(t_1-\bar{t}_1)(t_2-\bar{t}_2) - \frac{1}{2\tau_2^2}(t_2-\bar{t}_2)^2 \right] .$$

These assumptions with regard to the frequency distributions do not imply very serious restrictions to generality since the scales in which the attributes are measured are still at our discretion, meaning that these scales may be so adapted as to make at least either the s- or the t-distribution normal. The assumptions are, moreover, to some extent supported by the general experience that many human characteristics show distributions similar, at least, to the Gauss' distribution. Nevertheless, it should be fully recognized that this is one of the additional points about which empirical evidence will have to say the last word. As will be understood from (6.1) and (6.2), both frequency distributions are characterized by:

(I) the average values of the degrees of the attributes ($\bar{s}_1, \bar{s}_2$ and $\bar{t}_1, \bar{t}_2$);

---

[10] *Cf.* section 6.

(II) their standard deviations (σ_1, σ_2 and τ_1, τ_2)

and

(III) the coefficients of correlation between the "degrees" in the demand and the supply distribution (r_s and r_t).

This means that three forms of divergence between the distributions are admitted. In plain language, and by way of example, this means that there may be differences in average intelligence between requirements and availabilities, and differences in the dispersion of intelligence (and the same for, say, the ability to guide others). In addition, the way in which these abilities are combined on the demand side may differ from the supply side. There may be a relatively strong demand for the combination of the two, whereas the combination may be less frequent among the people who are available.

In order to simplify our calculations we choose the units for t_1 and t_2 so as to make $\tau_1 = \tau_2 = 1$. Since s_1 and s_2 are expressed in the same units as t_1 and t_2, this may also be interpreted by saying that our symbols s_1, s_2, $\bar{s}_1$, $\bar{s}_2$, t_1, t_2, $\bar{t}_1$, $\bar{t}_2$ and σ_1, σ_2 represent the ratios of each of these to the corresponding τ_i.

The essence of the process of income formation may now be reformulated by saying that an income scale brings about a choice by each individual with regard to his "job", resulting in a correspondence between s-sets and t-sets illustrated by (5.3) and (5.4), and that this correspondence will have to be such as to transform the t-distribution into an s-distribution identical with the given demand distribution. This identity is another expression for equality, in each compartment, of demand and supply. The procedure may be illustrated geometrically. Graph 1 shows the frequency distribution of t_1 and t_2, i.e. the supply side. On the frequency surface some curves of constant frequency densities f_1, f_2, f_3 have been drawn. Graph 2 shows the corresponding distribution of s_1 and s_2. Our income scale has to be one that will make the individuals around t_1^*, t_2^* choose a job around s_1^*, s_2^*, and so on for each point in the t_1-t_2-plane, in such a way that corresponding points in the s- and the t-plane have the same frequencies. This does not mean that the frequency densities—i.e. the distances of the points t_1^* t_2^* and s_1^* s_2^* to the horizontal plane—are equal, but that the product of this distance and the surface elements are equal, that is:

$$n\,(\overset{*}{t}_1\overset{*}{t}_2)\,d\overset{*}{t}_1\,d\overset{*}{t}_2 = m\,(\overset{*}{s}_1\overset{*}{s}_2)\,d\overset{*}{s}_1\,d\overset{*}{s}_2.$$

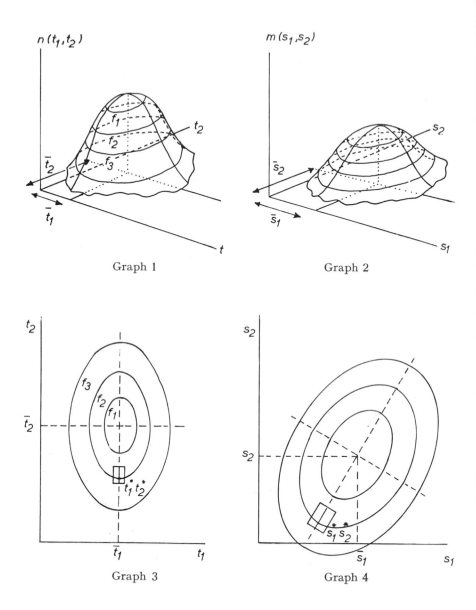

Graph 1

Graph 2

Graph 3

Graph 4

The surface elements have been represented by the small rectangles drawn in graphs 3 and 4, where the projections of the curves of constant density on the horizontal plane have been drawn. These are ellipses, with the axes parallel to the coordinate axes when there is no correlation between the attributes, and an arbitrary position of the axes when there is correlation. The case represented by the graphs is characterized by $r_t = 0$ and $r_s > 0$.

The t-surface has to be "deformed" so as to coincide with the s-surface, otherwise there will not be equilibrium in all compartments of the market.

The proces may now be shown algebraically. As is usual in mathematical problems of this type, we start by making an assumption about the shape of the function λ. We assume it to be of the form (5.5), where still the numerical values of the coefficients $\lambda_{00} \ldots \lambda_{02}$ are open. We try to find values for these coefficients which "do the job". If we are not able to find such values, our assumption (5.5) has to be abandoned. If it can be shown that there is only one solution, and our assumption appears to be a solution, then it will be the solution.

Trying, then, our solution (5.5), the transformation between t and s will be given by (5.6) and (5.7). Substituting these values for t_1 and t_2 in (6.2) must then yield a frequency distribution in s_1, s_2 identical with (6.1). Indicating by t_1' and t_2' the deviations of t_1 and t_2 from their averages:

$$(6.3) \qquad t_1' = t_1 - \bar{t}_1 \qquad t_2' = t_2 - \bar{t}_2$$

using similar symbols s_1' and s_2', and writing for the sake of simplicity,

$$(6.4) \qquad 1 - \omega_3' \lambda_{20} = x \qquad 1 - \omega_3'' \lambda_{02} = z$$

$$(6.5) \qquad \omega_3' \lambda_{11} = y \qquad \frac{\omega_3''}{\omega_3'} = \frac{\omega_1}{\omega_2} = a,$$

we get the transformation

$$(6.7) \qquad \begin{aligned} t_1' &= x s_1' - y s_2' \\ t_2' &= - a y s_1' + z s_2'. \end{aligned}$$

and the result of its application on $n(t_1, t_2)$:

$$-2(1-r_t^2) \times \text{ exponent of } n(t_1, t_2) = t_1'^2 + 2r_t t_1' t_2' + t_2'^2$$

$$= s_1'^2(x^2 - 2axyr_t + a^2y^2) + s_1' s_2'(-2xy + 2r_t xz + 2r_t ay^2 - 2ayz)$$

$$(6.8) \hspace{3cm} + s_2'^2 (y^2 - 2yzr_t + z^2).$$

This expression has to be identical to $-2(1-r_s^2) \times$ the exponent of $m(s_1, s_2)$ which, for simplicity's sake, we write as

$$(6.9) \hspace{3cm} \varrho_1^2 s_1'^2 + 2r_s \varrho_1 \varrho_2 s_1' s_2' + \varrho_2^2 s_2'^2$$

$$(6.10) \hspace{1cm} \text{where } \varrho_1 = \frac{1}{\sigma_1} \sqrt{\frac{1-r_t^2}{1-r_s^2}} \quad \text{and} \quad \varrho_2 = \frac{1}{\sigma_2} \sqrt{\frac{1-r_t^2}{1-r_s^2}}.$$

Our unknown coefficients x, y and z have to satisfy the conditions following from a comparison between (6.8) and (6.9):

$$(6.11) \hspace{1cm} x^2 + 2ar_t xy \hspace{2cm} + a^2 y^2 \hspace{2cm} = \varrho_1^2$$

$$(6.12) \hspace{1cm} -2 \hspace{0.5cm} xy - 2r_t xz - 2r_t ay^2 - 2ayz \hspace{1cm} = -2r_s \varrho_1 \varrho_2$$

$$(6.13) \hspace{3cm} y^2 + 2r_t yz + z^2 = \varrho_2^2.$$

In addition to these conditions to be satisfied by x, y and z, two other conditions will have to be satisfied by the coefficients λ_{10} and λ_{01}; these follow from applying (5.6) and (5.7) to the average values of $\bar{s}_1$ and $\bar{s}_2$. Such an application must yield, as its result, the average values of $\bar{t}_1$ and $\bar{t}_2$, since otherwise the exponent of $n(t_1, t_2)$ after transformation would show non-quadratic terms in s_1 and s_2 which are not present in the exponent of $m(s_1, s_2)$. Hence:

$$(6.14) \hspace{2cm} \bar{t}_1 = (1 - \omega_3' \lambda_{20}) \bar{s}_1 - \omega_3' \lambda_{11} \bar{s}_2 - \omega_3' \lambda_{10}.$$

$$6.15) \hspace{2cm} \bar{t}_2 = - \omega_3'' \lambda_{11} \bar{s}_1 + (1 - \omega_3'' \lambda_{02}) \bar{s}_2 - \omega_3'' \lambda_{01}.$$

Since, generally speaking, five unknowns can be solved from five equations, it appears that our assumption (5.5) yields a possible solution.

The solution may be undertaken in two stages, since the three unknowns x, y and z appear in (6.11)–(6.13) only and can therefore be solved first; (6.14) and (6.15) will then yield λ_{10} and λ_{01}. Apparently, λ_{00} is then still underdetermined; this coefficient only changes, by its variation, the general level of incomes, but not its distribution. This general level will follow from the condition that no more income can be paid out than has been produced. It may be said to be determined by the general level of productivity.

In order to understand the nature of our solution, we have to give it an explicit, instead of the implicit form we have before us.

For the sake of still further simplification we will now make the assumption that $r_t = 0$, *i.e.* that the attributes are chosen so as to show no correlation on the supply side. Since it is always possible, by a mathematical transformation of $n(t_1, t_2)$, to obtain this state of affairs, there is again no loss of generality.[11]

Equations (6.11)–(6.13) now reduce to:

$$\text{(6.16)} \qquad x^2 + a^2 y^2 \qquad\qquad = \varrho_1^2$$

$$\text{(6.17)} \qquad\qquad xy \quad + ayz \quad = r_s \varrho_1 \varrho_2$$

$$\text{(6.18)} \qquad\qquad\qquad y^2 \quad + z^2 = \varrho_2^2,$$

which it is not difficult to solve. Writing (6.17) in the form

$$\text{(6.19)} \qquad\qquad x + az = \frac{r_s \varrho_1 \varrho_2}{y}$$

and eliminating y between (6.16) and (6.18):

$$\text{(6.20)} \qquad\qquad x^2 - a^2 z^2 = \varrho_1^2 - a^2 \varrho_2^2$$

we derive from (6.19) and (6.20)

$$\text{(6.21)} \qquad\qquad x - az = \frac{\varrho_1^2 - a^2 \varrho_2^2}{r_s \varrho_1 \varrho_2} \, y.$$

Adding up (6.19) and (6.21) yields:

$$\text{(6.22)} \qquad\qquad 2x = \frac{\varrho_1^2 - a^2 \varrho_2^2}{r_s \varrho_1 \varrho_2} \, y + \frac{r_s \varrho_1 \varrho_2}{y}$$

This may be used to eliminate x from (6.16). Using capital letters to indicate squares, *i.e.*

---

[11] I owe this remark to Mr. J. A. HARTOG. In terms familiar to the statistician the procedure means that factor analysis is applied to the attributes so far used and a number of factors equal to the number of attributes is introduced in their place.

(6.23) $$Y = y^2; \quad P_1 = \varrho_1^2; \quad P_2 = \varrho_2^2; \quad A = a^2; \quad R_s = r_s^2,$$

we get for Y the equation:

(6.24) $$Y^2[(P_1 - AP_2)^2 + 4AR_sP_1P_2] - 2(P_1 + AP_2)R_sP_1P_2$$
$$+ R_s^2 P_1^2 P_2^2 = 0.$$

The solutions are:

(6.25) $$Y = \frac{R_s P_1 P_2}{P_1 + AP_2 \pm 2\sqrt{AP_1P_2(1-R_s)}}$$

or:

(6.26) $$y^2 = \frac{\omega_2^2 r_s^2}{\omega_1^2 \sigma_1^2 + \omega_2^2 \sigma_2^2 \pm 2\omega_1\omega_2\sigma_1\sigma_2\sqrt{1-r_s^2}} \frac{1}{1-r_s^2}$$

It follows that

(6.27) $$x^2 = \left[\frac{1}{\sigma_1^2} - \frac{\omega_1^2 r_s^2}{\omega_1^2 \sigma_1^2 + \omega_2^2 \sigma_2^2 \pm 2\omega_1\omega_2\sigma_1\sigma_2\sqrt{1-r_s^2}} \right] \frac{1}{1-r_s^2}$$

and

(6.28) $$z^2 = \left[\frac{1}{\sigma_2^2} - \frac{\omega_2^2 r_s^2}{\omega_1^2 \sigma_1^2 + \omega_2^2 \sigma_2^2 \pm 2\omega_1\omega_2\sigma_1\sigma_2\sqrt{1-r_s^2}} \right] \frac{1}{1-r_s^2}.$$

We thus have found a set of solutions to our problem.

7. INTERPRETATION OF RESULTS

These results may now be used for a reconnaissance and a verbal interpretation. We start by assuming that also on the demand side there is no correlation between the attributes, *i.e.* $r_s = 0$. Our solution then reduces to:

(7.1)
$$
\begin{cases}
x = 1 - \dfrac{\omega_3}{\omega_1} \lambda_{20} = \dfrac{1}{\sigma_1} & \text{or} \quad \lambda_{20} = \dfrac{\omega_1}{\omega_3}\left(1 - \dfrac{1}{\sigma_1}\right) \\[2ex]
y = \omega_3'\lambda_{11} \quad\; = 0 & \text{or} \quad \lambda_{11} = 0 \\[2ex]
z = 1 - \dfrac{\omega_3}{\omega_2} \lambda_{02} = \dfrac{1}{\sigma_2} & \text{or} \quad \lambda_{02} = \dfrac{\omega_2}{\omega_3}\left(1 - \dfrac{1}{\sigma_2}\right) \\[2ex]
& \qquad\;\; \lambda_{10} = \dfrac{\omega_1}{\omega_3}\left(\dfrac{\bar{s}_1}{\sigma_1} - \bar{t}_1\right) \\[2ex]
& \qquad\;\; \lambda_{01} = \dfrac{\omega_2}{\omega_3}\left(\dfrac{\bar{s}_2}{\sigma_2} - \bar{t}_2\right)
\end{cases}
$$

Remembering what was said about the units used, we may rewrite these formulae for the case where τ_1 and τ_2 are not chosen equal to 1:

$$(7.1')\begin{cases} \lambda_{20} = \dfrac{\omega_1}{\omega_3}\left(1 - \dfrac{\tau_1}{\sigma_1}\right) \\[2ex] \lambda_{02} = \dfrac{\omega_2}{\omega_3}\left(1 - \dfrac{\tau_2}{\sigma_2}\right) \\[2ex] \lambda_{10} = \dfrac{\omega_1}{\omega_3}\left(\dfrac{\bar{s}_1}{\sigma_1} - \dfrac{\bar{t}_1}{\tau_1}\right) \\[2ex] \lambda_{01} = \dfrac{\omega_2}{\omega_3}\left(\dfrac{\bar{s}_2}{\sigma_2} - \dfrac{\bar{t}_2}{\tau_2}\right) \end{cases}$$

The result is interesting enough. It appears that an income scale would be possible where log l is a quadratic function of the "degrees" s_1 and s_2 but without a "mixed term". This means that, generally, income has to depend on the degrees of the attributes of the contributions. The size of the coefficients, which are indicative of the extra remuneration wanted if a higher degree is required, depends on certain "tensions" again, namely, for the linear terms in (5.5), on the tensions between average required and average available degrees[11a]; and for the quadratic terms on the tensions between the dispersions of the required and the available degrees. If the dispersion in the required degrees is larger than that in the degrees available, there will be a positive quadratic term, meaning that successive equal increases in required degrees will have to be remunerated by increasing additional percentage income increases. If the dispersion in the required degrees is smaller than that in the degrees available, successive equal increases in required degrees can be remunerated with decreasing additional percentage income increases. These scales do not depend on the requirements made for the other degree.

Such interdependence will, however, have to be introduced as soon as $r_s \neq 0$. We may therefore say that the "mixed term" $\lambda_{11}s_1s_2$ is necessary because of possible correlation between the required degrees if such correlation is not available on the supply side. It is, in addition, noteworthy that in this case the solutions are no longer unique but that there are two sets of solutions, corresponding to the + and the — signs in our formulae (6.26), (6.27) and (6.28).

The results just obtained may be given a still further interpretation.

[11a] Both expressed in terms of their own dispersion.

We may ask to what extent or under what circumstances income distribution is equivalent to paying a certain price for each of the attributes used to classify jobs and abilities. At least three cases may be distinguished. In order to speak of a price of the attributes, we must have the situation where everybody's income is the sum total of, for each attribute, the product of quantity and price. Quantity, here, stands for the corresponding degree, and this situation would exist only if our income scale were linear. In this strictest sense we cannot therefore speak of the existence of a price, *i.e.* one price, for each attribute. We may, however, somewhat widen our concept of price and—as a second case—accept a different price for larger and for smaller "quantities". Our quadratic income scale without the mixed term $\lambda_{11}s_1s_2$ represents such a situation. Income may still be considered as the total of two amounts, one for the attribute 1 and one for the attribute 2; but each amount is not proportional any longer to the "quantity" s of the attribute. Finally, in the third case to be considered, there is our income scale with a mixed term; in this case one cannot speak at all of a price of an attribute: it not only depends on the quantity of the attribute considered, but also on the quantity of other attributes.

Finally, we may come back to the basic question of our essay, namely, whether the illustrative results obtained imply any hope of arriving at an explanation of the observed income distribution. There would indeed seem to be such a hope, since the income scale found will, under certain circumstances, lead to a logarithmic normal distribution of incomes. This applies when the quadratic terms in our scale vanish, *i.e.* when the dispersions in degrees required do not differ from those in degrees available. In that case, even with a large number of attributes, the logarithm of income can be represented as the sum total of a number of terms, each normally distributed. Such a sum is itself normally distributed and hence the frequency formula defended by Van der Wijk and by Gibrat would result. When quadratic terms appear, the distribution will be distorted, but the main shape need not be very much affected. Again this calls for empirical studies.

8. SOME GENERALIZATIONS

It is possible to remove some of our over-simplifying assumptions and so to generalize our model. First, a stochastic element may be introduced which, according to the observations published by the U.S. Employment Services,[12] plays a very real role. It may be assumed that an individual bases his occupation on assumed values of his attributes rather than on his real attributes. This element of deviation between the supposed values of the t_i and the real values may be brought into our model by the introduction of variables v_i (with means $\bar{v}_i$ and standard deviations φ_i) that have to be added to the supposed value of t_i in order to arrive at the real value u_i. The process of income formation will be based on the supposed values and nothing needs to be changed in the preceding formulae. In order, however, to establish the statistical relations between the real values u_i of t_i and s_i we will have to add the variable v_i:

$$(8.1) \qquad\qquad u_i = t_i + v_i.$$

This will account for a stochastic relation between u_i and s_i instead of a functional relation.

Next we will *remove our assumption that demand for productive contributions is inelastic.* Instead we will now assume that the distribution of demand will change if a change in relative remunerations occurs. What will be the consequences of a flatter income scale, that is, a decrease in the income differentials between more and less qualified contributions? Evidently, it will become more advantageous for the organizers of production to employ relatively more qualified and relatively less unqualified "workers". The demand distribution, that is, will shift away from unqualified towards more qualified occupations. The averages $\bar{s}_i$ will increase with decreasing values of the λ's. There may also be a concentration on qualified "workers", meaning that the standard deviations σ_i diminish. Both phenomena happen not only because the same products will now be produced with relatively more qualified contributors, but also because the demand for products will shift towards and concentrate upon quality products which can now be obtained at relatively more attractive prices. An interesting question is whether, with complete equality in incomes, the demand for relatively unqualified workers will completely vanish, meaning that the standard deviations σ_i would tend to zero. This is probably not the case

---

[12] U.S. Employment Services, *op. cit.*

since there is also a considerable degree of complementarity between more and less qualified work. There will always be a need for a certain quantity of relatively simple jobs too.

From these considerations we deduce that the relation between the two distributions may be a simple one or it may be more complicated. The simplest case would be that σ_i would be independent of the parameters λ of the income scale, while

$$(8.2) \qquad \bar{s}_1 = \bar{s}_{10} - \bar{s}_{11}\lambda_{10}$$

$$(8.3) \qquad \bar{s}_2 = \bar{s}_{20} - \bar{s}_{21}\lambda_{01}.$$

Thanks to the structure of our solution this would only affect the formulae for λ_{10} and λ_{01}, which would now become:

$$(8.4) \qquad \lambda_{10} = \frac{\omega_1(\bar{s}_{10} - \bar{l}_1\sigma_1)}{\omega_3\sigma_1 + \omega_1\bar{s}_{11}}$$

and

$$(8.5) \qquad \lambda_{01} = \frac{\omega_2(\bar{s}_{20} - \bar{l}_2\sigma_2)}{\omega_3\sigma_2 + \omega_2\bar{s}_{21}}.$$

Since we must assume that $\bar{s}_{11} > 0$ and $\bar{s}_{21} > 0$, the new values will be lower than the previous ones, illustrating that a certain elasticity of demand facilitates the adaptation of supply to demand.

Very probably, however, also the σ_i will be affected by the income scale and, in addition, not only λ_{10} and λ_{01} but the other λ's as well will exert some influence. In a general way we therefore assume that

$$(8.6) \qquad \sigma_1 = \sigma_{10} + \sigma_{11}\lambda_{10} + \sigma_{12}\lambda_{01} + \sigma'_{13}\lambda_{20} + \sigma'_{14}\lambda_{02}$$

$$= \sigma_{100} - \sigma_{13}x - \sigma_{14}z,$$

where

$$(8.7) \qquad \sigma_{100} = \sigma_{10} + \sigma_{11}\lambda_{10} + \sigma_{12}\lambda_{01} + \frac{\sigma'_{13}}{\omega'_3} + \frac{\sigma'_{14}}{\omega''_3}$$

and that similar formulae for σ_2 apply.

Our formulae become much more complicated and a general solution will not be attempted. For the case where $r_s = 0$ the solution may be undertaken in two stages; in our formulae (7.1) we may substitute (8.6):

$$(8.8) \qquad x = \frac{1}{\sigma_{100} - \sigma_{13}x - \sigma_{14}z}; \quad z = \frac{1}{\sigma_{200} - \sigma_{23}x - \sigma_{24}z},$$

from which x and z may be solved. It may be observed that the additional relations of the type (8.6) do not invalidate equations (6.11) to
(6.13) inclusive and that hence, for $r_s = 0$, it remains true that $x = 1/\sigma_1$
and $z = 1/\sigma_2$, or that for λ_{20} and λ_{02} to be zero $\sigma_1 = \sigma_2 = 1$.

9. DEVELOPMENT OF INCOME DISTRIBUTION AND POSSIBILITIES TO INFLUENCE IT

The theory so far presented is static. It assumes the two distributions
m and n to be given. They need not, however, be constant. Their coefficients may show movements; these movements may be exogenous or
endogenous. They may also be subject to political influence or they
may be independent from such influence. Each of these cases deserves
some further illustration.

Exogenous movements may be movements in the physical and
psychological conditions of the population and its technical development. The latter will continually lead to higher demands on the skill
of at least the supervising categories of jobs; and all types of education
will try to catch up with these demands or even to surpass them.

Endogenous movements in our context are movements caused by
the situation with regard to income distribution of the immediate past.
Perhaps the best example may be the role of wealth in income distribution. To-day's incomes will change to-morrow's wealth distribution and
to-morrow's wealth distribution will be partly responsible for to-morrow's income distribution. Interesting attempts have been made to
schematize this inderdependence and to single out the influence exerted
on income distribution by inheritance.[13] The complete mechanism of
income distribution and its development would have to be a combination of the influences of wealth and of personal abilities.

The question of whether, by a conscious policy, we can influence
income distribution without disrupting equilibrium in the various compartments of our market is of particular importance in the present
phase of social development. That question is the key to further social
reform which, in its turn, is the only way of eliminating the all-impor-
tant "social problem". Our illustrative formulae suggest that a de-

---

[13] A. W. HAMMING, unpubl. calculations on the effect of inheritance on the
distribution of wealth.

crease of inequality will be dependent on the possibilities of reducing the "tensions" between required and available attributes. For the purpose of policy design, a subdivision of attributes into attributes that can or that cannot "easily" be changed recommends itself. "Easy" changes may be either cheap or quick or both; difficult changes are those requiring much energy and time. The process of education itself shows the same components. The interesting corollary of our model is that equality of incomes does not require equality of capacities of all individuals but only the correspondence of the distribution of capacities to the distribution required.[14]

In our simplest model, considered in sections 6 and 7, this means τ_1 and τ_2 would have to be adapted to the given values of σ_1 and σ_2. In the more general model discussed in section 8, σ_1 and σ_2 are not given, but are themselves dependent on the distribution of incomes; any move towards a more equal distribution will reduce their values. The τ's have then to be adapted to the reduced values of the σ's; it may of course prove impossible for the τ's to adapt themselves completely. Again, the last word will have to come from empirical studies on both the demand and the supply side of the market.

10. THE NEED FOR CO-ORDINATION OF STATISTICAL DATA IN THE FIELDS CONCERNED

In the preceding discussion the paucity of statistical information relating to the phenomena discussed has been repeatedly stressed. It is this lack of relevant information which prevented us from offering a theory tested as to its degree of realism. This made the theory only illustrative of possible explanations and at the same time obliges us to go first to the facts. Now, the facts have been investigated in many ways and by a large number of research workers. We already referred to job evaluation and to school and army tests. What is wanted foremost, is a co-ordinated survey of our scattered knowledge; and in the second place, a filling up of the most evident lacunae. Formulated in an over-simplified way, what we want is job evaluation for the economy as a whole, indicating frequencies at the same time; and a test

---

[14] For a further elaboration of these suggestions *cf.* JAN TINBERGEN, *Economic Policy: Principles and Design*, Amsterdam, 1956, section 6.4.

of the population along the same lines. Finally, we want systematic data, again expressed in the same concepts, about the costs, in energy and time, and results of education. It is such a co-ordinated program of research which the Central Planning Bureau of the Netherlands, with the collaboration of a group of experts in these fields, is going to undertake.

THE THEORY OF THE OPTIMUM REGIME*

CONTENTS

---

* Although the precise influence exerted on him by the various authors on welfare economics cannot be easily traced, the author wants to express his gratitude to William J. Baumol, Abram Bergson, Gérard Debreu, J. Marcus Fleming, Ragnar Frisch, J. de Villiers Graaff, Harold Hotelling, Nicholas Kaldor, Tjalling C. Koopmans, Oskar Lange, Abba P. Lerner, James E. Meade, Nancy Ruggles, Pàul A. Samuelson, Tibor de Scitovsky and Robert H. Strotz for the contributions they made to his understanding, if any, of the subject matter.

1. INTRODUCTORY

This article attempts to summarize what seems to be the position of a large number of western economists on the question of the "best" economic regime. It has been written with a double purpose. On the one hand it seemed worth while to reformulate a set of doctrines that have emerged from various discussions in order to see where we stand and to make up our minds where further research is needed. On the other hand it seemed necessary that economists clarify, to a larger public, their views on a topic which plays a predominant role in the world's largest controversy to-day; I mean the one between communist and non-communist opinion. Although this controversy, according to most western citizens, is primarily about political organization—democracy *versus* dictatorship—most communists put the emphasis in a different place. Moreover, quite a few westerners seem to see a close correspondence between the question of political regime and the one of economic regime. I am now referring to those rightist citizens who identify dictatorship with "socialism" and democracy with "capitalism" and in addition consider "socialism" and "capitalism" as two opposed economic systems without any intermediate forms. The question of the economic regime therefore plays an important role in the controversy between communists and non-communists.

This question is a subject on which many non-economists have very definite opinions and in fact the larger part of the discussion about it is being carried on by non-economists. The economist is inclined to refer to these discussions—in newspapers, pamphlets, parliamentary and international gatherings—as "popular" discussions. These popular discussions are often black-and-white in nature and are often conducted by people who are accustomed to think that they are right in some absolute sense and their opponents wrong. Their opinions tend to be extreme. They seem to overlook the important fact that economic regimes of whatever kind have, to a considerable degree, common tasks and objectives. They also often seem to overlook the existence of a large number of intermediate and mixed types of economic systems and policies and the fact that actual economic regimes and policies are not fixed, but rather continuously changing; that, in other words, economic reality is less black or white than are the systems discussed. It may well be that the best economic regime is somewhere in between and much less difficult to determine than the optimum political structure.

In the current political situation there are considerable dangers involved in this attitude of popular opinion. In a world which is already rapidly becoming less stable, a further, and partly unjustified, concentration of political views around two opposite poles may hasten the process towards self-annihilation already set in motion by political and military developments. There is a desperate need for stabilizing forces and it is the author's conviction that the economist's "message" is just such a stabilizing force, however modest. It is for this reason that a wider public should be aware of the existence of a large number of economists who do not share the popular black-white opinions with regard to the economic order.

Against this background it seems useful indeed to relate a number of concepts and statements, mostly from the realm of "welfare economics" and to reformulate them so as to represent what could be called a "general theory of the optimum regime". The objectives of such a general theory are:

(i) to present a realistic picture of the main decisions that have to be taken in order to choose a regime;

(ii) to show the relationships between these decisions and some of the fundamental data of a society;

(iii) to appraise a number of well-known popular arguments and to eliminate some widespread misunderstandings;

(iv) thereby to offer a basis for discussion between the representatives of different regimes;

(v) to make it clear that there are some formidable unsolved problems more worthy of discussion than a number of more popular but futile arguments, and finally

(vi) to present a program for further basic research likely to be more valuable than much current short-term research.

The contents of this article present, of course, only an outline.

Although the author believes that he summarizes what seems to be the position of a large number of western economists, he is well aware that on certain points he is deviating from the usual approach. This is true particularly for section 2.2. However, the specific attitude taken there toward the comparability of individual welfare levels does not affect the main conclusions, but gives a more definite interpretation to some vague and multi-dimensional concepts which are quite commonly used.

2. STRUCTURE OF THE PROBLEM

2.1. CONCEPT, DATA AND UNKNOWNS

For our purpose we may say that an economy is characterized by its *actors*[1] and by the *actions* of these actors. The actors have to be subdivided into *natural* and *institutional* actors. Natural actors are the consuming and the producing units which approximately may be identified with families and enterprises, respectively. Institutional actors are all those which at first sight do not appear to be necessary for the process of production, distribution and consumption; *e.g.* the state, local authorities, social insurance agencies, cartels, trade unions *etc.* By an economy's *regime* we will understand its order or its institutions and these terms may cover two things. On the one hand they indicate certain procedures or a certain behaviour, on the other hand certain organizations; for these latter we will stick to our term institutional actors. The procedures and behaviour not only refer, moreover, to the institutional actors but also to the natural actors. An institution of a certain regime may be the income tax. The corresponding organization or institutional actor is the tax authority; but the behaviour implied not only covers the actions of this authority but clearly also the corresponding actions of the taxpayers. It must be stressed that an economy is defined only when its institutions are specified; this seems to be overlooked by quite a few welfare economists.[2]

The *actions* of the actors, or the *economic process*, may also be subdivided into natural actions, such as production, exchange and con-

---

[1] I prefer the word actor rather than transactor, although the two terms would seem to be synonymous.

[2] This applies particularly to the authors adhering to the compensation principle.

sumption and institutional actions such as government measures, paying taxes, monopoly pricing etc.

The problem of the *optimum regime* can now be stated by a specification of its data and its unknowns. As *data* we consider a number of physical and psychological characteristics (or coefficients) of the society considered and of possible institutions. Physical data are *e.g.* the characteristics of the production processes available, such as production functions (implying input-output relations of any type). Psychological data are the preferences of the consuming units, usually expressed in terms of their utility functions. We will, in addition, consider as given the social utility or welfare function by which the society's rulers are guided. The origin of such a social welfare function will be discussed because it is exactly at this point that our procedure deviates from the one usually followed. Among the data we list also the characteristics of a number of possible institutions. Such characteristics include their method of operation—a qualitative datum implying the instruments they use—and the "costs" their operation entails. Such costs may be material and psychological costs (aversion). Instruments may be such things as taxes, subsidies, wage and price systems *etc.*; like material costs they are of a quantitative nature. However their quantitative aspects (extent, level *etc.*) are not among the data, but among the unknowns.

The *unknowns* of the problem of the optimum regime are twofold. First, the institutions of the regime are unknown and secondly, the quantitative aspects (or numerical values) of the instruments involved are unknown. Both have to be chosen in such a way as to maximize the social welfare function. It is necessary to emphasize that, as a consequence, the qualitative and the quantitative unknowns are closely interrelated and that as a rule, a solution cannot be obtained without due regard to the quantitative aspects of the problem.

2.2. THE COMPONENTS AND SHAPE OF THE SOCIAL WELFARE FUNCTION

The problem of the optimum regime cannot be given a clear meaning unless we define the social welfare function. As economists know, this involves some theoretical difficulties of which the practical politician is only partly aware. In formulating short-run policy these difficulties can often be avoided by reasonable compromises between the opposed interests. For long-term policy and even more for the choice of an economic order they cannot be disregarded since the ultimate aims of economic activity are involved. The problems alluded to are those of the relationship between individual and social welfare.

Not so much controversy will exist with regard to the list of *components* or *elements* entering into welfare, both individual and social. It will be generally accepted that welfare depends on the means to satisfy needs and these needs may be subdivided in the following way:

(1) individual needs: (a) material   ((i) general level
                            [goods]   ((ii) distribution over time
                        (b) non-material [education, culture]

(2) social needs: (a) material [distribution between individuals
                                     and groups]
                        (b) non-material [justice, freedom]

Some of the most important examples of the means to satisfy the various needs have been indicated in the square brackets. Accordingly the choice of the economic order will be based on what each conceivable order has to offer with regard to supplying the population with goods, both their general level and their distribution over time and among individuals, with regard to education, to the "equality of chances", to human relations and to the numerous types and intensities of freedom and so on. Since the necessary counterpart for the satisfaction of needs is productive effort, the disutility of making such efforts is also part of welfare components.

More theoretical difficulties—and practical controversies—are encountered when these various components must be given their relative weights. These weights have to be derived in one way or another from individual preferences, but these preferences are not identical for all individuals. Hence we will have to consider, first, these individual preferences and, secondly, how diverging preferences can be reconciled. In order not to complicate the argument unnecessarily, we will, in our examples, restrict ourselves to two components, *i.e.* the quantity of goods consumed and the quantity of effort made (both the general level and the distribution among individuals). However we will also mention some of the complications due to other components.

Individual preferences are usually described with the aid of *utility functions*, which express the level ω_i of utility experienced by an individual i as a function of the quantity of goods consumed x_i and the quantity of productive effort made a_i; both per unit of time:

$$(2.21) \qquad\qquad \omega_i = \omega_i(x_i, a_i)$$

All economists accept the principle that indifference curves corresponding with constant values of ω_i can be observed, but it should be admitted immediately that actual observations are primitive and only partial. Lack of adequate measures for the various types of productive effort is the main reason.[3]

Theoretical difficulties arise in two areas: *measurability* and *interpersonal comparability* of utility. Most economists deny that utility can be measured and that comparisons between individuals can be made without the introduction of some ethical principle. It will be clear that, if utility could be measured, interpersonal comparisons would also be possible. The author does not want to exclude this possibility for the future. Comparability, however, does not require measurement. One may get by with the *explicit introduction of ethical principles*. The author prefers to do so immediately instead of trying to build up welfare economics without resorting to such principles.

Upon inspection of possible alternatives, the most appropriate ethical principle seems to be the principle of *"basic equality of man"*, pronounced by philosophers of very different background, although usually in a rather vague way. It will be applied in two ways in this essay. In a general way it will be assumed that individuals have *identical utility functions* into which *observable parameters* enter only as sources of differences between individuals. Or, in other words, differences are introduced only to the extent that we can observe them. More specifically whenever this can help us to define our choice, we will introduce, a *"principle of least differences"*, implying that where the nature of our problem allows us some latitude in our choice of utility functions, we will choose functions which are of the same shape

---

[3] The few observations available refer to indifference maps between the quantities of some types of goods rather than to maps between x_i and a_i. This one-sided interest for goods as distinct from productive effort is typical of economic science.

and have the smallest possible differences between coefficients but which are still compatible with our observations.

Apart from these two ways of applying the philosophy of basic equality we will use another device that will be of some help. We shall restrict ourselves to such variables in the utility function that we think are relevant to the problems to be treated. This applies first of all to the number of commodities to be included. This number we will some-times restrict to as little as one even, when differences of taste for different goods seem to be irrelevant. In any society with free consumer choice, for example, there is a good deal of irrelevance in this respect, since everybody can spend his income in the way he prefers. Much more relevant for questions of income distribution are the variables defining the nature of the productive effort supplied by the individuals considered.[4]

A simple illustration of the application of our ethical principle seems in order. As before, let us choose two variables only, consumption x_i and the quantity of effort supplied a_i.

Our *first example* illustrates the general application. First we assume identical utility functions for all individuals. These functions are based on biological and psychological assumptions, and contain parameters with a well-defined meaning, such as calorie intake to remain fit or the effort a man is able to make under specified conditions. Examples will be given later (*cf.* this section, below).[5]

In a *second illustration* we will not specify the observable parameters of the utility function but simply assume that all coefficients occurring in the function may be different for different individuals. Writing the function as

$$\omega_i = \omega_i^{10} x_i + \omega_i^{01} a_i + \omega_i^{20} x_i^2 + \omega_i^{11} x_i a_i + \omega_i^{02} a_i^2$$

as a first approximation, where the ω_i with superscripts are coefficients, we can determine from observed values of x_i, a_i on various indifference curves the values of as many coefficients as we think it proper to introduce. Since the equations from which these values of the coefficients have to be determined are essentially of the form

$$(2.22) \qquad \omega_i^{10} x_i' + \omega_i^{01} a_i' + \ldots = \omega_i^{10} x_i'' + \omega_i^{01} x_i'' \ldots$$

(where x_i', a_i' and x_i'', a_i' are two observed points on the same indifference

---

[4] *Cf.* J. TINBERGEN, "On the Theory of Income Distribution", *Weltw. Archiv* 77 (1956) p. 10.

[5] An example will also be found in J. TINBERGEN, *loc. cit.*

curve), the ω_i-coefficients are indeterminate: any set of values satisfying the observations can be replaced by a proportional set. This is a typical degree of freedom in the choice of a utility function. The corresponding arbitrariness in the comparison between two individuals can be removed by our principle of least differences. In order to avoid another element of arbitrariness, represented by the choice of units of x_i and a_i, our principle may be stated in relative terms, *i.e.* that the sum total of the squares of the *relative* deviations in the coefficients between the individuals considered should be a minimum.

Turning now to the *social welfare function* Ω, there seem to be two main ways to estimate it which are worthwhile to distinguish; one is to construct Ω from some average preferences to be derived from the study of individual ω_i's, the other to use the ω_i themselves as the elements of Ω. This latter procedure is usually adhered to and has considerable advantages. The simplest possible form for Ω would then seem to be:

$$(2.23) \qquad\qquad \Omega = \Sigma\omega_i.$$

This form has been often mentioned by way of illustration. It can only be given a precise meaning if either (i) all ω_i are identical, or (ii) ω_i is measurable or (iii) some rule is made for choosing among the variety of ω_i existing in the case of non-measurability. Since (i) is contrary to observation and (ii) is at best a future possibility, only (iii) remains. Our principle of least differences seems to be an appropriate rule.

It should be kept in mind, however, that (2.23) is not the only possible shape of Ω. It may be said to represent—with the reservations implied by our rule—the total "happiness" in the society studied and also (when divided by the number of individuals) the average happiness. No separate weight is given, in this Ω, to the *distribution of utility* among individuals. Remarkably enough, already (2.23) leads to rather "equalitarian" consequences with regard to the optimum state of affairs. It will be clear that an introduction of the distribution of utility may well reinforce such consequences. Our conclusions with regard to this subject therefore tend to be understated.

Our argument will be illustrated by some examples. In them we have used particular cases of ω_i in that we have assumed that:

(2.24) $$\omega_i = \omega(x_i, \sigma_i) + \varphi(a_i, \tau_i).$$

This means that (i) ω_i is an additive function of x_i and a_i respectively and that (ii) differences between individuals can be represented by two parameters, one (σ_i) referring to the taste for goods and the other (τ_i) to the appraisal of effort. We have been even more specific in considering two special cases of (2.24), to be called *parabolic* and *hyperbolic* utilities. Parabolic utility functions will be represented by:

(2.25) (P) $$\omega_i = \sigma_i \frac{x_i^{1-\omega}}{1-\omega} - \tau_i \frac{a_i^{\varphi+1}}{\varphi+1}$$

where now ω and φ are numbers.

Hyperbolic utility functions will be represented by

(2.26) (H) $$\omega_i = -\frac{1}{x_i - x^0} - \frac{1}{a_i^0 - a_i}$$

The meaning of the various parameters is:

In example (P) the marginal utility of goods is $\sigma_i x_i^{-\omega}$; high values of σ_i represent ascetic individuals, low values materialistic ones, while $-\omega$ is the elasticity of marginal utility with regard to the quantity of goods consumed; similarly, high values of τ_i represent weak, low values strong people and φ is the elasticity of marginal disutility of effort with regard to the "quantity" of effort. It will be understood that τ_i/σ_i only is measurable and not σ_i and τ_i separately.

In example (H) one might conceive of x^0 as the subsistence minimum (assumed equal for all individuals concerned) and a_i^0 as the maximum effort the individual is able to supply.

2.3. INSTITUTIONS, INSTRUMENTS AND COSTS

In this section a description will be given of the most important institutions that seem to determine present-day societies of various types and between which a choice must be made or whose size has to be chosen in order to define an economic order. Such a description is necessary if our approach is to be realistic; it is also necessary for the analytical reasons set out in section 2.1. Our restriction of the discussion to the most important institutions is based on the desire to deal with only the main features of the problem of the optimum regime.

The following institutions will be discussed:

I. Public authorities, including possible public enterprises.

 II. Lower authorities.

III. Private enterprises.

IV. Markets.

 V. Social Insurance Institutions.

VI. Production Councils.

Some of these institutions are, partly at least, competing with others; thus, public authorities may take the place of private enterprises and *vice versa*; public authorities thought of as one centralized agency may take the place of lower authorities and *vice versa*; they may also take over the role of markets. Social Insurance Institutions as well as Production Councils may take over part of the activities of private enterprises etc. It might have been possible to choose different and more abstract institutions in order to arrive at a more symmetrical discussion of alternatives, but it seems preferable to stick to concrete institutions known from practical discussions. In more abstract terms, a choice has to be made as to:

 (i) the degree of public ownership and the tax system;

 (ii) the degree of (de)centralization both in administration and

 (iii) in production;

 (iv) exchange systems and their degree of (de)centralization;

 (v) the insurance system and its degree of (de)centralization;

(vi) types of social control.

For simplicity's sake we have omitted from our list a number of important institutions about which there seems to be less controversy in to-day's world, *e.g.* trade unions and schools. In a more general treatment of our problem they should, of course, be included.

Each institution is characterized by a certain number of instruments and by certain costs their activities imply. The instruments of public authorities are manifold; those of other institutions are less numerous. They will be briefly listed in the subsequent sections. In a way it may be said that public authorities are a bundle of (partial) institutions; we already mentioned the (income) tax authorities as a possible example of such a partial institution. As already stated, the costs of a certain institution do not only imply the material costs but also certain psychological costs. The latter exist not only when there is an aversion against the operations of the institution (say, rationing), but also when the probability of conflicts and hence friction is large. That may be the case when the instruments used are not clearly defined. Costs also occur when the efficiency of management is impeded as a consequence of the rules under which, say, a public enterprise operates.

2.4. Description of Institutions and Their Main Instruments

2.41. *Public Authorities*

The institution of public authorities is characterized, first of all, by the elements of authority, *i.e.* the capacity to impose, in the name of the community, certain patterns of conduct. This power can be used to establish law, order and security, to inform and to educate, to regulate certain economic activities, to protect the weak or the short-sighted and to levy taxes. Next, public authorities have the particular capacity to diverge, in their actions, from the profit principle and to base their decisions on the general interest. In doing so they can even operate a number of their units at a deficit. On the "cost" side it should be added that the efficiency of public units may be less than the efficiency of privately operated units, depending on their organization.

As already stated, public authorities represent a complicated set of institutions that may be subdivided into four main groups:

1 Financial institutions: (a) spending authorities
                                   (b) tax authorities
2 Productive institutions: (a) services, producing law and order, security, information and regulation;
                                   (b) enterprises, producing goods and services for sale.

Among the instruments of these sub-institutions the following stand out:

1a Criteria for subsidies, expenditures on investment;
1b Rates of various types of taxes;
2a Rules of regulation in regulated markets, information about development targets;
2b Prices and production of public enterprises, system of selection of students.

2.42. *Lower Authorities*

Public authorities are not a single centralized body, as is so often suggested by the phrase "the state". In reality they are a multitude of units, each of which has at least some autonomy. In each country there are the ministries, their directorates *etc.*; there are provinces and municipalities or whatever other names they have; there are enterprises and agencies for special purposes. And, in addition to those which exist in individual countries, there are now coming into being supra-national authorities.

Some of the instruments of economic policy handled by the authorities are handled in a centralized way, *i.e.* by one decision at the centre (*e.g.* federal tax rates); others are handled in a more or less decentralized way (discount rates of reserve banks in the United States, electricity rates in many countries, local taxes *etc.*).

2.43. *Private Enterprises*

This institution is characterized by the direct link between effort and income. The smaller the enterprise, the more direct is the relationship. The owner of a private enterprise must behave more or less according to the profit principle, *i.e.* to strive for maximum profit, although these profits should be interpreted in a wide sense. As a consequence of his status he has the possibility to invest, to exert power and to hand over part of his accumulated assets to his children.

The private enterprise not only stands at variance with public enterprises but, in another context, also with cartels, trusts or corporations, which represent, in the field of private activity, the more centralized forms.

The main instruments of the private enterprise are the volume of its production and inputs, and its investments. Under certain conditions their prices also are instruments at their command.

2.44. *Markets*

Markets as an institution may be said to be characterized by the virtual absence of an institutional actor. They represent, in their idealized form, the most decentralized form of exchange of products and services. Yet certain types of markets may need some actor as is illustrated by the auction system. In modern times, due to tendencies towards monopolistic competition, free competition may even have to be enforced by a fairly elaborate acting agency (*e.g.* the High Authority of the European Coal and Steel Community or the State Mediators in charge of the Dutch wage policy). The more a market tends towards monopolism, the more reason there is to speak of the market as an actor, namely, the sales organization trying to maintain monopoly.

In the case of a "regulated" market the apparatus necessary for its operation becomes even larger. It may then involve a system of price regulation and even of rationing. The most regulated form of marketing may be one based on discrimination, such as *e.g.* a system of multiple exchange rates, or the supply of cheap meals to factory workers. Here there is a substantial actor, implying the presence of fairly high costs.

The most important instrument of a market is its rate system. The uniform flat rate is by no means the only conceivable system as is illustrated by electricity rates, by season tickets *etc.*

2.45. *Social Insurance Institutions*

These might have been considered part of public authorities, but because of their autonomous status they have been singled out. As producers of social security they play a very important role in present-day life. They are authorized to collect contributions and to pay out benefits. Their costs are not merely their visible costs of administration; their existence exerts a double psychological influence on all workers. On the one hand, the feeling of security probably acts in a positive way to produce loyalty to the regime; on the other hand, this same feeling may well reduce productivity.

The main instruments of social insurance institutions are their contribution and benefit rates.

2.46. *Production Councils*

This name has been chosen to indicate any form of co-determination of workers or workers' representatives in the economic process. The common feature of these institutions is that they satisfy an important

psychological need. It is difficult to assess their influence. Councils
may be bipartite, when workers and entrepreneurs are represented,
or tripartite, when public authorities are also represented. They may
exist at various levels, *i.e.* at the enterprise, the industry and the
national level. Their competence may be different and may range from
advising on labour matters as a minimum to full responsability for the
broad lines of production and income distribution.

3. MODELS OF THE PROCESS OF PRODUCTION AND DISTRIBUTION

1. TYPES OF VARIABLES AND RELATIONS INCLUDED

The problem of the optimum regime in its general form is extremely
complicated. It not only covers almost everything in the field of economics but in addition a considerable number of aspects of a more
general sociological nature. The contribution economic thinking can
make to its solution should not be overestimated. Whatever contribution can be made should be based on clear and explicit *specifications
of the problem*, that is, on well-defined models of the process of production and distribution. Clarity can be obtained, as a rule, only at the
cost of some loss of generality, perhaps even a considerable loss of
generality. For various reasons the traditional method of decreasing
abstraction may be useful. In this chapter some models will be presented which, in the author's opinion, give some rigour to the statements to be made later.

In general, models must be defined by first listing the variables
included and secondly, the relationships assumed. These latter have
to bear on the given characteristics of production and distribution
anyhow and possibly on the characteristics of such institutions as are
considered given.

The two main groups of *variables* are those relating to quantities of
goods produced and consumed and to "quantities" of effort made.
The latter quantities will be partly in the nature of intensities, partly
in the nature of "extensities", such as the number of hours worked.
The number of variables in each category depends on the number of
types distinguished and on the number of persons and of producing
units. Thus, for each commodity, the quantities produced in each
establishment and the quantities consumed by each person (or family)

are among our variables. Indicating individuals by a lower index i, the type of good by a superscript j behind and the enterprise by a lower index h in front of the main symbol x for quantities of goods, we have the following variables:

x_i^j quantity of good j consumed by individual i;

$_hx^j$ quantity of good j produced in establishment h;

In a simple approach we may use the variable a to indicate the quantity of labour supplied without specifying between types of labour and let

a_i mean the quantity supplied by individual i;

$_ha^j$ the quantity used in establishment h for the production of commodity j.

A somewhat more realistic approach may be made with the aid of the same variables on the effort side but assuming differences in productivity.

A still better approach would seem to be one where types of effort are described by a multidimensional vector indicating the "scores" of each type in a number of criteria.[6]

The *relationships* are, first of all, the *technical relations* characterizing production. In our models we will assume that the quantities $_hx^j$ produced of good j in enterprise h are a function $_h\xi^j$ of the quantities of labour applied. Without differentiation between types of labour this relation is:

$$(3.11) \qquad\qquad _hx^j = {}_h\xi^j({}_ha^j).$$

Differentiating between the labour supplied by various individuals we may generalize this into:

$$(3.12) \qquad\qquad \xi(\pi_1 a_1 + \pi_2 a_2 + \ldots),$$

where a_i represents the quantity of labour of individual i and π_i a productivity coefficient.

The function ξ may take various shapes and either show constant, or variable returns.

In addition to the production relations there will be relations governing the *distribution* of the goods produced and the effort applied

---

[6] J. TINBERGEN, *loc. cit.*

between the individuals composing the economy. As long as no particular institutions are assumed to exist the only relations to be taken account of will be *balance equations* expressing equality of total demand and total supply.

3.2. Two-Person Models (2P and 2H)

In order to illustrate some of the basic problems it is convenient to use models containing only two persons, where social and personal differences will be represented by a difference in a parameter (*cf.* section 2.2) between the two persons only. The parameters entering into the utility functions are σ_i and τ_i in the case of parabolic and x^0 and a_i^0 in the case of hyperbolic functions. The corresponding models will be indicated as models 2P and 2H, respectively. It will be assumed, moreover, that there is only one enterprise which uses the labour of both individuals and that the product obtained $(x_1 + x_2)$ depends on the total quantity of effort applied $(a_1 + a_2)$ in the following way:

$$(3.21) \qquad x_1 + x_2 = (a_1 + a_2)^\xi.$$

As will be understood, x_1 and x_2 represent the quantities of the product consumed by individual 1 and 2, respectively. The notation chosen for total production and total effort already implies that the balance equations are satisfied.

3.3. Models with an Arbitrary Number of Persons, Goods and Enterprises, but One Homogeneous Factor of Production (N)

Here the full notation developed in section 3.1 will have to be used and the relations between the variables include production functions as well as balance equations. The former will be written as:

$$(3.31) \qquad {}_hx^j = {}_h\xi^j({}_ha^j), \quad h = 1 \ldots \ H; \ j = 1 \ldots J.$$

The latter are:

$$(3.32) \qquad \sum_i a_i = \sum_h \sum_j {}_ha^j$$

$$(3.33) \qquad \sum_i x_i^j = \sum_h {}_hx^j, \quad j = 1 \ldots J,$$

This model will be called model N.

3.4. Generalizations and Specifications

Incidentally, generalizations will be discussed, without being worked out in full detail. Among the generalizations are the following assumptions:

(I) Productivity may differ between individuals; this has already been illustrated by expression (3.12);

(II) There may be a larger number of factors of production;

(III) Production may depend on inputs not only of the industry itself but of other industries ("external economies or diseconomies").

For the two-person models a number of different specifications will be considered, expressing varying properties of the production functions as well as the utility functions.

As will be set out below, some problems require the introduction, *a priori*, of specifications for institutions. These will be given whenever needed during the treatment of these problems.

4. ON THE SOLUTION OF THE PROBLEM OF THE OPTIMUM REGIME

4.1. Methods of Solution

As usual in such matters, the more rigorous methods can only be applied to precisely defined and hence simplified models of reality, whereas the complications of reality can only be dealt with in a looser type of argument. Some remarks may be made about both. Scientifically the most satisfactory solution to our problem can be given only by what I shall call the *direct method*. This consists of expressing the conditions for maximum social welfare (Ω) in mathematical equations and *interpreting these equations as the operation of a regime*, which, when specified, would then be the optimum regime. The success of the direct method evidently depends on whether such an interpretation can be given. The interpretation must pay due regard to the costs of any regime it suggests. It is a weak spot of welfare economics, that these costs are often neglected. An interesting example is the *compensation principle*, which does not take us very far for the same reason. If an interpretation cannot be given, we are left with *indirect methods* only. These consist, in principle, of specifying a regime, calculating the value of Ω and choosing, among the regimes considered, the one with the highest Ω obtained. It clearly depends on the regimes specified whether this method brings us near to "the" solution or keeps us far from it. We cannot be sure that a better but unknown regime does not exist. We may call the solution found in this way the *"best attainable" regime*.

In order to deal with complications we are unable to express in terms of a model we shall often have recourse to looser arguments which at best can be presented as "small variations" from some situation provisionally accepted as an optimum. It goes without saying that the variations will have to be small and that the important choices will therefore have to be made first.

The optimum regime will be characterized by a number of institutions and instruments. Those occurring in it will be called *relevant* institutions and instruments, other instruments will be called irrelevant. It may be vaguely understood already that instruments which do not help to bring about effects essential to the optimum state will turn out to be irrelevant. Thus instruments discriminating between subjects or objects which, according to the social welfare function, should not be discriminated between, will turn out to be irrelevant, *e.g.* discrimination between black-haired and red-haired individuals or discriminations around a political frontier which has no economic meaning whatsoever. From our definition it follows that the proof that an instrument is relevant can be given only in cases where the direct method as defined above applies. As soon as it does not apply we can only find out whether or not the instrument occurs in the best attainable solution. Such instruments will be called *semi-relevant*.

4.2. The Main Choices to Be Made

In the subsequent sections it will be attempted to apply, first of all, the direct and some indirect methods. This will provide us with some provisional and tentative conclusions regarding the main aspects of our problem. We will then try to sketch further possible lines of argument which, although they are of the looser type, suggest directions for further research. For the general reader it may be helpful if we summarize, before we go into detail, the main choices which have to be made in order to define the optimum regime. In accordance with the items (i)–(vi) mentioned in section (2.3) they are, in our opinion, the following.

(I) Which productive activities (in the widest sense) should be carried out by the public sector and which by the private one? What taxes should be raised and at what level, what subsidies should be granted?

(II) What public tasks should be carried out in a centralized way and which ones should be left to lower authorities?

(III) How should production be spread over separate units, what size should they have and how should their location be spread?

(IV) What system of pricing and exchange should be chosen: regulated or not, flat rates or not, monopolies or not?

(V) What should be the rate system and the level of social insurance contributions and benefits?

(VI) What type of social control should be chosen?

4.3. CONCLUSIONS FROM THE DIRECT METHOD

4.31. *The Decentralization Thesis*

Some interesting conclusions can be drawn from an application of the direct method to simplified models. Model N and its generalizations or specifications provide us with a clue to the *size of the public sector*. The conditions for maximum social welfare follow from the solution of the following "maximum problem with side conditions":

$$\Omega\left(x_i^j, a_i\right) \equiv \sum_i \omega_i\left(x_i^j, a_i\right)$$

shall be a maximum with side conditions (3.31), (3.32) and (3.33). The ordinary Lagrangian method requires that

(4.31)
$$\sum_i \omega_i(x_i^j, a_i) + \lambda\{\sum_i a_i - \sum_h \sum_j {}_h a^j\} + \sum_j \mu^j\{\sum_i x_i^j - \\ - \sum_h {}_h x^j\} + \sum_h \sum_j {}_h v^j\{{}_h x^j - {}_h \xi^j({}_h a^j)\} \text{ max.}$$

Differentiation with regard to the various groups of variables yields:

(4.32)
$$\text{For } x_i^j: \quad \frac{\partial \omega_i}{\partial x_i^j} + \mu^j = 0 \quad i = 1 \ldots I; j = 1 \ldots J.$$

(4.33)
$$\text{For } a_i: \quad \frac{\partial \omega_i}{\partial a_i} + \lambda = 0 \quad i = 1 \ldots I.$$

(4.34)   For $_ha^j: -\lambda - _hv^j {}_h\xi'^j(_ha^j) = 0$ $h = 1 \ldots H; j = 1 \ldots J.$

(4.35)   For $_hx^j: -\mu^j + _hv^j = 0$ $h = 1 \ldots H; j = 1 \ldots J.$

This may be simplified into:

(4.36) $_h\xi'^j(_ha^j) = -\dfrac{\lambda}{\mu^j}$ $h = 1 \ldots H; j = 1 \ldots J.$

and

(4.37) $\dfrac{\dfrac{\partial \omega_i}{\partial a_i}}{\dfrac{\partial \omega_i}{\partial x_i}} = \dfrac{\lambda}{\mu^j}.$

These are some well-known and rather far-reaching statements. With the assumptions underlying this particular model the famous *"decentralization thesis"* of liberal economists can be proved. The maximum conditions (4.36) and (4.37) can in fact be interpreted as a regime of free competition between all enterprises and all individuals. They require that enterprises produce such a quantity that their marginal value product equals the wage rate and that individuals buy so much of each product that their marginal substitution rate with regard to labour equals the price ratio of that particular product and labour, provided we consider λ as the price of labour and $-\mu^j$ as the price of good j. With the assumptions of this model there would be no need of a sector of public enterprises. This, however, is completely due to the limitations on the validity of the assumptions. We shall therefore discuss some generalizations and specifications of model N calling for a revision of this famous thesis.

4.32. *External Effects*

Let us introduce the well-known phenomenon of external effects, *i.e.* the dependence of the productivity of industry j on the volume of production of industry 1, say. For simplicity's sake we assume that $H = 1$ for industry 1, *i.e.* that there is only one enterprise in that industry. The maximum condition for Ω with regard to a^1 without external effects was, according to (4.34):

(4.38) $-\lambda - v^1\xi'^1(a^1) = 0.$

If now the production functions for the other industries are dependent on a^1, the condition runs:

$$(4.38') \qquad\qquad -\lambda - \sum_h \sum_j {}_h v^j \frac{\partial_h \xi}{\partial a^1} = 0.$$

For the other industries no change occurs, except that the production functions and their derivatives now depend also on a^1. The other industries therefore can still be run by a competitive individualistic system, but this is no longer true for industry 1. A private entrepreneur would, as before, behave according to (4.38). It is now in the general interest, however, that this industry is run according to the principle underlying (4.38'), *i.e.* taking into account the effects on the profits of all other industries. This can best be done by making it a public enterprise.[7]

4.33. *Increasing Returns*

Another important exception to the decentralization thesis refers to the industries for which increasing returns characterize production. Private enterprises cannot here behave according to equation (4.34) since this would imply marginal cost pricing and hence permanent losses. To be sure this might be overcome by a system of non-flat rates, to be discussed later (section 4.55). It is doubtful, however, whether such a system can be administered by private enterprises in a competitive system. It might be run by a monopolistic private enterprise, but there are other objections against such a solution (*cf.* also section 4.54).

We shall discuss later on some further arguments in favour of public enterprises and summarize our tentative conclusions in section 4.51.

4.34. *The Tax System*

From our models we can derive some further clues with regard to the *tax* system. In a negative way we can state that our *optimum conditions are incompatible either with indirect or with income taxes. Indirect taxes* would violate the equality between the marginal substitution rates on the demand and the supply side. For one single indirect tax on, say, tobacco this is clear since the equality with regard

---

[7] If the external effects only exist between two enterprises mutually, integration of these enterprises would be sufficient.

to other goods would be broken; for a general turn-over tax the equality with regard to labour would be invalidated. *Income taxes* too are incompatible with the maximum conditions. An income tax leaves the individual with part only of the revenue of his marginal effort and so "falsifies" his decisions as to where to choose the margin. This would not be true when the individual's supply of effort is fixed, however.[8]

Yet the optimum regime as defined by our equations (4.32)–(4.35) docs imply *income transfers*. There is no equation requiring the equality of an individual's income to his total expenditures. Some individuals and some enterprises will spend more than they earn, while other individuals and enterprises are obtaining more goods than they are able to buy with their earnings. The corresponding income transfers are known as *lump-sum transfers*, since the individuals' and the enterprises' marginal decisions are assumed not to be influenced by them.

They may be illustrated by the results of a few numerical applications of model 2P, computed for various values of the constants ω, φ and ξ occurring in this model. Since for $\xi \neq 1$ there appear entrepreneurial profits or losses, but no separate entrepreneur as a person has been introduced, it is assumed that in those cases profits are distributed to the two persons proportional to their labour income.

Two versions have been made, A and B. In version A $\sigma_1 = \sigma_2$, $\tau_1 = 1$, $\tau_2 = 1.3$, person 1 representing a strong and person 2 a weak individual. In version B $\tau_1 = \tau_2$, $\sigma_1 = 1$ and $\sigma_2 = 1/1.3$, person 1 now being an ascetic and person 2 a materialist. It will be understood that according to the usual attitude taken by economists no measurement (*i.e.* of indifference curves) can distinguish version A from version B. I have preferred to show both cases nevertheless (instead of applying my own "principle of least differences" between coefficients) hoping that future measurements may be available for distinguishing between them.

For both versions of model 2P the variables x_i and a have been calculated corresponding to two different "states", namely I, the welfare optimum (according to the "direct method") and II, the state of free competition (or the "individualistic order") without income transfer.

Some interesting features will be discovered in Table I. The occurrence of income transfers in state I follows from the fact that the ratio of the a's does not coincide with that of the x's, whereas in II it does. In case 5, where the wage

---

[8] Probably the most explicit treatment of the problem has been given by R. FRISCH, *"On Welfare Theory and Pareto Regions"*, Memorandum fra Universitetets Socialøkonomiske Institutt, Oslo, 17 August 1953 (also appeared in French in Économie Appliquée).

TABLE I

VALUES OF EFFFORT APPLIED (a) AND CONSUMPTION (x) OF THE TWO INDIVIDUALS 1 AND 2 FOR I THE WELFARE OPTIMUM AND II THE INDIVIDUALISTIC ORDER WITHOUT INCOME TRANSFERS*

A: Person 1 is "strong", person 2 is "weak"
B: Person 1 is an "ascetic", person 2 a "materialist"

Values of constants			Case no	I								II			
				A				B							
ω	φ	ξ		a_1	a_2	x_1	x_2	a_1	a_2	x_1	x_2	a_1	a_2	x_1	x_2
2	1	$\frac{1}{2}$	1	0.94	0.72	0.64	0.64	0.83	0.83	0.69	0.60	1.14	1.04	0.77	0.71
2	1	$\frac{3}{4}$	2	1.03	0.79	0.79	0.79	0.92	0.92	0 84	0.74	1.06	0.97	0.89	0.81
2	2	$\frac{2}{3}$	3	0.98	0.96	0.75	0.75	0.92	0.92	0.80	0.70	1.06	0.99	0.84	0.78
$\frac{1}{2}$	1	$\frac{2}{3}$	4	0.77	0.59	0.61	0.61	0.68	0.68	0.77	0.46	0.94	0.79	0.78	0.66
2	1	1	5	1.09	0.83	0.96	0.96	0.96	0.96	1.02	0.90	1.00	0.92	1.00	0.92

* I am indebted to Mr. Maarten Eisma for having made the computations.

rate is 1, this is most easily seen; here the a's are equal to the labour incomes. Transfers are, in version A, 0.13 and, in version B 0.06. The equality of x_1 and x_2 in version A, and of a_1 and a_2 in version B are due to the assumptions that tastes with regard to goods are identical in version A and with regard to effort in version B. They represent limiting cases in a way; had we used our principle of least differences between the coefficients of ω_1 and ω_2, we would have found an intermediary version, where $x_1 > x_2$ and $a_1 > a_2$. It is also to be noted that production and consumption as a whole are higher in state II than in state I. As compared with I, effort is undervalued leading to too much activity. Whereas in state II the weak or the materialist works less than the strong or the ascetic man and as a consequence has a lower consumption level too, in state I the strong man has to pass on part of his production to the weak and the materialist part of his production to the ascetic. In state II it can be shown that the strong man is better off than the weak in that he attains a higher level of ω; correspondingly the materialist is better off than the ascetic.

The lump-sum transfers are a very remarkable theoretical outcome. Upon specification of a model they can be calculated and they are, therefore, determinate. They represent, in our terminology, an institution and *their relevant instruments* can be also derived from the model.

This may be illustrated by model 2H. Taking, for simplicity's sake, the case of constant returns, or $\xi = 1$, we find that the optimum is determined by:

(4.39) $\Omega + \lambda\{x_1 + x_2 - (a_1 + a_2)\}$ max.

with $\Omega = -\dfrac{1}{x_1 - x^0} - \dfrac{1}{a_1^0 - a_1} - \dfrac{1}{x_2 - x^0} - \dfrac{1}{a_2^0 - a_2}$.

The conditions are:

$$\frac{1}{(x_1 - x^0)^2} + \lambda = 0 \qquad \frac{1}{(x_2 - x^0)^2} + \lambda = 0$$

$$-\frac{1}{(a_1^0 - a_1)^2} + V - \lambda = 0 \qquad -\frac{1}{(a_2^0 - a_2)^2} - \lambda = 0$$

$$x_1 + x_2 = a_1 + a_2$$

or: $x_1 - x^0 = x_2 - x^0 = a_1^0 - a_1 = a_2^0 - a_2$.

The solutions are:

$$x_1 = x^0 + \tfrac{1}{4}(a_1^0 + a_2^0 - 2x^0)$$

$$x_2 = x^0 + \tfrac{1}{4}(a_1^0 + a_2^0 - 2x^0)$$

$$a_1 = a_1^0 - \tfrac{1}{4}(a_1^0 + a_2^0 - 2x^0)$$

$$a_2 = a_2^0 - \tfrac{1}{4}(a_2^0 + a_2^0 - 2x^0)$$

From this we find the income transfers to be (since the price of labour is 1) $a_1 - x_1 = -(a_2 - x_2) = \tfrac{1}{2}(a_1^0 - a_1^0)$.

In this extremely simple case the relevant criteria for the income transfers appear to be the "maximum efforts" of the individuals introduced at the end of section 2.2, which may also be called their productive capacities. In a more general setup they might also depend on further characteristics of the individuals' utility functions and perhaps on other data. Since income is not a datum it will not be among the criteria.

Welfare economists have discovered this remarkable feature of the optimum situation a long time ago already, but its impact on practical economic policy has not been large. Many laymen have no idea of its existence and misinterpret the meaning of the optimum by emphasizing the importance of "self-responsibility", often identified even with the budget constraint for each individual. It may be observed in passing that a completely different "optimum" is obtained if such a system of individual budget constraints is added *a priori* to the maximum conditions.[9]

The reason why the influence of this remarkable feature of the optimum has not been large is to be found in the complete *neglect of its costs*, which probably are very high. In fact, the assessment of an individual's income, though not a simple matter as we know, is much more accessible to objective approaches than the assessment of his "capacities" to produce (with the exception of his physical or financial wealth). It therefore seems to be out of the question to administer, without incurring grave frictions, a system of lump-sum payments or subsidies. This means that, on a very important point, the interpretation of the theoretical optimum in terms of a practical regime breaks down and consequently also the direct method.

4.4. AN EXAMPLE OF THE INDIRECT METHOD[10]

We are thus forced to apply the indirect method and will illustrate the latter by an example. In view of the importance of some sort of income transfers we will try to find out to what extent the imposition of an *income tax* can improve the social welfare of an individualistic order and move such an order in the direction of the optimum—obtained by neglecting the cost of lump-sum transfers. We will assume that, amending our model 2H with $\xi = 1$, consumption x_i depends on earned income a_i in the following way:

$$(4.41) \qquad\qquad x_i = \gamma a_i + \gamma_0.$$

This implies that a tax is paid equal to $a_i - x_i = (1 - \gamma) a_i - \gamma_0$. Individuals are assumed to maximize their ω_i, as is usually assumed for an individualistic order, and it will be assumed that taxes add up to zero, since transfers only are considered. (The costs of administering the income tax seem to represent a small percentage of national income.)

---

[9] The simplest way to do so in a two-person model is to add the condition $x_1/a_1 = x_2/a_2$. It will be easily found what the consequences for the optimum are. They may even be interpreted as violating the free choice of the individual with regard to the extent of his effort.

[10] This example was mentioned in the author's contribution to Essays in Honour of Professor Zeuthen (Til Frederik Zeuthen, Copenhagen 1958), p. 351.

We hence get the following system of equations:

(4.42) $x_i - \overset{0}{x} = \gamma(a - a_i)$ $i = 1,2$

(4.43) $x_1 + x_2 = \gamma(a_1 + a_2) + 2\gamma_0$

(4.44) $x_1 + x_2 = a_1 + a_2,$

to which we have to add equations (4.41). Equation (4.42) follows from maximizing ω_i under the side condition (4.41). The solutions appear to be, writing δ for $\sqrt{\gamma}$:

(4.45)

$$a_1 = \frac{\overset{0}{x}}{1+\delta} + \tfrac{1}{2}\overset{0}{a_1} + \tfrac{1}{2}\frac{\delta-1}{\delta+1}\overset{0}{a_2}$$

$$a_2 = \frac{\overset{0}{x}}{1+\delta} + \tfrac{1}{2}\frac{\delta-1}{\delta+1}\overset{0}{a_1} + \tfrac{1}{2}\overset{0}{a_2}$$

and

$$x_1 = \overset{0}{x} + \delta(\overset{0}{a_1} - a_1)$$

$$x_2 = \overset{0}{x} + \delta(\overset{0}{a_2} - a_2),$$

which can be expressed in the data with the aid of (4.45).

Applying the indirect method now, we choose γ *in such a way as to maximize* Ω. Writing

$$\overset{0}{a_1} + \overset{0}{a_2} - 2x_0 = \eta,$$

and

$$\frac{\overset{0}{a_1} - \overset{0}{a_2}}{\eta} = a$$

we find

(4.46) $$\frac{\Omega}{4\eta} = -\frac{(\delta+1)^2}{\delta}\,\frac{1}{1-a^2\delta^2}$$

From this it appears that the optimum value of δ (in the sense of the indirect method, *i.e.* assuming an income tax of the type indicated as given) depends on a, which represents the ratio between $\overset{0}{a_1} - \overset{0}{a_2}$ and $\overset{0}{a_1} + \overset{0}{a_2} - 2x_0$. As extreme examples we mention that for $a = 0$ we find $\delta = 1$, meaning that no income tax should be raised, while for $a = \infty$ we find $\delta = 0$, meaning that incomes after tax should be equal. An intermediary case, leading to $\gamma = 0.5$, will be obtained when we choose

$$a_1^0 = 1.3; \quad a_2^0 = 1; \quad x^0 = 0.77.$$

As the final step in applying the indirect method, we have calculated, for this case, the values of Ω obtained under (I) an individualistic order without income tax, (II) the same order with income tax of the type specified at the optimum level, and (III) the theoretical optimum regime. The results are the following.

TABLE II

VARIABLES AND UTILITY LEVELS IN THREE DIFFERENT STATES, MODEL 2H

	x_1	x_2	a_1	a_2	ω_1	ω_2	Ω
(I) individualistic order	1.035	0.885	1.035	0.885	—7.6	—17.4	—25.0
(II) ditto, plus income tax	0.97	0.88	1.01	0.84	—8.4	—15.4	—23.8
(III) theoretical optimum	0.96	0.96	1.11	0.81	—10.5	—10.5	—21.0

The figures show us that no income transfers exist under (I), since $a_i = x_i$, and that there are substantial income transfers (0.15) under (III); the transfers under (II) are very modest (0.04) and so is the increase in Ω obtained by them (from —25.0 to —23.8).

An extremely simplified model like our model 2H cannot prove very much. It illustrates, however, that an *income tax may be among the "semi-relevant instruments"* and that its optimum rate may be substantial.

4.5. SUGGESTIONS REGARDING THE MAIN CHOICES

Partly on the basis of the more rigorous methods so far illustrated and partly on the looser type of argument announced in section 4.1, we will now make a number of suggestions about the main choices to be made in order to determine the optimum regime, as listed in section 4.2.

4.51. *Size of the Public Sector and Nature of Taxes*

In section 2.41 we indicated the complex nature of the institution summarized as "public authorities" and the main groups of sub-institutions. We will take up the sub-institutions one by one and discuss the factors which determine their optimum size.

(1a) Total *expenditure* will be the sum of expenditure on the factors of production needed for the production of services typical to government, listed under 2(a) in section 2.41 and of expenditure on subsidies, investment *etc*. For a country in need of development the last item may be very important. On the one hand there are types of investment, particularly those in the *infrastructure*, which can hardly be undertaken by private investors, since they are not easily operated on a profit basis. Construction of roads and canals is one outstanding example, irrigation and other activities for the improvement of agriculture another. In addition there may be important tasks with regard to education, not only on behalf of development, but also with a view to a redistribution of income.[11]

On the other hand, the amount of capital needed will, in an under-developed country, surpass the free supply of capital and must be obtained through *forced savings*. The main institution which can impose forced savings by taxing people more than is needed for current expenditure is the state.

(1b) About the most appropriate *tax structure* our purely theoretical arguments are somewhat negative. In principle, the income tax as well as general indirect taxes are incompatible with optimum conditions. We are then left with retributions for the services supplied by the government, with specific indirect taxes on goods deemed harmful to the population (alcoholic beverages, tobacco *etc*. and possibly subsidies for goods the government thinks particularly healthy) and, perhaps, with taxes on wealth or assets. However because of the cost of collecting certain types of taxes, theory will have to yield to practice on certain points, as was illustrated in the case of the income tax. It should, in addition, not be forgotten that the theory does require a type of income transfers ("lump-sum" payments and subsidies) which would be difficult to organize and that this reduces the strength of any argument derived from the direct theoretical method. From the evidence supplied by the indirect method, we found that an income tax may be justified, even at rather high levels.

(2a) The production of *services* typical to government under any

---

[11] *Cf.* J. TINBERGEN, *loc. cit.*

circumstances need not be discussed at any length; some remarks to be given under (2b) will also apply here.

There will be a need for *regulations* in a number of markets which, because of their structure, are continuously threatened by instabilities. Agricultural markets are usually of this type because of low elasticities of demand as well as supply and because of the hazards of weather conditions.

(2b) With regard to the *productive* sub-institutions of the state our foregoing analysis (sections 4.32 and 4.33) suggests that a number of activities have to take place in the public sector. These are:

(a) activities with external effects on a considerable number of industries, and

(b) activities showing increasing returns.

In brief, the reasons why these activities should be publicly operated are that those of category (a) would not be operated in the right way when subject to private profit considerations and that those of category (b) would either produce permanent losses to their private operators or threaten the general interest by monopolistic tendencies.

The activities under (a) imply a number of "basic activities" for any government, such as the organization of security, external as well as internal, including perhaps even certain aspects of social security; the maintenance of law and of sound monetary conditions and a good deal of education. Category (a) could also be extended to include the production of certain goods and services used by so many industries that an interruption of their supply might endanger the economy: energy, water, transportation. This applies more particularly in periods of general scarcity of goods.

Activities (b) imply partly the same activities and, in addition, a number of heavy industries.

While the above argument is based on the concern for optimum production decisions, another argument in favour of bringing industries into the public sector is that of eliminating "unearned income" and thus decreasing the inequality of income distribution.

A general argument against expanding the public sector may be a lack of efficiency as apparent in a number of public services. It depends a good deal on the details of its organization whether or not a public enterprise is less efficient than a private one.

The precise frontier between the public and the private sector thus depends on a number of detailed data, among which are the types of industries a country has, the degree of scarcity of goods in general, the organization of public enterprises and the level of efficiency in private production.

Under almost all circumstances a number of typical small-scale industries, including agriculture and retail trade, are more appropriately taken care of by the private sector. Even though some of the auxiliary functions of these industries, such as the purchase of supplies and the selling of products in the case of agriculture, can be carried out by collective agencies such as cooperatives, the production process proper usually is conducted more successfully in privately-owned enterprises.

4.52. *The Degree of Centralization in Administration*

Administration, in our terminology, consists of handling a number of instruments of public policy and does not include public production in the narrower sense, as conducted in enterprises. The choice before us can be made separately for each instrument. It is a choice between one central agency, dealing with that instrument and a number of autonomous local agencies. By a central agency we shall also understand an agency with local branches, when these branches have no autonomy. The problem can be handled at a national level, but also for the world at large.

There is an *a-priori argument in favour of decentralization:* it means more freedom, less friction and lower costs. This argument will be overruled, however, in a number of cases where it can be shown that decentralized administration by its nature leads to biased decisions or is less efficient. It will be biased when the effects of the instruments it handles are to be found outside its own realm. Each instrument may be said to have a certain action radius. This radius is indicative of the natural sphere for decentralized control. Smaller units would lead to erroneous decisions since they would be based on part of the effects only. Decentralized administration will be inefficient if there are economies of scale requiring bigger optimal units. The action radius and optimum size will therefore be among the important data on which to base the degree of decentralization.

Accordingly a number of questions of a purely local interest should be left to local authorities; local security, prices of local energy supply and transportation, local cultural matters may be examples. Unfortunately however, there are very few things, that do not influence a wider community. Bad management of local affairs may not directly affect other communities, but it will, as a bad example, have indirect effects. There will be a need therefore at least to subject local decisions to certain general rules or limits between which a free choice can be made.

Such administrative matters as *economic policy* generally will have to be conducted in a rather centralized way. A regulation of the *wheat* market, to quote one example, must be undertaken on a world-wide scale. The *coal* market may be left to smaller units since the bulk of coal does not move so far. Even *financial policy*, however, though apparently a national matter, influences the economic position of other countries so much that it cannot be considered a subject for complete national autonomy.

It is interesting to observe that once big agglomerations—like a big nation, or a big trust—have come into existence, their actions are influencing others so much that these actions should be made subject to an even more centralized system of administration—in our two examples a supranational agency or a government respectively. Had they not come into existence, a decentralized system might have remained possible: in a world of small nations no danger exists for anybody to impose an "optimum tariff" tending to exploit other nations; in a world of competitive enterprises no antitrust laws are needed.

4.53. *The Degree of Centralization in Production*

This question has been dealt with in section 4.51 to a considerable extent already. It may be repeated that it was the fundamental discovery of liberal economics that, under specified conditions, important portions of production can be dealt with in independent units; these may be private enterprises, but they may also be public enterprises or cooperative ones. In this section we will consider two further aspects of this question, namely *what size* the units should have and where they should be *located*. In determining the size the concept of *optimum size* gives useful information. For many industries there is a fairly clearly determined size for which costs of production are a minimum and this will then be the preferred size. There will even be a tendency for free competition to approach this size, although smaller sizes will often persist because of a strong preference for independence among producers and because of the uneven distribution of wealth.

The optimum size depends partly on the costs of transporting the product to the consumers and this may mean that it depends also on the density of the population. Here the factor of location enters the picture. Questions of location are seldom treated in economics and even less so in welfare economics. The particular shape the question takes when approached from the viewpoint of the optimum regime is whether *movement through space of either capital goods or population* can help to maximize social welfare. The problem of depressed areas or of underdeveloped countries is today's practical form of it. It is now felt that some of the forces of external effects and of increasing returns are responsible for an over-concentration of production units which may have to be counteracted. On a world-wide scale the dimensions of the problem are so large to make this a major policy question, affecting the relations between nations and even races, and with repercussions on the question of the proper degree of centralization in administration. It can be maintained that a satisfactory solution of this problem of location involves a greater development of underdeveloped countries and that for its realization more or stronger international agencies are needed.

4.54. *The System of Exchange*

Goods and services must not only be produced and consumed but they have to be exchanged as soon as some degree of the division of labour makes it advantageous. There are many conceivable ways of exchanging goods. They may be rationed and allocated in a more or less centralized way. They may be sold at uniform prices to everybody concerned or there may be price discrimination. The prices may be different in structure: they may be *"flat rates"*, meaning that the buyer pays the seller a sum which is proportional to the quantity bought; or the buyer may pay a *non-flat rate, e.g.* a lump sum (season tickets) or a combination of a lump sum and a proportional sum. Finally the prices may be calculated in a different way, *e.g.* so as to imply monopoly profits or so as to be equal to marginal costs.

Our model N (*cf.* section 4.3) illustrates the possibility of relying on *free markets* for the exchange of goods and services. Equations (4.36) and (4.37) can be interpreted as the behaviour of both producers and consumers in such markets.

Our model N further suggests that there is *no scope for price discrimination*. In fact equation (4.37) states that the (relative) price vector should be the same for all individuals. In other words: whatever subsidies or taxes must be granted or levied can be dealt with as income corrections.

Model N also suggests that *flat rates are not the ideal price structure*. Lump-sum payments are very characteristic of the optimum regime, when they can be organized. Electricity rates provide an interesting example. Lump-sum payments may even involve the reconciliation of two principles, that of marginal-cost pricing and that of self-sufficiency of enterprises. But, as stated before, there has to be a workable criterion for determining the size of the lump-sum payments. And if every citizen had to pay lump sums to every enterprise, a huge simplification could be made by combining all these payments into a single tax. However, we have already discussed the difficulty of finding the proper criterion, when we discussed the tax system. This whole complex of problems contains some interesting arguments in favour of public enterprise.

All models of welfare economics arrive at the conclusion that *monopoly prices* have to be rejected. But again the costs of preventing them from being charged may interfere with the practical side of administering anti-monopoly policies.

4.55. *The System of Social Insurance*

Three sets of questions will be treated briefly, dealing with the coverage, the financing and the organization of social insurance.

The questions of *coverage* are: Which risks are to be covered and at what level of benefits? There seems to be a consensus about the desirability of covering unemployment (as far as existent), sickness and "hospitalization", accidents, death of breadwinner and old-age. Doubts exist as to the coverage of family allowances. The levels should be set so as to safeguard the victims in a real way but not to tempt them to be inactive. Since most risks can be objectively stated, this latter argument applies mainly to unemployment benefits. These might be made dependent on the economic situation and thus could rise and fall with the level of unemployment. A benefit of 80% of wages seems to be an upper limit.

Social insurance can be *financed* out of contributions from workers, employers and the state. The higher the former two, the more they act as a tax on employing labour, which can be used as an instrument of anti-cyclical policy. The higher the public contribution, the larger the possibilities for redistribution of income are. There seems to be little scope in distinguishing between workers' and employers' contribution, since they are both *paid* by the employer and *borne* by the worker.

With regard to the *organization* of social insurance the question of private *vs* public agencies should be mentioned first. Here the usual arguments about private *vs* public operation apply. When operated by public bodies, whether autonomous or not, the question about merging seems important. A maximum of merging all risks and a maximum of uniformity in rates seems advisable; but where risks or costs are clearly different, this should be reflected in the rates.

4.56. *Social Control*

As already observed (section 2.46), the institutions of social control are meant, first of all, as a means to satisfy certain psychological needs and are therefore on the border line of economics. They cannot, however, be separated from our general problem. The main problem is how to combine some real influence given to the workers with an efficient operation of production. The latter point is usually taken care of by restricting the number of representatives, their rights and the number of meetings, all of which tends to undermine the workers' confidence in the institution. This can only be maintained, on the one hand, if the representatives have the personal confidence of workers and, on the other hand, if a program of education is undertaken to help everybody understand the problems at stake. It seems that particularly for this aspect of the optimum regime the influence of the cultural traditions of each country must be considered.

5. SOME TENTATIVE CONCLUSIONS

5.1. UNSOLVED PROBLEMS; RESEARCH PRIORITIES

In this section some tentative conclusions will be formulated with regard to "the world's largest controversy". Before doing so we should, however, admit that the economist's view, as any scientific and human point of view, can be only provisional and that there are, in the subject matter under discussion, a number of unsolved issues calling for further research. They should be obvious after the foregoing discussion; but it may be useful to summarize them briefly.

We need much more empirical data about the main features of indifference surfaces, in particular about the influence exerted by changes in effort *versus* changes in income. Studies like the one undertaken by G. F. BREAK[12] should be conducted on a large scale. Next, we have to make up our minds—with the help of such extra-economic considerations as ethics—on the comparison of utilities of different individuals, or rather, social groups represented by individuals. This may help us to come to more practical ideas about the social welfare function.

Further, a more systematic study of the "costs", in the widest sense, of important institutions as well as the "cost laws" of various productive processes is still highly urgent. Finally, the potentiality of education as a means for increasing people's productive capacities is among the more important subjects to investigate.

This list, incomplete as it is, represents a good research programme, probably more useful than many effort-consuming current investigations on the details of the cyclical position, to give an example.

5.2. TWO STATEMENTS ABOUT THE OPTIMUM REGIME

For our discussion it seems that two general statements that can be tentatively made about the nature of the optimum regime are relevant. The first is that *the optimum regime*—even when one particular social welfare function is adhered to—depends on many structural data of the society considered and therefore *is different under different circumstances*. As we have seen, the size of the public sector has to depend on the extent of the activities showing external effects on other industries,

---

[12] G. F. BREAK, "Income Taxes and Incentives to Work", *The Amer. Econ. Rev.* XLVII (1957) p. 529.

and on the extent of the industries showing increasing returns. Income tax rates should depend, among other things, on the dispersion of productive capacities among the population. The degree of decentralization in production should depend on the optimum size of enterprises and on population density. We may add other examples, not discussed in the preceding sections. Government intervention with free consumption (*i.e.* rationing) may be necessary in situations of extreme scarcity. Government intervention with industrialization may depend on the initiatives taken by the population. Finally the optimum depends on the preferences of the population as a whole which may differ between peoples or between time periods.

The practical conclusion to be drawn is that what is the optimum regime for one country need not be the optimum regime for another country.

The second general statement is that *as a rule the optimum regime will not be some form of extreme.* It is very improbable that it will be characterized by

(I) either complete absence of the public or of the private sector;

(II) either complete centralization or complete decentralization in production, administration or exchange;

(III) complete equalization of incomes;

(IV) an entirely one-sided tax system, *etc.*

The general reasons why this is so are that usually the motivation for each type of means or of instrument depends on the size of certain structural constants which are so different between industries or social groups that it is very improbable that the same means should be used everywhere. The motivation for making an activity a public one depends, as we saw, on the existence of external effects or of increasing returns. It is highly improbable that all industries will have these characteristics. The degree of decentralization to be applied in various fields of administration depends on what we called the action radius of the various instruments; it is very improbable that all of these would be very large or very small. Again, complete equalization of incomes would entail many consequences incompatible with other elements of social welfare, such as a high level of production or a high level of growth. Finally, the case for one single tax is so specific that it hardly ever exists. For all these and several other reasons the optimum regime will practically never coincide with an entirely one-sided regime. Where such a regime exists, it will as a rule not be an optimum. The reason for the existence of extremist regimes will be discussed in the next section.

It follows from our last statement that the optimum regime will as a rule shift only slowly and that sudden changes in regime are indicative of a deviation between the actual and the optimum regime, either before the change, or after it, or in both cases. Sudden changes anyhow should be avoided under the present conditions of a complicated and very sensitive system of production and exchange.

5.3. Factors Making for Deviations Between the Optimum and the Actual Regime

Looked at from the point of view of the economist, deviations between a regime in actual existence and what the economist thinks to be the optimum may be due to differences of opinion between the economist and the politicians in power as to:

(a) the operation of the economic mechanism;

(b) the aims of economic policy.

Differences of opinion as to the operation of the mechanism may be classified—assuming that by definition the economist knows better about this subject than the politician—as errors on the politician's side. These errors may be incidental or systematic; the latter will be called doctrinaire deviations. Incidental errors may arise because of *misunderstandings* about economic statements. Thus, the famous decentralization thesis discussed in section 4.31 (the Pareto thesis) has been given many popular formulations which are completely false. It is not generally known that as a rule the optimum requires income transfers. Many do not know that the decentralization thesis does not apply in the case of external effects or increasing returns. On the other hand, the consequences of a complete equalization of incomes by decree are not known by many popular discussants and were not known in the U.S.S.R. around 1920. There is a host of less fundamental issues where erroneous policies are followed for lack of understanding of their consequences. These will not be discussed now.

Doctrinaire deviations occur when a political group adheres to a more or less outspoken system of thought including economic theories which have been found to be too simple to explain economic reality. The most typical examples are the liberalist and the Marxist systems, often showing deviations on opposite sides of what most economists nowadays consider an equilibrated view, although not necessarily always. Both may be said to be productivists, *i.e.* overemphasizing the importance of high production at the detriment of distributional aspects. The typical examples of their doctrinaire opinions refer to the size of the public sector and to the freedom to be given to management. Here they stand at the opposite extremes as is indeed well known.

Differences of opinion between the economist and a politician about the *aims* of economic policy can exist when the economist discovers inconsistencies in a politician's aims. Such may be the case when various forms of *shortsightedness* are responsible for the basic aims of a policy. Thus, future well-being may be neglected by some political systems, while it may be overemphasized by others to the detriment of present well-being. Or, politicians may be too shortsighted in a geographical sense, neglecting the interests of citizens outside their own geographical unit. Finally, the relative importance attached by certain politicians to the various elements of utility may differ from what can be observed to be the case for the citizens. It would be too easy for the economist to say that all this is not of his concern. The frontier of what is accessible to scientific analysis is shifting continually. It is the contention of the present author that we can push this frontier further and need not accept as given all that some politicians would formulate as aims. Inconsistent aims can be rejected.

The ethical principles needed to give a meaning to the social welfare function cannot be a permanent excuse for not discussing them. The author invites economists, politicians and philosophers to formulate alternatives to his proposal. Once we can measure utility, there may be another forward shift of the frontier.

5.4. Differences Between Aims of Political Systems

To a certain extent the great controversy may be said to be due to differences in aims of policy. As far as economic policy is concerned, such differences may take the form of representing the interests of different groups or classes of the population. When only part of the population has voting rights this phenomenon will be a natural result. It may occur even when voting rights are general, if it is possibile for one single group or class to take office. Thus, schematically it can be said that some political parties represent the interests of workers and others those of capital owners. Nowadays, however, this statement will apply to some hidden aims rather than to most of the aims defended in public. Competition between parties forces most political programmes to take into account the interests of a large number of groups. A closer analysis of the details of programmes shows that a considerable portion of the programmes of all parties is identical. The differences are magnified by our habit of emphasizing the differences, the time may have come to emphasize what is common to all.

5.5. Is There a Basis for Discussion?

If it is true that the aims of various economic regimes are not so very different and if it is true that quite a few of the differences of opinion on the operation of the economic system are biased, we can hope for converging ideas rather than diverging. Doctrinaire ideas about the operation of the economic system will in the long run be disadvantageous to those who hold them. Actions will be more successful when based on reality than when based on unrealistic assumptions. If there really is a more or less clearly defined optimum regime, actual regimes will have to move towards this optimum. If it exists it can be successfully discussed between the representatives of different opinions.

Is this a utopia? Or can we trace changes in the real world supporting our point of view? In the author's view there are a number of events in the chronicles of economic policy of these last thirty years that do support our thesis. As early as in the twenties communist policy did away with a number of dogmas until then adhered to. They were forced to recognize the necessity of management; they themselves broke the regular sequence of feudalism – capitalism – socialism by starting socialism (or at least attempting to establish it) in a largely feudal country; at a certain stage they denied another automatism sofar believed in, when deciding themselves on the rate of investment in the Russian economy. They stopped attempts at a complete equalization of incomes. After the Second World War, to quote another example, rationing of consumer goods was abolished. More recently, changes have been made in the economic structure of Yugoslavia and Poland, and even in Russia, which are of particular importance. In all three countries a considerable degree of decentralization in production decisions has been introduced. Production volume is no longer prescribed to the individual enterprise in Yugoslavia and Poland, but the decision is made at the plant level. In Yugoslavia free price formation has even been accepted.

In the same period the economic regime of Western countries also changed profoundly. The public sector was extended, the governments accepted responsibility for the level of employment, social insurance was extended, development was made a conscious concern of economic policy and "plans" for the economy as a whole were introduced, which were intended to serve as background information to producers and government. It is particularly interesting to note that the plans of the communist countries which for a long time were of a completely different character are, through the latest developments, changing their nature in the direction of the freer type of plans of the west.

If, then, there is a logical basis for discussion, what should be discussed? The answer is that it would be easier to say what should not be discussed. There is a common interest to discuss, in a far less emotional way than is usual in political documents so far, almost everything covered in this essay. The technical tool needed will be, first of all, a common language—not a simple matter if one reads some of the communist scientific publications. Then a careful and patient summing up and scrutiny of the aims of economic policy in general and development planning in particular. Finally, a discussion on the objective consequences, in various environments, of certain means of economic policy or institutions of economic regime. It is the author's hope that his views are shared by a number of colleagues on both sides of the iron curtain.

BIBLIOGRAPHY OF JAN TINBERGEN

i. Books, Pamphlets, Reports and Essays

Minimumproblemen in de natuurkunde en de ekonomie, Amsterdam, J. H. Paris. 1929. XIII + 68 pp. (Dissertation Leiden).

Het nut van statistiese analyse voor het bedrijf, Amsterdam, N.V. de Arbeiderspers, 1931. 15 pp. (Openbare les Amsterdam).
Also: *De Socialistische gids,* 1931, p. 697-707.

"In hoeverre kan het regelen van den omvang der voortbrenging of van het aanbod van bepaalde goederen door producenten al dan niet met medewerking van de Overheid, bevorderlijk worden geacht voor de volkswelvaart"? 's-Gravenhage, M. Nijhoff, 1932. 31 pp. *(Prae-advies voor de Vereeniging voor de Staathuishoudkunde en de Statistiek).*

De Konjunktuur, Amsterdam, N.V. de Arbeiderspers, 1933. 194 pp. *(Nieuwe intern. Bibliotheek 6).*
"Het waarnemen van maatschappelijke verschijnselen", in: *De uitdrukkingswijze der wetenschap,* 1933. p. 1-13. (Lecture, February 13, 1933).

Statistiek en wiskunde in dienst van het konjunktuuronderzoek, Amsterdam, N.V. de Arbeiderspers, 1933. 24 pp. (Rede uitgesproken bij de aanvaarding van het ambt van buitengewoon hoogleeraar aan de Nederlandsche Handels-Hoogeschool te Rotterdam).

"Is te verwachten, dat de maatregelen van President Roosevelt zullen bijdragen, en zoo ja, in welke mate, tot een blijvende vermindering der werkloosheid in de Vereenigde Staten van Noord-Amerika? 1934, 21 pp. *(Prae-*advies Nat. Vereen. tegen de werkloosheid). Also: *Tijdschrift van de Ned. Werkloosheids-Raad,* 1934, pp. 329-350.

"Socialisme", in: *Waar gaan wij heen?* Amsterdam, H. Meulenhoff, 1934, p. 86-152.

"De economische zijde van het ordeningsvraagstuk" in: *Ordening.* Delft, 1935, p. 17-29. (Verslag van de voordrachten gehouden op 14, 15 en 16 januari 1935 voor het Delfts hogeschoolfonds).

Conjunctuurbeheersing, Amsterdam, 1935, 38 pag. (Verslag van een voordracht gehouden te 's-Gravenhage met de daarna gevolgde gedachtenwisseling in een bijeenkomst op 23 november 1935 te Amsterdam ter gelegenheid van het 10-jarig bestaan van het Algemeen Verbond van Accountants).

"Kan hier te lande, al dan niet na Overheidsingrijpen, een verbetering van de binnenlandse conjunctuur intreden, ook zonder verbetering van onze exportpositie"? *Prae-adviezen voor de Vereeniging voor de Staathuishoudkunde en de Statistiek,* 's-Gravenhage, 1936, p. 62-108.

"Über den Wert mathematischer Konjunkturtheorien", in: *Beiträge zur Konjunkturlehre. Festschrift zum zehnjährigen Bestehen des Institutes für Konjunkturforschung,* Hamburg, 1936, S. 198-224.

Grondproblemen der theoretische statistiek, Haarlem, F. Bohn N.V., 1936, VII + 174 pag. *(Volksuniversiteits-Bibliotheek 66).*

306   BIBLIOGRAPHY OF JAN TINBERGEN

"L'élasticité de la demande des produits des industries agricoles", in: *Ve Congrès International technique et chimique des industries agricoles*, Schéveningue, 1937, p. 462-476 (Comptes Rendus).

An econometric approach to business cycle problems, Paris, Hermann and Cie., 1937, 75 pag. (*Actualités scientifiques et industrielles.* 525: *Impasses économiques II.*)

"Vertragingsgolven en levensduurgolven", in: *Strijdenskracht door Wetensmacht*, Amsterdam, 1938, p. 143-150. (Opstellen aangeboden aan S. de Wolff, ter gelegenheid van zijn 60e verjaardag.)

Les fondements mathématiques de la stabilisation du mouvement des affaires, Paris, Hermann et Cie., 1938, 114 pag. (*Actualités scientifiques et industrielles.* 632. *Economie théorique et statistique économique 2.*)

"Arbeidsproductiviteit en werkgelegenheid. Berekeningen betreffende den samenhang tusschen de werkgelegenheid en haar bepalende factoren, in: *Onderzoek naar de blijvende werkloosheid*, 's-Gravenhage, Landsdrukkerij, 1939. Bijlage III. p. 181-194 resp. p. 195-230 (Rapport van de commissie ingesteld bij beschikking van den voorzitter van den Hoogen Raad van Arbeid 18 december 1936).

A method and its application to investment activity, Geneva, League of Nations, 1939, 164 pag. (*Statistical testing of business cycle theories. Vol. 1.*)

Une méthode et son application au mouvement des investissements. Genève, Soc. des nations, 1939, 178 pag. (*Vérification statistique des théories des cycles economiques*, I).

Business cycles in the United States of America. 1919-1932, Geneva, League

of Nations, 1939. 244 pag. (*Statistical testing of business cycle theories. Vol. II.*)

Les cycles économiques aux Etats Unis d'Amérique de 1919 à 1932, Genève, Soc. des Nations, 1939. 267 pag. (*Vérification statistique des théories des cycles économiques. III.*)

Technische ontwikkeling en werkgelegenheid, Amsterdam, Noord-Hollandsche Uitgevers Maatschappij, 1940, 111 pag. (*Uit leven en wetenschap*, 3.) 2de druk 1941.

— — en J. B. D. DERKSEN. "Nederlandsch Indië in cijfers", in: *Daar werd wat groots verricht.* Samengesteld en verzorgd onder leiding van W. H. VAN HELSDINGEN, Amsterdam, Elsevier, 1941, p. 508-525.

Het streven naar efficiency en de werkgelegenheid, Purmerend. 's-Gravenhage 1941. 34 pag. (Publicatie Nederlandsch Instituut voor Efficiency. 199.)

Econometrie; werkwijzen en resultaten van econometrisch onderzoek, Gorinchem, 1941. VIII + 115 pag. (Noorduyn's wetenschappelijke reeks. 1). Translated into Danish, German, English, French, Hungarian and Polish.

"An acceleration principle for commodity stockholding and a short cycle resulting from it", in: *Lange et aleds. Studies in mathematical economics and econometrics*, Chicago, 1942. p. 255-267.

Economische bewegingsleer, Amsterdam, N.V. Noord-Hollandsche Uitgevers Maatschappij. 1943, 274 pag. (Translated into English and Spanish.)

De les van dertig jaar; economische ervaringen en mogelijkheden, Amsterdam, 1944, 257 pag. (Elseviers economische bibliotheek.)

International economic co-operation (translated into English by P. H. BREITENSTEIN AND E. INGLIS ARKELL), Am-

sterdam, 1945, 208 pag. (Elseviers economische bibliotheek). 2e druk: *International economic integration.*

Enkele problemen van centrale planning
's-Gravenhage, 1945, 14 pag. (Publicatie Nederlandsch Instituut voor Efficiency 247)

— — en F. M. BARON VAN ASBECK,
J. H. W. VERZIJL en anderen; *Bouwstof
voor de oplossing van na-oorlogsche
vraagstukken*, Den Haag, Martinus
Nijhoff, 1946, 120 pag.

Redelijke inkomstenverdeling, Haarlem,
De Gulden Pers, 1946, 80 pag.

"Unstable equilibria in the balance of
payments", in: *Economic research and
the development of economic science and
public policy*, New York, 1946, p. 133-
142.

Beperkte concurrentie, Leiden, 1946,
152 pag. (*Capita selecta der economie*, 1.)

"Nederland in de twintigste eeuw", in:
Hecht verbonden in lief en leed, Amsterdam, Elsevier, 1946, p. 1-44.

*Some remarks on the problem of dollar
scarcity*, Washington Congress Econometric society. 1946, 11 pag.

KEUS, H. J. en TINBERGEN, J. "Prae-
adviezen over de vraag: Gesteld, dat
men te zijner tijd het huidige systeem
van geleide economie geheel of gedeel-
telijk door een stelsel van vrije economie zal willen vervangen, welke voor-
waarden moeten dan zijn vervuld en
welke maatregelen zullen daartoe moeten worden genomen respectievelijk in-
getrokken." 's-Gravenhage, 1947, 119
pag. met bijlagen. (*Prae-adviezen voor
de Vereeniging voor de Staathuishoudkunde en de Statistiek*).

— — and J. B. D. DERKSEN; "Recent
experiments in social accounting:
flexible and dynamic budgets," in:

The econometric society meeting, Septem-
ber 1947, Washington, 1949, p. 195-204.

"Welke mogelijkheden en middelen bestaan er tot het in evenwicht brengen
van de betalingsbalans van Nederland
na afloop van de Marshallhulp onder
gelijktijdig streven naar een overwe-
gend vrij en internationaal handels-
betalingsverkeer? Den Haag, 1949, 53
pag. (*Prae-advies voor de Vereeniging
voor de Staathuishoudkunde en de Statistiek.*)

"The reformulation of current business
cycle theories as refutable hypotheses",
in: *Conference on business cycles*, National bureau of economics research,
1949, 19 pag. (Special conference series,
New York 1950, no. 2.)

De grenzen der ordening, Voorburg,
1950, 12 pag. (Serie vraagstukken van
heden en morgen, no. 16). (Reprint
N.E.I. no. 1).

"The possibility of price and exchange
adaptation," in: *Tracing a new international balance*, Leiden, Stenfert
Kroese, 1950, p. 1-17. (International
Study Conference, June 1950. Netherlands School of Economics, Rotterdam.

Business cycles in the United Kingdom,
1870-1914. Amsterdam, Noord-Hollandsche Uitgevers Maatschappij, 1951,
139 pag. (*Verhandelingen der Koninklijke Nederlandse Akademie van Wetenschappen. afd. Letterkunde, Serie 57 no.
4.*)

— — en G. STUVEL, "National budget",
in: *Handbuch der Finanzwissenschaft*,
herausgegeben von W. Gerloff und F.
Neumark, Tübingen, J. C. B. Mohr.
1942, S. 537-553.

*Rapport van de Commissie sanering zee-
visserij*, 's-Gravenhage, 1952, 125 pag.
(Commissie - Tinbergen).

A. A. VAN AMERINGEN, H. J. HOFSTRA, G. M. NEDERHORST, J. TINBERGEN EN J. M. DEN UYL. *Onder Lieftincks bewind. Het financiëel-economisch beleid na de oorlog*, Amsterdam, N.V. de Arbeiderspers, 1952, 64 pag.

On the theory of economic policy, Amsterdam, Noord-Hollandsche Uitgevers Maatschappij, 1952, 78 pag. (*Contributions to economic analysis* No. 1.)

LIPS, J., D. B. J. SCHOUTEN AND J. TINBERGEN, *The financial aspect of macro-economic models*, Intern. Monet. Fonds. 1958, 13 pag.

MAAS H. J., H. VAN ROESSE E.A., "Algemene aspecten van de industrialisatie", in: *Industrialisatie*, Delft, Waltman, 1953, p. 59-70.

"Het economisch aspect", in: *Het Deltaplan; afdamming zee-armen. Praeadviezen door* A. G. MARIS, J. TINBERGEN en G. H. L. ZEEGERS. Haarlem, Nederlandsche Maatschappij voor Nijverheid en Handel, 1954. pp. 29-53.

Nederlands economische positie vandaag en morgen, Middelburg, 1954, 17 pag. (rede uitgesproken op de algemene ledenvergadering van het Verbond van Nederlandsche Werkgevers op 21 october 1954 te Middelburg).

Centralization and decentralization in economic policy, Amsterdam, North. Holl. Publ. Comp., 1954. 80 pag. (*Contributions to economic analysis no. 6.*)

"De betekenis van het plan voor de Nederlandse volkshuishouding" in: *Herwonnen welvaart. De betekenis van het Marshallplan voor Nederland en de Europese samenwerking*,'s-Gravenhage, 1954, 219 pag. (Ministerie v. Buitenlandse Zaken.)

"Rapport Nederland algemeen", in: *Les problèmes sociaux au niveau de l'entreprise et de l'économie nationale. Actes du congrès du centenaire de la S.E.P. tenu à Bruxelles les 23, 24, et 25 septembre*, 1955, tome 1, p. 491-502.

Prijzen in een hoogconjunctuur. Feiten en wensen, Amsterdam 1956. 18 pag. (Inleiding gehouden op de gecombineerde ledenvergadering van de raad voor het grootwinkelbedrijf, 3 nov. 1955 te Utrecht.)

Economic policy; principles and design, Amsterdam, N.Holl. Publ. Co., 1956, XXVIII + 276 pag.

"Bevolkingsgroei en mechanisatie als factoren van de vraag naar energie", in: *Bevolkingsgroei en energie-verbruik*, Assen, Gorcum en Camp, 1958, p. 24-34. (Symposium der universiteit van Amsterdam gehouden in de zomer van 1957.)

Les problèmes fondamentaux de l'économie européenne contemporaine, 1958. 12 pag.

"Should the income tax be among the means of economic policy." *Festskrift til* Frederik Zeuthen, København, 1958, p. 351-362.

II. PERIODICALS

"Over de mathematies-statistiese methoden van konjunktuur-onderzoek", *De Ekonomist*, Haarlem, 76 (1927) 11, p. 711-723.

"Opmerkingen over ruiltheorie", *De Socialistische Gids*, Amsterdam, 13 (1928) I p. 431-445. II p. 539-548.

"De roulering in het werklozenleger", *De Economist*, Haarlem, 77 (1928) p. 772-782.

"Konjunkturforschung und Variations-rechnung", *Archiv für Sozialwissen-schaft und Sozialpolitik*, Tübingen, 61 (1929) 3 p. 533-541.

"Het ekonomiese getij" (naar aanlei-ding van S. de Wolff: Het economisch getij, bijdrage tot de verklaring van het conjunctuurverschijnsel) *De Socialis-tische Gids*, Amsterdam, 14 (1929) p. 849-858.

"Kopen op afbetaling; ekonomiese overwegingen", *De Socialistische Gids*, Amsterdam, 14 (1929) p. 993-999.

"Het verband tussen den aardappel-oogst en den prijs en den uitvoer van aardappelmeel, "*De Nederlandsche Con-junctuur*, 's-Gravenhage, (1930) 1 (mrt.) p. 18-26.

"Mathematiese psychologie", *Mensch en maatschappij*, Amsterdam, 6 (1930) p. 342-352.

"Bestimmung und Deutung von An-gebotskurven. Ein Beispiel", *Zeit-schrift für Nationalökonomie*, Wien, (1930) 5, p. 669-779.

"Structuur- en conjunctuurverloop in de katoenindustrie", *De Nederlandsche Conjunctuur*, 's-Gravenhage, (1930) 3. (sept.) p. 12-23.

"De werkloosheid", *De Socialistische Gids*, Amsterdam, 15 (1930) p. 817-823.

"Scheepsbouw en conjunctuurver-loop", *De Nederlandsche Conjunctuur*, 's-Gravenhage, (1931) 1 (mrt.) p. 14-23.

"Ein Schiffbauzyklus? "*Weltwirtschaft-liches Archiv*, Hamburg, 34 (1931 II) p. 152-164.

"Oorzaken en bestrijding der werkloos-heid", *De Socialistische Gids*, Amster-dam, 16 (1931) p. 169-180.

"De landbouwcrisis. Prae-advies uit gebracht voor de socialistiese vereni-ging ter bevordering van de studie van maatschappelijke vraagstukken", *De Socialistische Gids*, Amsterdam, 16 (1931) I en II p. 300-313, III p. 384-393.

"Het nut van statistiese analyse voor het bedrijf", *De Socialistische Gids*, Amsterdam, 16 (1931) p. 697-707.

"Ein Problem der Dynamik", *Zeit-schrift für Nationalökonomie*, Wien, 3 (1932) 2 p. 169-184.

"De structurele beweging van enkele belangrijke economische verschijnse-len", *De Nederlandsche Conjunctuur*, 's-Gravenhage, (1932) 2 (juni) p. 13-18.

"Struktuurwerkloosheid", *De Socialis-tische Gids*, Amsterdam, 17 (1932) p. 409-421.

"Het loonvraagstuk" (de diss. van J. G. J. C. Nieuwenhuis), *De Socialistische Gids*, Amsterdam, 17 (1932) p. 723-727.

—— en DR. TH. VAN LUYTELAER, "De koffievalorisaties: geschiedenis en re-sultaten," *De Economist*, Haarlem, 81 (1932) 7/8 p. 517-538.

"Prijsvorming op de aandelenmarkt", *De Nederlandsche Conjunctuur*, 's-Gra-venhage, (1932) 4 (dec.) p. 12-23.

"L'Utilisation des équations fonction-nelles et des nombres complexes dans les recherches économiques", *Econo-metrica. Journal of the econometric so-ciety*, Chicago, 1 (1933) 1, p. 36-52.

"The notions of horizon and expectan-cy in dynamic economics", *Econome-trica*, Chicago, 1 (1933) 3, p. 257-264.

"De beteekenis der voorraden voor het conjunctuurverloop", *De Nederland-sche Conjunctuur*, 's-Gravenhage, (1933) 1 (mrt.) p. 11-20.

"Vraag en aanbod van scheepsruimte", *De Nederlandsche Conjunctuur*, 's-Gravenhage, (1933) 1 (mrt.) p. 25-31.

"De invloed van de werkloosheid op het loonpeil", *De Nederlandsche Conjunctuur*, 's-Gravenhage, (1933) 2 (juni) p. 11-13.

"Verminderende meeropbrengsten", *De Economist*, Haarlem, 82 (1933) 6, p. 481-491.

"De wisselwerking tussen loon en werkgelegenheid", *De Nederlandsche Conjunctuur*, 's-Gravenhage, (1933) 3 (sept.) p. 10-26.

"Over de ekonomie der werkverruiming", *De Socialistische Gids*, Haarlem, 18 (1933) p. 556-573.

"Annual survey of significant developments in general economic theory", *Econometrica. Journal of the econometric society*, Chicago, 2 (1934) 1. p. 13-36.

— — and H. W. METHORST, "Les recherches relatives à la conjuncture au Bureau Central de Statistique des Pays-Bas", *Revue de l'Institut International de Statistique*, 's -Gravenhage, 2 (1934) 1, p. 37-55.

"Scheepsruimte en vrachten", *De Nederlandsche Conjunctuur*, 's-Gravenhage, (1934) 1 (mrt.) p. 23-35 (met medewerking van B. G. F. BUYS).

"Der Einfluss der Kaufkraftregulierung auf den Konjunkturverlauf", *Zeitschrift für Nationalökonomie*, Wien, 5 (1934) 3. p. 289-319.

"De invloed van de conjunctuur op de arbeidsproductiviteit", *De Nederlandsche Conjunctuur*, 's-Gravenhage, (1934) 2 (juni), p. 13-20.

"De vraag naar korte kredieten en de rentestand", *De Nederlandsche Conjunctuur*, 's-Gravenhage, (1934) 3 (aug.) p. 18-31.

"La politique des salaires, les cycles économiques et les mathématiques", *Revue des sciences économiques*, Bruxelles, 10 (1935) febr.

"De politiek van Roosevelt", *De Socialistische Gids*, Amsterdam, 20 (1935) 2, p. 87-97.

"Cijfers betreffende het conjunctuurverloop in de Vereenigde Staten, 1919-1932", *De Nederlandsche Conjunctuur*, 's-Gravenhage, (1935) 1 (febr.) p. 14-24.

"Suggestions on quantitative business cycle theory", *Econometrica. Journal of the econometric society*, Chicago, 3 (1935) 3, p. 241-308.

"Omwegproductie", *De Economist*, Haarlem, 84 (1935) 6, p. 461-480 en 478.

"Quantitative Fragen der Konjunkturpolitik", *Weltwirtschaftliches Archiv*, Hamburg, 42 (1935 I) p. 316-399.

"Winsten, koersen en investeringen", *De Nederlandsche Conjunctuur*, 's-Gravenhage, (1935) 3 (aug.) p. 14-21.

"Winstmarge, investeering en productie", *De Nederlandsche Conjunctuur*, 's-Gravenhage, (1935) 4 (nov.) p. 15-19.

"Resultaten van verschillende vormen van conjunctuurpolitiek", *De Socialistische Gids*, Amsterdam, 20 (1935) 10, p. 625-637. Prae-advies te houden in de najaarsvergadering van de Sociale Vereeniging ter Bevordering van de studie van Maatschappelijke Vraagstukken op 10 november 1935 te Amsterdam. Zie ook geschriften S.V.M.V. no. 7.

"Die Preise im Konjunkturverlauf", *Zeitschrift für Nationalökonomie*, Wien, 7 (1936) p. 104-109.

"Sur la détermination statistique de la position d'équilibre cyclique", *Revue de l'Institut International de Statistique*, 's-Gravenhage, 4 (1936) 2, p. 173-189.

"Is het conjunctuurevenwicht reeds overschreden? Enige cijfers en lijnen betreffende Nederland, de Vereenigde Staten, Engeland, Duitschland en Zwitserland", *De Nederlandsche Conjunctuur*, 's-Gravenhage, (1936) 3 (aug.) p. 12-19.

"Conjunctuurpolitiek en prijsstabilisatie", *De Economist*, Haarlem, 85 (1936) 6, p. 443-456.

"De loondispariteit tussen Nederland en 't buitenland voor de devaluatie", *De Economist*, Haarlem, 85 (1936) p. 739.

"Einige Grundfragen der mathematischen Konjunkturtheorie", *Archiv für Mathematische Wirtschafts und Sozialforschung*, 3 (1937) p. 1 en 83.

"Über die Sekundärwirkungen zusätzlicher Investitionen", *Weltwirtschaftliches Archiv*, Hamburg, 45 (1937 I) p. 39-57.

"Econometrie en technische economie", *De Ingenieur*, Utrecht, 52 (1937) p. 20-34. Voordracht gehouden voor de afd. van technische economie van het Kon. Inst. van Ingenieurs op 23 jan. 1937 te Den Haag.

"Conjunctuurpolitiek en internationale verhoudingen", *De Economist*, Haarlem, 86 (1937) 2, p. 81.

"Over enige socialistische conjunctuurtheorieën (n.a.v. Natalie Moszkowska 'Zur Kritik moderner Krisentheorien')", *De Socialistische Gids*, Amsterdam, 22 (1937) 3, p. 99-104.

—— en A. ROMBOUTS, "Statistische bepaling van de vraagfunctie van electrische energie voor licht, huishoudelijk verbruik en verwarming", *Economisch-Technisch Tijdschrift*, Maastricht, 17 (1937) 6, p. 104-111.

"De mogelijkheid van economische calculatie in een volledig gesocialiseerde maatschappij" (n.a.v. Hayek, Collectivist economic planning), *De Socialistische Gids*, Amsterdam, 22 (1937) 10, p. 611-616.

"Eine volkswirtschaftliche Theorie der öffentlichen Investitionen". Naar aanleiding van het gelijknamige boek van Hans Richter - Altschäffer, *Weltwirtschaftliches Archiv*, Hamburg, 46 (1937 II) p. 27-31.

"Recherches économétriques sur l'importance de la bourse dans l'activité générale aux Etats-Unis", *X-Crise (Centre polytechnique d'études économiques)*, 49 (1938) juillet, p. 25-41.

"On the theory of business cycle control", *Econometrica. Journal of the econometric society*, Chicago, 6 (1938) 1, p. 22-39.

"Statistical evidence on the acceleration principle", *Economica, London. The London school of economics and political science*. New series 5, (1938) p. 164-176.

—— en A. ROMBOUTS, 'Seizoenbewegingen. Toepassing van de methoden van Wald en Zaycoff", *De Nederlandsche Conjunctuur*, 's-Gravenhage, (1938 3 (aug.) p. 74-86;

—— en B. V. D. MEER, "De woningbouw in Amsterdam", *De Nederlandsche Conjunctuur*, 's-Gravenhage, (1938 3 (aug.) p. 87-100.

—— en DR. TH. V. LUYTELAER, "De Braziliaansche koffiepolitiek en haar gevolgen in de jaren 1927-1937", *De Economist*, Haarlem, 87 (1938) 9 p. 586-602.

"De uitwerking van extra-investeringen. Antwoord aan A. Bijl", *De Economist*, Haarlem, (1938) 9. p. 658-661.

—— en B. VAN DER MEER, "Enige cijfers betreffende de tekorten op de rijksrekeningen en -begrootingen", *De Nederlandsche Conjunctuur*, 's-Gravenhage, (1938) 4 (nov.) p. 115-116.

—— en B. VAN DER MEER, ,,Verloop van het saldo-tegoed der spaarbanken", *De Nederlandsche Conjunctuur*, 's-Gravenhage, 9 (1938) 4 (nov.), p. 128-140.

—— en J. B. D. DERKSEN, "Productiekosten in Nederland en enkele andere landen", *De Nederlandsche Conjunctuur*, 's-Gravenhage, 10 (1939) 1 (febr.), p. 50-52.

—— and P. DE WOLFF, "A simplified model of the causation of technological unemployment", *Econometrica. Journal of the econometric society*, Chicago, 7 (1939) 3, p. 193-207.

"Henri Schultz' levenswerk: Statistische bepaling van vraagcurven", *De Economist*, Haarlem, 88 (1939) 4, p. 299-308.

—— en P. J. VERDOORN, "De vraag naar personenvervoer per spoor", *De Nederlandsche Conjunctuur*, 's-Gravenhage, 10 (1939) 2 (mei), p. 79-89.

"Econometric business cycle research", *The Review of Economic Studies*, London, (1939)/40) p. 73-90. Ook opgenomen in: *Readings in business cycles theory*, London, Allen and Urwin 1950.

—— en J. J. J. DALMULDER, "De factoren, welke het koersverloop van aandelen bepalen", *De Nederlandsche Conjunctuur*, 's-Gravenhage, 10 (1939) 3 (aug.), p. 111-123.

"Oorzaken van de werkloosheid en bestrijding op lange termijn", *Het Gemeenebest*, 's-Gravenhage, 2 (1939) p. 271-280.

"Contingentering of invoerrechten (de voorstellen tot wijziging der tariefwet),"

Socialisme en Democratie, Amsterdam, 1 (1939) p. 326-328.

—— en DR. O. BAKKER, "Het werkloosheidsrapport van de commissie Van der Waerden. Een verweer," *De Economist*, Haarlem, 88 (1939) 9, p. 643-654.

"The dynamics of share-price formation", *The Review of Economics and Statistics*, Cambridge, Mass., 21 (1939) 4 (nov.) p. 153-160.

—— en A. L. G. M. ROMBOUTS, "De samenhang tussen de prijzen van ingevoerde grondstoffen en die van afgewerkte producten in Nederland", *De Nederlandsche Conjunctuur*, 's-Gravenhage, 10 (939) 4 (nov.), p. 150-165.

"Meer begrip voor de werking van het economisch systeem", *Het Gemeenebest*, 's-Gravenhage, 3 (1940) p. 18-22.

—— en A. L. G. M. ROMBOUTS, "Statistische metingen van Keynes begrippen 'propensity to consume' en 'propensity to save' voor Nederland", *De Nederlandsche Conjunctuur*, 's-Gravenhage, 11 (1940) 1 (febr.), p. 21-26.

—— en F. SNAPPER, "Verdere beschouwingen over de conjunctureele werking der overheidsfinanciën. Eenige cijfers betreffende de conjunctureele werking van de belastingen en de winsten der overheidsbedrijven", *De Nederlandsche Conjunctuur*, 's-Gravenhage, 11 (1940) 1 (febr.), p. 27-30.

—— en J. B. D. DERKSEN, "Enkele der belangrijkste directe oorzaken van de fluctuaties in het nationale inkomen", *Maandschrift van het Centraal Bureau voor de Statistiek*, Den Haag, 35 (1940) 5/6, p. 691-701.

"De invloed van werktijd, loon en rentestand op de arbeidsproductiviteit", *De Economist*, Haarlem, 89 (1940) 7, p. 385-394.

"Unstable and indifferent equilibria in economic systems", *Revue de l'Institut International de Statistique*, 's-Gravenhage, 9 (1941) 1/2, p. 36-50.

"Over enkele econometrische tekortkomingen", *De Economist*, Haarlem, 90 (1941) 4 p. 226-235.

"Het verband tussen dividenden en aandeelkoersen in 1941 en in vroegere jaren", *Maandschrift van het Centraal Bureau voor de Statistiek*, 's-Gravenhage, 36 (1941) 8/9 p. 768-772.

"Indifferente en labiele evenwichten in economische stelsels", *De Economist*, Haarlem, 90 (1941) II, p. 561-584.

"Does consumption lay behind incomes"? *The Review of Ecobomics and Statistics*, Cambridge, 24 (1942) 1 (febr.) p. 1-8.

"Professor Douglas' production function", *Revue de l'Institut International de Statique*, 's-Gravenhage, 10 (1942) 1/2, p. 37-48.

"Critical remarks on some business cycle theories", *Econometrica. Journal of the Econometric Society*, Chicago, 10 (1942) 2, p. 129-146.

"Zur theorie der langfristigen Wirtschaftsentwicklung", *Weltwirtschaftliches Archiv*, Hamburg, 55, (1942 I) p. 511-549.

"De groei van den voorraad van eenige soorten kapitaalgoederen in zes landen van omstreeks 1870", *Maandschrift van het Centraal Bureau voor de Statistiek*, 's-Gravenhage.
I (1870-1910) 37 (1942) 2/3, p. 20-213
II (1914-1918) 37 (1942) 5/6 p. 470-472
III (1919-1939) 37 (1942) 8/9, p.737-749.

"Berekeningen over de sociale waarde van den grond", *Maandschrift van het Centraal Bureau voor de Statistiek*, 's-Gravenhage, 38 (1943) 1.

"Het verloop op langen termijn van de rentestanden", *Maandschrift van het Centraal Bureau voor de Statistiek*, 's-Gravenhage, 38 (1943) 2/3 p. 117-124.

"Over verschillende soorten evenwichten en de conjunctuurbeweging", *De Economist*, Haarlem, 92 (1943) 3, p. 129-147.

"Verdere metingen van de vervangingselasticiteit", *Maandschrift van het Centraal Bureau voor de Statistiek* 's-Gravenhage, 38 (1943) 5/6, p. 295-303.

"Ligevaegtstyper og konjunkturbevaelgelse", *Nordisk Tidsskrift for Teknisk Økonomi*, København, 10 (1944) p. 45-63.

—— en J. B. D. DERKSEN, "Berekeningen over de economische betekenis van Nederlandsch-Indië voor Nederland", *Maandschrift van het Centraal Bureau voor de Statistiek*, 's-Gravenhage, 40 (1945) 10/12, p. 210-216.

"De noodzaak van internationale planning", *Socialisme en Democratie*, Amsterdam, 3 (1946) 2 p. 42-44.

"De plaats van de econoom in de maatschappij", *Wording*, II (1946) p. 189-191.

'Wiskundige methoden in gebruik bij de statistiek, welke van toepassing zijn bij het onderzoek van hygiënische vraagstukken", *De Ingenieur*, Utrecht 58 (1946) 18, p. 914-920.

"Some measurements of elasticities of substitution", *The Review of Economics and Statistics*, Cambridge, 28 (1946) 3 (aug.), p. 109-116.

"Het Nederlandsche welvaartsplan", *De Ingenieur*, Utrecht, 58 (1946) 31 A 297-A 306 en A 320.

"Wijk, Jacob van der. In memoriam", *Socialisme en Democratie*, Amsterdam, 13 (1946) p. 237-239.

"De derde weg (tussen vrije en gebonden economie)", *Socialisme en Democratie*, Amsterdam, 3 (1946) 12, p. 369-372.

"International economic co-operation" *Erasmus Speculum Scientiarum*, Aarau, (Zwitserland), 1 (1947) 1.

"The Netherlands central economic plan for 1947", *Revue Suisse d'Economie Politique et de Statistique*, Bern, 83 (1947) 1, p. 19-29).

"Quelques estimations de l'influence des contingentements 1933-1938 sur l'emploi aux Pays-Bas", *Revue de l'Institut International de Statistique*, 's-Gravenhage, 15 (1947) 1/4, p. 2-18.

"The use of correlation analysis in economic research", *Ekonomisk Tidskrift, Uppsala*, 49 (1947) 3, p. 173-192.

"Central planning in the Netherlands", *The Revue of economic studies*, London, 15 (1947/48) 38, p. 70-77.

"Problems of central economic planning in the Netherlands", *National Økonomisk Tidskrift*, Stockholm, 85(1947) p. 96.

"Enkele opmerkingen over de verdeling der arbeidsinkomens, nieuwe reeks, *Mededelingen der Koninklijke Nederlandse Akademie van Wetenschappen, afd. Letterkunde*, Amsterdam. 10 (1947) 8, p. 199-214.

"Some problems in the explanation of interest rates", *The Quarterly Journal of Economics*, Harvard University, Cambridge, 61 (1947) p. 397-438.

"Observations sur le problème de la rareté du dollar", *Revue d'Economie Politique*, Paris, 58 (1948) 1, p. 36-56.

"De schommelingen van de invoer 1923-1938", *Statistische en Econometrische Onderzoekingen*, Utrecht, 3 (1948) 2, p. 52-60.

"On a method of statistical business cycle research; a reply", *The Economic Journal*, London, 50 (1948) 197, p. 141-154. Also: *Readings on business cycles and national income* A. H. HANSEN and R. V. CLEMENCE, London, 1953.

"Carmiggelt, Jan. Ter nagedachtenis", *Socialisme en Democratie*, Amsterdam, 5 (1948) p. 323-325.

"S. de Wolff als econoom", *Socialisme en Democratie*, Amsterdam, 5 (1948) p. 401-405.

"Modelli di commercio internazionale", *Giornale degli Economisti e Annali di Economia*, Padova, 7 (1948) 11/12, p. 627-648.

"Planning for viability", *The Way Ahead*, 's-Gravenhage, 2 (1949) p. 38-61.

"Contribuição da econometria para a compreensao do mecanismo de transferência", *Revista Brasileira Economia*, Rio de Janeiro, 3 (1949) 1, p. 71-91.

"The equalisation of factor prices between free-trade areas", *Metroeconomica*, Bologna, 1 (1949) 1, p. 38-47.

"De uitgaven van de gemeenten en de economische politiek der overheid", *Bestuurswetenschappen*, 's-Gravenhage, (1949) 4, p. 197-204. Overdruk Centraal Planbureau no. 3.

"Government budget and central economic plan", *Public Finance: Openbare Financiën*, Haarlem, 42 (1949) 3, p. 195-205. Overdruk C.P.B. no. 5.

"Long-term foreign trade elasticities", *Metroeconomica*, Bologna, 1 (1949) 3, p. 174-185.

"Le mécanisme des cycles vu par un économètre", *Economique Appliquée*, Paris, 2 (1949) 3/4 p. 417-428.

"Some remarks on the problem of dollar scarcity", *Econometrica. Journal of the Econometric Society*, Chicago, 17 (1949) suppl. juli p. 73-97.

—— and J. B. D. DERKSEN, "Recent experiments in social accounting flexible and dynamic budgets", *Econometrica. Journal of the Econometric Society*, Chicago, 17 (1949), suppl. juli p. 195-204. (Proceedings of the international statistical conferences).

"Du système de Pareto aux 'modèles' modernes", *Revue d'Economique Politique*, Paris, 59 (1949) 2, p. 642-652.

"Möglichkeiten und Grenzen der Anwendung mathematischer Verfahren in der Wirtschaftswissenschaft", *Zeitschrift für die Gesamte Staatswissenschaft*, Tübingen, 105 (1949) 4, p. 638-652.

"Anomalien im Zahlungsbilanzmechanismus", *Weltwirtschaftliches Archiv*, Hamburg, 63 (1949 II) p. 153-177.

"Wesen und Bedeutung der Oekonometrie," *Zeitschrift für Oekonometrie*, Mainz, 1 (1950) 1, p. 5-13.

"Economic policy in the Netherlands", *Statsøkonomisk Tidsskrift*, Oslo, 64 (1950) 1-2, p. 70-80.

"De algemene economische aspecten van de belastingen", *Maandschrift economie*, Tilburg, 15 (1950/51) 1/2 p. 83-89.

"Werkgelegenheidspolitiek", *Financiëel Economisch Kwartaaloverzicht, Amsterdamsche Bank N.V.*, Amsterdam, (1950) no. 80 p. 1-7.

"Ökonometrie und Statistik in ihrer gegenseitigen Beziehung", *Allgemeines Statistisches Archiv*, München, 34(1950) p. 109-113.

"Optimisme en pessimisme t.a.v. de betalingsbalans", *Socialisme en Democratie*, Amsterdam, 7 (1950) 1, p. 1-4.

"De betekenis van de loonpolitiek voor de werkgelegenheid", *De Economist*, Haarlem, 98 (1950) 3, p. 161-172. Overdruk C.P.B. no. 8. Also: *International economic papers o.d.t. The significance of wage policy for employment*.

Nationale en internationale maatregelen ten behoeve van de volledige werkgelegenheid, 98 (1950) p. 338-350.

Recherches statistiques sur la conjoncture et sur la structure, 25 (1950) 82, p. 53-61.

"In hoeverre kunnen economische stellingen zonder wiskunde worden bewezen?", *Mededelingen der Koninklijke Nederlandse Akademie van wetenschappen, afd. Letterkunde* 13 (1950) 10, p. 283-293.

A. H. ALBREGTS, J. TINBERGEN, A. M. GROOT E.A.: "Opvoering productiviteit", *Verkeer en vervoer*, 's-Gravenhage, 5 (1951) p. 67-83.

"Economic fluctuations in the United States 1921-1941", *Zeitschrift für Oekonometrie*, Mainz, 1 (1951) 2, p. 23-96.

"Some neglected points in demand research", *Metroeconomica*, Bologna, 3 (1951) 2, 49-54.

"De sociale betekenis van de techniek", *De Ingenieur*, Utrecht, 63 (1951) 4, p. A.33-A.38.

"Het loon- en prijsrapport van de Sociaal-Economische Raad", *De Economist*, Haarlem, 99 (1951) 4, p. 315-317.

"Les aspects néerlandais du problème de l'équilibre international en longue période", *Revue Economique*, Paris, (1951) 3, p. 298-303.

316   BIBLIOGRAPHY OF JAN TINBERGEN

"Schumpeter and quantitative research in economics", *The Review of Economics and Statistics*, Cambridge, 33 (1951) (mei) 2, p. 119-111.

"Dirigisme et liberté dans le cadre de l'intégration économique de l'Europe", *Anais do instituto superior de ciências económicas e financeiras*, Lisboa, 20 (1952) p. 5-13.

"Financing social insurance out of premiums or out of income tax", *Archive of Economic and Social Sciences*, Athens, 32 (1952) p. 71-77.

"Emigratie: een besparing", *Maatschappijbelangen*, Haarlem, 116 (1952) 2, p. 35-37.

"Ökonometrische Modelle und die Wirtschaftspolitik", *Allgemeines Statistisches Archiv*, München, 36 (1952) 2, p. 119-129.

"The influence of productivity on economic welfare", *The Economic Journal*, London, 62 (1952) 245 p. 68-86. Overdrukken C.P.B. no. 17.

"De quelques problèmes posés par le concept de structure économique", *Revue d'Economie Politique*, Paris, 62 (1952) 1/2 p. 27-46.

ORCUTT, GUY H.: "Toward partial redirection of econometrics. Comments by J. Tinbergen", *The Review of Economics and Statistics*, Cambridge, 34 (1952) 3, p. 205.

"On the theory of economic integration", *Les Cahiers de Bruges*, Bruges, quarterly, (1952) 4, p. 292-303, Franse tekst (1952) 4, p. 304-309.

"Goudriaans analytische economie", *De Economist*, Haarlem, 100 (1952) p. 401-410.

"Investeringen, betalingsbalans en welvaart", *De Ingenieur*, Utrecht, 64 (1952) 13, p. A.135-A.139.

"The relation between internal inflation and the balance of payments", *Quarterly Review. Banca Nazionale del Lavoro*, Roma, 5 (1952) 23 p. 187-194.

Efficiency and future of economic research", *Kyklos; Internationale Zeitschrift für Sozialwissenschaften*, Bern (1952) 4, p. 309-319.

"De economist en het sociale vraagstuk", *De Economist*, Haarlem, 100 (1952) 12, p. 1010-1024.

"Capital formation and the five-year plan", *The Indian Economic Journal*, Bombay, 1 (1953) 1, p. 1-5:

—— and H. M. A. VAN DER WERFF, "Four alternative policies to restore balance of payments equilibrium: a comment and an extension", *Econometrica. Journal of the Econometric Society*, Chicago, 21 (1953) 2, p. 332-335.

"Planification et liberté dans l'analyse économique générale et l'expérience des Pays-Bas", *Revue Economique*, Paris, (1953) 2. p. 245-261.

"Fäystyöllisygsja rahatalou dellinen tasapaina Hollannissa: eräs yrikys nüden sopenttamiseksi", *Kansantaloudellinen Aikakauskirja*, Helsinki, 4 (1953) p. 7 with Eng. summ.

Import and export elasticities; some remarks, (Int. Stat. Conferences in India, dec. 1951) *Bulletin International Statistical Institute*, Calcutta, 33 (1953) p. 215-226.

"Algunas tecnicas aplicables a planes de desarrollo (some techniques of development planning)", *Boletin del Banco Central de Venezuela*, Caracas, 14 (1954) 110/112 p. 14-25.

"De voorspelling en de beïnvloeding van de conjunctuur" *Socialisme en Democratie*, Amsterdam 11 (1954) 3 p. 169-177.

"Prognose der niederländischen Wirtschaftslage für das Jahr 1954", *Zeitschrift für die Gesamte Staatswissenschaft*, Tübingen, 110 (1954) 4, p. 578-614.

—— und D. B. J. SCHOUTEN: "Die Anwendung des Nationalbudgets zur kritischen Beurteilung der Währungslage", *Wirtschaftsdienst*, Hamburg, 34 (1954) 4, p. 199-207. Intern. Ec. Papers. 1955 no. 5.

"Over de theorie der economische politiek. Repliek op H. S. Houthakker: Het mechanisme der economische politiek". *De Economist*, Haarlem, 102 (1954) 6, p. 241-249.

"Rechtvaardigheid en solidariteit", *Socialisme en Democratie*, Amsterdam, 11 (1954) 6/7, p. 413.

"Krappe arbeidsmarkt; een tijdelijk verschijnsel dat tijdelijke maatregelen vraagt", *De zakenwereld*, Haarlem, 32 (1954) 29, p. 676-678.

"The functions of mathematical treatment: Mathematics in economics, discussion of Mr. Novicks article", *The Review of Economics and Statistics*, Cambridge, 36 (1954) 4 (nov.), p. 365-369.

"Professor Tinbergen antwoordt Dr. Keus naar aanleiding van zijn art. 'Schijn bedriegt'," *De zakenwereld*, Haarlem, 32 (1954) 35, p. 821.

"Modèles statistiques à l'usage de la politique économique", *Cahiers du Séminaire d'Econométrie*, Paris, (1955) 3, p. 31-37.

"Economische aspecten van het ontwikkelingsvraagstuk geïllustreerd aan de problemen in India", *Socialisme en Democratie*, Amsterdam, 12 (1955) 7, p. 455-460.

"Revaluatie of loonsverhoging; voordracht voor de afd. technische economie v.h. K. I. v. I. 18 januari 1955", *De Ingenieur*, Utrecht, 67 (1955) 39, A477-A482.

"Vijftig jaar economische ontwikkeling in de wereld", *De vakbeweging*, Amsterdam, (1956), no. 1, 10 januari.

"Problems concerning India's second five year plan", *Public finance; Openbare financiën*, Haarlem, 11 (1956) 2, p. 103-110.

"De quelques problèmes de développement à long terme", *Bulletin d'Information et de Documentation de la Banque Nationale de Belgique*, Bruxelles, 31 (1956) 3, p. 177-184.
Reprint series N.U.I. no. 3.
Ook in: *Tijdschrift voor documentatie en voorlichting*.

"On the theory of income distribution" *Weltwirtschaftliches Archiv*, Hamburg, 77 (1956 I) p. 10-31. Reprint series C.P.B. no. 49.

"De economie der Beneluxlanden voor 1940 en na 1945", *De Zakenwereld*, Haarlem, 34 (1956) 17 p. 27-32.

"The optimum rate of saving", *The Economic Journal*, London, 66 (1956) 264, p. 603-609. Ook: Reprint series NES no. 1.

"De toegenomen betekenis van onderwijs en opvoeding voor de socialistische beweging", *Socialisme en Democratie*, Amsterdam, 13 (1956) 11, p. 486-489.

"Welfare economics and income distribution", *The American Economic review, Papers and Prodeecings*, Menasha, 47 (1957) 2, p. 490-503.

"The optimum choice of technology", *Pakistan Economic Journal*, Dacca, 7 (1957) 2, p. 1-7.

J. TINBERGEN, G. L. BACH, HARRY G. JOHNSON, LORRIE TARSHIS, "Comments on the economics of governor Stevenson's program paper: Where is the money coming from?" *The Review of economics and statistics*, Cambridge, (1957) 2 (mei) p. 134-142.

"De internationale taak van de sociaaldemocratie", *Socialisme en Democratie*, Amsterdam, 14 (1957) 2, p. 84-89.

"Customs unions: influence of their size on their effect", *Zeitschrift für die Gesamte Staatswissenschaft*, Tübingen, 113 (1957) 3, p. 404-415.

"The use of a short-term econometric model for Indian economic policy", *Sankhyā; the Indian Journal of Statistics*, 17 (1957) 4, p. 337-344.

"An international economic policy," *The Indian Journal of Economics*, Allahabad (India), 38 (1957) 148, p. 11-16.

"The appraisal of road construction, two calculation schemes", *The Review of Economics and Statistics*, Cambridge, 39 (1957) 3 (aug.), p. 241-249. Reprint series N.E.I. no. 5.

"Internationale socialistische politiek", *Socialisme en Democratie*, 14 (1957) 11, p. 666-671.

"Choice of technology in industrial planning", *Industrialization and Pro-ductivity. Bulletin United Nations*. New York, 1 (1958) 1, p. 24-33.

"Les distorsions et leur correction", *Revue d'Economie Politique*, Paris, 68 (1958) 1, p. 256-263

"Enkele beginselen der economische politiek", *De Economist*, Haarlem, 106 (1958) 2, p. 120-122.

"Internationale socialistische politiek anno 1958", *Socialisme en Democratie*, Amsterdam, 15 (1958) 2, p. 102-105.

"Quantitative economics in the Netherlands. Model building for economic policy", *Higher Education and Research in the Netherlands*, The Hague, 2 (1958) 3, p. 3-7.

"Ontwikkelingsprogrammering", *Mededelingenblad van Afgestudeerden der Nederlandsche Economische Hoogeschool*, Rotterdam, 6 (1958) 8, p. 8-13.

"Meer economisch begrip tussen Oost en West", *Wending*, 13 (1958) 8, p. 531.

"Mogelijkheden en grenzen der econometrie" *Rosta economica*, Amsterdam, 6 (1958) 26, p. 2-3.

"The economic principles for an optimum use of space", *Les Cahiers de Bruges, quarterly*, Bruges, (1958) 11, p. 15-18.